THE BEST OF GERALD DURRELL

Lee Durrell is a well-known conservationist in her own
right. She was married to and worked with Gerald
Durrell for many years.

THE BEST OF
Gerald Durrell

CHOSEN BY
Lee Durrell

HarperCollins*Publishers*

HarperCollins*Publishers*
77–85 Fulham Palace Road,
Hammersmith, London W6 8JB

This paperback edition 1998

1 3 5 7 9 8 6 4 2

First published in Great Britain by
HarperCollins*Publishers* 1996

ISBN 0 00 638764 0

Set in Linotype Minion by
Rowland Phototypesetting Ltd,
Bury St Edmunds, Suffolk

Printed and bound by
Caledonian International Book Manufacturing Ltd, Glasgow

To all those who were inspired by Gerry's books to
do something for the wild animals, plants and places of
his 'magical world' . . .

and to the new readers who will follow suit

ACKNOWLEDGEMENTS

While I was gallivanting around Madagascar and North America in the autumn of 1995, James Rogers read through Gerry's works and took copious notes. Then we sat at his kitchen table and discussed this book while Gooch snoozed peacefully on the rug on the radiator. Thanks, James, for your time and thought.

CONTENTS

THERE ARE SO MANY REASONS why I am delighted to have been asked to write the foreword for this anthology of Gerald Durrell's writings. Perhaps, most importantly, it is because it reflects a most remarkable man with a unique talent for communicating through the written word, the financial result of which went to create a new concept in zoos for the breeding of endangered species.

One of my memories of Gerry's books is of *My Family and Other Animals* on a train journey to Liverpool, where my occasional involuntary bursts of laughter caused a mixture of quizzical, amused, annoyed or possibly envious looks. It was impossible not to laugh out loud at descriptions of his pets, their behaviour and their effect on various members of his family.

Catch Me a Colobus introduced me to Gerry's travels. Here he used the natural humour of the stories to gently underline the complexities of the relationship between species and their environment and man's responsibilities in that balance.

The Jersey Wildlife Preservation Trust and its Zoo have set examples to the world of education and practice of breeding, reintroducing and maintaining endangered species, but it was the observations, skill and determination of one man who made that possible. This book reflects that man, with items selected by his able and equally determined widow Lee, who has been such an important member of the team at Les Augrès Manor and has so willingly taken on Gerry's lifetime work.

Gerry's work is not finished and all of us understand the need to continue and spread the support for the work of the Jersey Wildlife Preservation Trust. This book is part of that support.

Anne

H. R. H. THE PRINCESS ROYAL,
PATRON OF THE JERSEY
WILDLIFE PRESERVATION TRUST

PREFACE

MY FIRST ENCOUNTER with Gerald Durrell was in south-eastern Madagascar in the mid seventies – in the attic of the missionary's house where I lived after a hurricane had destroyed my tiny bungalow. The day the hurricane struck was also the day that a military coup toppled the government of Madagascar. Neither communications nor international flights were working, and so I was facing an indefinite sojourn in the country, although I had just finished a year and a half of my PhD studies there and was more than ready to come home. However, I had just checked out *My Family and Other Animals* from the mission library. As I read it by lantern light on a straw pallet with my closest companion, a baby fruit bat, by my side, life didn't seem so grim. In fact, as described by Gerry, life was glorious, full of animals, sunshine and happiness, and I laughed and laughed, to the obvious bewilderment of the little bat clinging to my arm.

My next encounter with Gerry was two years later when I was finishing graduate school in the States. By then I knew that he had written many books, not only delightful descriptions of the animals he had met around the world, but also moving accounts of what was happening to them as their world shrank under the rising tide of human population. And I knew that he had set up, on the island of Jersey in the English Channel, a breeding sanctuary for the most threatened species. Imagine my excitement when some professors decided to throw a party for this eminent author and conservationist when he visited our university, and invited me! When my hero walked into the room, the whole place suddenly shone with his megawatt personality, and I talked to no one else but Gerry that evening. The rest, as they say, is history: I visited Jersey (quickly correcting my notion that the whole island was a breeding centre for endangered animals – forgive me, fellow Islanders!), became engrossed in the workings of Gerry's Jersey Zoo and Wildlife Preservation Trust, travelled with Gerry to Canada, France, Costa Rica and back to my beloved Madagascar, added the finishing touches to my PhD thesis as he looked over my shoulder in a castle in Spain, and

1

we were married in the garden of my parents' home in Tennessee, on a lawn of violets and wild strawberries surrounded by blossoming azaleas and dogwoods.

If this all sounds like a fairy tale, well, quite frankly, it was, and it continued to be so. Together we visited many countries, wrote several books and hosted a number of television programmes, all activities to do with wildlife and the people trying to protect it. Our occasional bolt-hole was a little cottage in southern France, in the *garrigue*, where we cooked for our friends with the thyme and rosemary growing wild on the hillside and watched caterpillars turn into butterflies and red squirrels gorge themselves on pine nuts. But always we returned to Jersey, to the Jersey Zoo, head-quarters of the Wildlife Preservation Trust that Gerry had set up way back in 1963, and to the wonderful animals there and our extraordinary team of people who look after them.

But there would be no fairy tales without wicked witches, and for Gerry the wickedness lay in the threats to the animal kingdom. Why should animal species suffer at human hands? Animals, plants, humans themselves and the natural environments in which they all live were and are being menaced, not by human malevolence, but by human ignorance and, sometimes, greed. Gerry saw this earlier than most people, and began not just to talk about it, but to do something about it.

For more than four decades he publicized the environmental crisis, par-ticularly as it was affecting his beloved animals. He shaped his own organiz-ation into a leader of modern zoos, demonstrating the vital role zoos can and should play in the conservation struggle. His writings about animals, so engaging and so thoughtful, inspired countless readers, young and old, to join the fray. Many of them are now professional conservationists, while others champion the cause in other ways from small to grand, but never insignificant.

Gerry's writings are, for the most part, autobiographical, and so it seemed obvious to arrange my selections of the best of them in the order in which his extraordinary life unfolded. They were written, of course, in a different sequence and at various times. He would write during a spare moment on a ship taking him to or from exotic lands, or when finances were tight and he had to put bread and butter on the table, or after sufficient reflection led him to develop his earlier ideas. But to my untrained eye, each is like the other in terms of craft and style, and so I never considered presenting his writings in a literary evolutionary order. I feel that his inimitable way of expressing himself emerged full-blown with his first published book, *The Overloaded Ark* (1953). Actually, he wrote his very first book as a child on Corfu – a pacy tale of cliff-hangers, he told me, in which he rescued various members of his family from the perils of jungle and desert on a daily basis. Unfortunately, that manuscript was lost during the war, but perhaps this is not a tragic blow to literature, for Gerry was so very much more than a writer.

Three themes run through Gerry's writings and life. One is central, the pivot around which the other two revolve. It is his sheer and total delight in discovering the natural world and the animals which populate it. Gerry had the ability to express this and share it with others by virtue of his immense and often quirky powers of observation. His accounts of animals have sometimes been criticized as anthropomorphic. Yes, they are, and unashamedly so! This was Gerry's unique way of getting his readers and listeners to 're-connect' with animals, restoring a link which, in his view, had become dangerously tenuous, given that we – humans and animals – are all living organisms which must somehow get along together on the same planet.

The second theme is his view of people and their behaviour. You could say his accounts are 'zoomorphic', for he often describes humans in animal terms, but he takes just as much delight in observing the foibles of humans as those of animals. The expression of both is enriched by his own brand of humour and wit, sometimes sarcastic, even caustic, but in the end always underpinned by true insight or deserved gentleness.

But on one matter – his third theme – Gerry was not gentle: he became outraged and furious on seeing the natural world despoiled and its creatures destroyed, and he tried to rectify the situation in the way he knew best, providing a loving sanctuary for threatened animals until they were able to go back to their wild homes.

Before meeting Gerry, his family, friends and animals through his writings, let him tell you in his own words just why he was the person he was. In this passage he is being typically modest, attributing it all to luck.

FROM THE AMATEUR NATURALIST:

All of us are born with an interest in the world about us. Watch a human baby or any other young animal crawling about. It is investigating and learning things with all its senses of sight, hearing, taste, touch and smell. From the moment we are born we are explorers in a complex and fascinating world. With some people this may fade with time or with the pressures of life, but others are lucky enough to keep this interest stimulated throughout their lives.

I can never remember the time when I was not intrigued and excited by everything about the world and, in particular, the other animals that inhabited the world with me. One of my very first recollections was when I was two years old. I went for a walk along a mountain road in India accompanied by my ayah. There had been heavy rain some time during the day, and the earth smelt rich and moist. At a bend in the road my ayah met two friends, a man and a woman, and I remember that the woman was wearing a brilliant magenta-coloured sari that shone like an orchid against the green undergrowth alongside the road. I soon lost interest in what they were talking about and made my way to a ditch nearby where I discovered, to my delight, two huge khaki-coloured slugs brought out by the rain. They were slowly wending their way along the ditch, leaving glittering trails of slime behind them. I remember squatting down and watching them, enraptured, seeing how they slid over the earth without any legs to propel them. I remained captivated by these two creatures until my ayah came over to see what I was doing and pulled me away from them, saying that I should not watch such dirty things. To me, they were not only fascinating but, in their own way, as pretty as my ayah's friend in her beautiful sari.

Throughout my life – and I have seen a great number of creatures all over the world – it has always astonished me that people can look at an animal or plant and say 'Isn't that loathsome?' or 'Isn't it horrible?' I think that a true naturalist must view everything objectively. No creature is horrible. They are all part of nature. You may not want to curl up in bed with a rattlesnake or a stinging nettle, and you may find it irritating (as I once did) when giant land snails invade your tent and eat all your food, but these organisms have just as much right in the world as we have.

When I was five or six, the next step in my career as a naturalist was collecting woodlice or ladybirds and carrying them around in matchboxes in my pocket. Then when my family and I went to live on the Greek island of Corfu my interest in natural history really blossomed. I found the island had a whole array of wonderful wildlife, and so I not only made collections of things, like butterflies and beetles, but I also kept them alive and studied them. At any one time I would have in my room or in the garden a varied assortment of creatures ranging from eagle owls to scorpions and from tortoises to sea horses. I was extremely lucky in having as a mentor and friend Dr Theodore Stephanides, who had, and still has, an encyclopaedic knowledge of the natural world. It was he who gave me my first 'professional' piece of equipment when I was eight years old – a pocket microscope. A whole new world was opened up for me and I discovered that ordinary ponds and ditches were full of minute creatures, so that every puddle became a teeming jungle of tiny life.

Later I became a professional animal collector for zoos, and I travelled in places as far removed from each other as Patagonia and the Cameroons, from Guyana to Malaysia. Over the years I have been lucky enough to meet a magnificent selection of wildlife. I have lain on a beach in South America surrounded by huge carunculated elephant seals, some of them snoring loudly, others – if you got too close – rearing up two metres high in a shower of shingle, threatening you with open mouths and deep bellows. In the tropical forests of South America I have captured electric eels a metre and a half long, capable of stunning prey almost their own length with a charge of electricity. In the cloud forests of Costa Rica I have watched the beautiful flight of the quetzal, with his metre-long golden-green tail glittering like a banner as he flew across the clearings between the trees, and on the other side of the world I have spent an exciting – if somewhat dangerous – half-hour at night trying to capture a black mamba, one of the deadliest of African snakes, which had escaped from one of my cages. I have had great fun being introduced to and playing with a duck-billed platypus that looked like Donald Duck in a fur coat, but at the same time I get enormous pleasure by simply looking out of my kitchen window and watching the sparrows bustling about in the hedge beneath.

A naturalist is lucky in two respects. First, he enjoys every bit of the world about him and has a much more enriched life than someone who is not interested in nature. Second, he can indulge his hobby in any place at any time, for a naturalist will be fascinated to watch nature struggling to exist in the midst of a great city as well as observe its riotous splendour in a tropical forest. He can be equally interested and moved by the great herds on the African plains or by the earwigs in his back garden.

PART ONE

———◆·❖·◆———

1925–1945

'The child is mad, snails in his pockets!'
LAWRENCE DURRELL, C. 1931

Born in India, a toddler and youngster in London and Bournemouth, Gerry moved with his family to the Greek island of Corfu when he was eight years old. The subsequent sojourn was the most important experience of his life. He compared his arrival in Corfu to Dorothy's first sight of Oz, when she stepped through the door of a black-and-white house into a Technicolor universe. Here his passion for animals and thirst for knowledge of the natural world developed rapidly, and his child's innocent perspective on the people closest to him has given a million readers unlimited pleasure.

FROM MY FAMILY AND OTHER ANIMALS:

The villa was small and square, standing in its tiny garden with an air of pink-faced determination. Its shutters had been faded by the sun to a delicate creamy-green, cracked and bubbled in places. The garden, surrounded by tall fuchsia hedges, had the flower-beds worked in complicated geometrical patterns, marked with smooth white stones. The white cobbled paths, scarcely as wide as a rake's head, wound laboriously round beds hardly larger than a big straw hat, beds in the shape of stars, half-moons, triangles, and circles, all overgrown with a shaggy tangle of flowers run wild. Roses dropped petals that seemed as big and smooth as saucers, flame-red, moon-white, glossy, and unwrinkled: marigolds like broods of shaggy suns stood watching their parent's progress through the sky. In the low growth the pansies pushed their velvety, innocent faces through the leaves, and the violets drooped sorrowfully under their heart-shaped leaves. The bougainvillaea that sprawled luxuriously over the tiny front balcony was hung, as though for a carnival, with its lantern-shaped magenta flowers. In the darkness of the fuchsia hedge a thousand ballerina-like blooms quivered expectantly. The warm air was thick with the scent of a hundred dying flowers, and full of the gentle, soothing whisper and murmur of insects. As soon as we saw it, we wanted to live there – it was as though the villa had been standing there waiting for our arrival. We felt we had come home.

Having lumbered so unexpectedly into our lives, Spiro now took over complete control of our affairs. It was better, he explained, for him to do things, as everyone knew him, and he would make sure we were not swindled.

'Donts you worrys yourselfs about anything, Mrs Durrells,' he had scowled; 'leaves everythings to me.'

So he would take us shopping, and after an hour's sweating and roaring he would get the price of an article reduced by perhaps two drachmas. This was approximately a penny; it was not the cash, but the principle of the thing, he explained. The fact that he was Greek and adored bargaining was, of course, another reason. It was Spiro who, in discovering that our money had not yet arrived from England, subsidized us, and took it upon himself to go and speak severely to the bank manager about his lack of organization. That it was not the poor manager's fault did not deter him in the least. It was Spiro who paid our hotel bill, who organized a cart to carry our luggage to the villa, and who drove us out there himself, his car piled high with groceries that he had purchased for us.

That he knew everyone on the island, and that they all knew him, we soon discovered was no idle boast. Wherever his car stopped, half a dozen voices would shout out his name, and hands would beckon him to sit at the little tables under the trees and drink coffee. Policemen, peasants, and priests waved and smiled as he passed: fishermen, grocers, and café-owners greeted him like a brother. 'Ah, Spiro!' they would say, and smile at him affectionately as though he was a naughty but lovable child. They respected his honesty, his belligerence, and above all they adored his typically Greek scorn and fearlessness when dealing with any form of Governmental red tape. On arrival, two of our cases containing linen and other things had been confiscated by the Customs on the curious grounds that they were merchandise. So, when we moved out to the strawberry-pink villa and the problem of bed-linen arose, Mother told Spiro about our cases languishing in the Customs, and asked his advice.

'Gollys, Mrs Durrells,' he bellowed, his huge face flushing red with wrath; 'whys you never tells me befores? Thems bastards in the Customs. I'll take you down theres tomorrows and fix thems: I knows thems alls, and they knows *me*. Leaves everythings to me – I'll fix thems.'

The following morning he drove Mother down to the Customs shed. We all accompanied them, for we did not want to miss the fun. Spiro rolled into the Customs-house like an angry bear.

'Wheres these peoples things?' he inquired of the plump little Customs man.

'You mean their boxes of merchandise?' asked the Customs official in his best English.

'Whats you thinks I means?'

'They are here,' admitted the official cautiously.

'We've comes to takes thems,' scowled Spiro; 'gets thems ready.'

He turned and stalked out of the shed to find someone to help carry the luggage, and when he returned he saw that the Customs man who had taken the keys from Mother was just lifting the lid of one of the cases. Spiro, with a grunt of wrath, surged forward, and slammed the lid down on the unfortunate man's fingers.

'Whats fors you open it, you sonofabitch?' he asked, glaring.

The Customs official, waving his pinched hand about, protested wildly that it was his duty to examine the contents.

'Dutys?' said Spiro with fine scorn. 'Whats you means, dutys? Is it your dutys to attacks innocent foreigners, eh? Treats thems like smugglers, eh? Thats what you calls dutys?'

Spiro paused for a moment, breathing deeply, then he picked up a large suitcase in each great hand and walked towards the door. He paused and turned to fire his parting shot.

'I knows you, Christaki, sos donts you go talkings about dutys to me. I remembers when you was fined twelve thousand drachmas for dynamitings fish. I won't have any criminal talkings to *me* abouts dutys.'

We rode back from the Customs in triumph, all our luggage intact and unexamined.

'Thems bastards thinks they owns the islands,' was Spiro's comment. He seemed quite unaware of the fact that he was acting as though he did.

Once Spiro had taken charge he stuck to us like a burr. Within a few hours he had changed from taxi-driver to our champion, and within a week he was our guide, philosopher, and friend. He became so much a member of the family that very soon there was scarcely a thing we did, or planned to do, in which he was not involved in some way. He was always there, bull-voiced and scowling, arranging things we wanted done, telling us how much to pay for things, keeping a watchful eye on us all, and reporting to Mother anything he thought she should know. Like a great, brown, ugly angel he watched over us as tenderly as though we were slightly weak-minded children. Mother he frankly adored, and he would sing her praises in a loud voice wherever we happened to be, to her acute embarrassment.

'You oughts to be carefuls whats you do,' he would tell us, screwing up his face earnestly; 'we donts wants to worrys your mothers.'

'Whatever for, Spiro?' Larry would protest in well-simulated astonishment. 'She's never done anything for us . . . why should we consider her?'

'Gollys, Master Lorrys, donts *jokes* like that,' Spiro would say in anguish.

'He's quite right, Spiro,' Leslie would say very seriously; 'she's really not much good as a mother, you know.'

'Donts says that, *donts says that*,' Spiro would roar. 'Honest to Gods, if I hads a mother likes yours I'd gos down every mornings and kisses her feets.'

So we were installed in the villa, and we each settled down and adapted ourselves to our surroundings in our respective ways. Margo, merely by donning a microscopic swim-suit and sun-bathing in the olive-groves, had collected an ardent band of handsome peasant youths who appeared like magic from an apparently deserted landscape whenever a bee flew too near her or her deckchair needed moving. Mother felt forced to point out that she thought this sun-bathing was rather *unwise*.

'After all, dear, that costume doesn't cover an awful lot, does it?' she pointed out.

'Oh, Mother, don't be so old-fashioned,' Margo said impatiently. 'After all, you only die once.'

This remark was as baffling as it was true, and successfully silenced Mother.

It had taken three husky peasant boys half an hour's sweating and panting to get Larry's trunks into the villa, while Larry bustled round them, directing operations. One of the trunks was so big it had to be hoisted in through the window. Once they were installed, Larry spent a happy day unpacking them, and the room was so full of books that it was almost impossible to get in or out. Having constructed battlements of books round the outer perimeter, Larry would spend the whole day in there with his typewriter, only emerging dreamily for meals. On the second morning he appeared in a highly irritable frame of mind, for a peasant had tethered his donkey just

over the hedge. At regular intervals the beast would throw out its head and
let forth a prolonged and lugubrious bray.

'I ask you! Isn't it laughable that future generations should be deprived
of my work simply because some horny-handed idiot has tied that stinking
beast of burden near my window?' Larry asked.

'Yes, dear,' said Mother; 'why don't you move it if it disturbs you?'

'My dear Mother, I can't be expected to spend my time chasing donkeys
about the olive-groves. I threw a pamphlet on Christian Science at it: what
more do you expect me to do?'

'The poor thing's tied up. You can't expect it to untie itself,' said Margo.

'There should be a law against parking those loathsome beasts anywhere
near a house. Can't one of you go and move it?'

'Why should we? It's not disturbing us,' said Leslie.

'That's the trouble with this family,' said Larry bitterly: 'no give and take,
no consideration for others.'

'*You* don't have much consideration for others,' said Margo.

'It's all your fault, Mother,' said Larry austerely; 'you shouldn't have
brought us up to be so selfish.'

'I like that!' exclaimed Mother. 'I never did anything of the sort!'

'Well, we didn't get as selfish as this without *some* guidance.' said Larry.

In the end, Mother and I unhitched the donkey and moved it farther
down the hill.

Leslie meanwhile had unpacked his revolvers and startled us all with an
apparently endless series of explosions while he fired at an old tin can from
his bedroom window. After a particularly deafening morning, Larry erupted
from his room and said he could not be expected to work if the villa was
going to be rocked to its foundations every five minutes. Leslie, aggrieved,
said that he had to practise. Larry said it didn't sound like practice, but
more like the Indian Mutiny. Mother, whose nerves had also been somewhat
frayed by the reports, suggested that Leslie practise with an empty revolver.
Leslie spent half an hour explaining why this was impossible. At length he
reluctantly took his tin farther away from the house where the noise was
slightly muffled but just as unexpected.

In between keeping a watchful eye on us all, Mother was settling down
in her own way. The house was redolent with the scent of herbs and the
sharp tang of garlic and onions, and the kitchen was full of a bubbling
selection of pots, among which she moved, spectacles askew, muttering to

herself. On the table was a tottering pile of books which she consulted from time to time. When she could drag herself away from the kitchen, she would drift happily about the garden, reluctantly pruning and cutting, enthusiastically weeding and planting.

For myself, the garden held sufficient interest; together Roger and I learnt some surprising things. Roger, for example, found that it was unwise to smell hornets, that the peasant dogs ran screaming if he glanced at them through the gate, and that the chickens that leapt suddenly from the fuchsia hedge, squawking wildly as they fled, were unlawful prey, however desirable.

This doll's-house garden was a magic land, a forest of flowers through which roamed creatures I had never seen before. Among the thick, silky petals of each rose-bloom lived tiny, crab-like spiders that scuttled sideways when disturbed. Their small, translucent bodies were coloured to match the flowers they inhabited: pink, ivory, wine-red, or buttery-yellow. On the rose-stems, encrusted with greenflies, lady-birds moved like newly painted toys: lady-birds pale red with large black spots; lady-birds apple-red with brown spots; lady-birds orange with grey-and-black freckles. Rotund and amiable, they prowled and fed among the anaemic flocks of greenfly. Carpenter bees, like furry, electric-blue bears, zigzagged among the flowers, growling fatly and busily. Humming-bird hawk-moths, sleek and neat, whipped up and down the paths with a fussy efficiency, pausing occasionally on speed-misty wings to lower a long, slender proboscis into a bloom. Among the white cobbles large black ants staggered and gesticulated in groups round strange trophies: a dead caterpillar, a piece of rose-petal, or dried grass-head fat with seeds. As an accompaniment to all this activity there came from the olive-groves outside the fuchsia hedge the incessant shimmering cries of the cicadas. If the curious, blurring heat-haze produced a sound, it would be exactly the strange, chiming cries of these insects.

At first I was so bewildered by this profusion of life on our very doorstep that I could only move about the garden in a daze, watching now this creature, now that, constantly having my attention distracted by the flights of brilliant butterflies that drifted over the hedge. Gradually, as I became more used to the bustle of insect life among the flowers, I found I could concentrate more. I would spend hours squatting on my heels or lying on my stomach watching the private lives of the creatures around me, while Roger sat nearby, a look of resignation on his face. In this way I learnt a lot of fascinating things.

I found that the little crab-spiders could change colour just as successfully as any chameleon. Take a spider from a wine-red rose, where he had been sitting like a bead of coral, and place him in the depths of a cool white rose. If he stayed there – and most of them did – you would see his colour gradually ebb away, as though the change had given him anaemia, until, some two days later, he would be crouching among the white petals like a pearl.

I discovered that in the dry leaves under the fuchsia hedge lived another type of spider, a fierce little huntsman with the cunning and ferocity of a tiger. He would stalk about his continent of leaves, eyes glistening in the sun, pausing now and then to raise himself up on his hairy legs to peer about. If he saw a fly settle to enjoy a sun-bath he would freeze; then, as slowly as a leaf growing, he would move forward, imperceptibly, edging nearer and nearer, pausing occasionally to fasten his life-line of silk to the surface of the leaves. Then, when close enough, the huntsman would pause, his legs shift minutely as he got a good purchase, and then he would leap, legs spread out in a hairy embrace, straight on to the dreaming fly. Never did I see one of these little spiders miss its kill, once it had manoeuvred into the right position.

All these discoveries filled me with a tremendous delight, so that they had to be shared, and I would burst suddenly into the house and startle the family with the news that the strange, spiky black caterpillars on the roses were not caterpillars at all, but the young of lady-birds, or with the equally astonishing news that lacewing-flies laid eggs on stilts. This last miracle I was lucky enough to witness. I found a lacewing-fly on the roses and watched her as she climbed about the leaves, admiring her beautiful, fragile wings like green glass, and her enormous liquid golden eyes. Presently she stopped on the surface of a rose-leaf and lowered the tip of her abdomen. She remained like that for a moment and then raised her tail, and from it, to my astonishment, rose a slender thread, like a pale hair. Then, on the very tip of this stalk, appeared the egg. The female had a rest, and then repeated the performance until the surface of the rose-leaf looked as though it was covered with a forest of tiny club moss. The laying over, the female rippled her antennae briefly and flew off in a mist of green gauze wings.

Perhaps the most exciting discovery I made in this multi-coloured Lilliput to which I had access was an earwig's nest. I had long wanted to find one and had searched everywhere without success, so the joy of stumbling upon one unexpectedly was overwhelming, like suddenly being given a wonderful present. I moved a piece of bark and there beneath it was the nursery, a small hollow in the earth that the insect must have burrowed out for herself. She squatted in the middle of it, shielding underneath her a few white eggs. She crouched over them like a hen, and did not move when the flood of sunlight struck her as I lifted the bark. I could not count the eggs, but there did not seem to be many, so I presumed that she had not yet laid her full complement. Tenderly I replaced her lid of bark.

From that moment I guarded the nest jealously. I erected a protecting wall of rocks round it, and as an additional precaution I wrote out a notice in red ink and stuck it on a pole nearby as a warning to the family. The notice read: 'BEWAR – EARWIG NEST – QUIAT PLESE.' It was only remarkable in that the two correctly spelt words were biological ones. Every hour or so I would subject the mother earwig to ten minutes' close scrutiny. I did not dare examine her more often for fear she might desert her nest. Eventually the pile of eggs beneath her grew, and she seemed to have become accustomed to my lifting off her bark roof. I even decided that she had begun to recognize me, from the friendly way she waggled her antennae.

To my acute disappointment, after all my efforts and constant sentry duty, the babies hatched out during the night. I felt that, after all I had done, the female might have held up the hatching until I was there to witness it. However, there they were, a fine brood of young earwigs, minute, frail, looking as though they had been carved out of ivory. They moved gently under their mother's body, walking between her legs, the more venturesome even climbing on to her pincers. It was a heart-warming sight. The next day the nursery was empty: my wonderful family had scattered over the garden. I saw one of the babies some time later: he was bigger, of course, browner and stronger, but I recognized him immediately. He was curled up in a maze of rose-petals, having a sleep and when I disturbed him he merely raised his pincers irritably over his back. I would have liked to think that it was a salute, a cheerful greeting, but honesty compelled me to admit that it was nothing more than an earwig's warning to a potential enemy. Still, I excused him. After all, he had been very young when I last saw him.

I came to know the plump peasant girls who passed the garden every morning and evening. Riding side-saddle on their slouching, drooping-eared donkeys, they were shrill and colourful as parrots, and their chatter and laughter echoed among the olive-trees. In the mornings they would smile and shout greetings as their donkeys pattered past, and in the evenings they would lean over the fuchsia hedge, balancing precariously on their steeds' backs, and smiling, hold out gifts for me – a bunch of amber grapes still sun-warmed, some figs black as tar striped with pink where they had burst their seams with ripeness, or a giant water-melon with an inside like pink ice. As the days passed, I came gradually to understand them. What had at first been a confused babble became a series of recognizable separate sounds. Then, suddenly, these took on meaning, and slowly and haltingly I started to use them myself: then I took my newly acquired words and strung them into ungrammatical and stumbling sentences. Our neighbours were delighted, as though I had conferred some delicate compliment by trying to learn their language. They would lean over the hedge, their faces screwed up with concentration, as I groped my way through a greeting or a simple remark, and when I had successfully concluded they would beam at me, nodding and smiling, and clap their hands. By degrees I learnt their names, who was related to whom, which were married and which hoped to be, and other details. I learnt where their little cottages were among the olive-groves, and should Roger and I chance to pass that way the entire family, vociferous and pleased, would tumble out to greet us, to bring a chair, so that I might sit under their vine and eat some fruit with them.

Gradually the magic of the island settled over us as gently and clingingly as pollen. Each day had a tranquillity, a timelessness, about it, so that you wished it would never end. But then the dark skin of night would peel off and there would be a fresh day waiting for us, glossy and colourful as a child's transfer and with the same tinge of unreality.

*   *   *

A tiny green grasshopper with a long, melancholy face sat twitching his hind legs nervously. A fragile snail sat on a moss sprig, meditating and waiting for the evening dew. A plump scarlet mite, the size of a match-head, struggled like a tubby huntsman through the forest of moss. It was a micro-scopic world, full of fascinating life. As I watched the mite making his slow progress I noticed a curious thing. Here and there on the green plush surface of the moss were scattered faint circular marks, each the size of a shilling. So faint were they that it was only from certain angles they were noticeable at all. They reminded me of a full moon seen behind thick clouds, a faint circle that seemed to shift and change. I wondered idly what could have made them. They were too irregular, too scattered to be the prints of some beast, and what was it that would walk up an almost vertical bank in such a haphazard manner? Besides, they were not like imprints. I prodded the edge of one of these circles with a piece of grass. It remained unmoved. I began to think the mark was caused by some curious way in which the moss grew. I probed again, more vigorously, and suddenly my stomach gave a clutch of tremendous excitement. It was as though my grass-stalk had found a hidden spring, for the whole circle lifted up like a trapdoor. As I stared, I saw to my amazement that it *was* in fact a trapdoor, lined with silk, and with a neatly bevelled edge that fitted snugly into the mouth of the silk-lined shaft it concealed. The edge of the door was fastened to the lip of the tunnel by a small flap of silk that acted as a hinge. I gazed at this magnificent piece of workmanship and wondered what on earth could have made it. Peering down the silken tunnel, I could see nothing; I poked my grass-stalk down, but there was no response. For a long time I sat staring at this fantastic home, trying to decide what sort of beast had made it. I thought that it might be a wasp of some sort, but had never heard of a wasp that fitted its nest with secret doors. I felt that I must get to the bottom of this problem immediately. I would go down and ask George [Gerry's tutor at the time] if he knew what this mysterious beast was. Calling Roger, who was busily trying to uproot an olive-tree, I set off at a brisk trot.

I arrived at George's villa out of breath, bursting with suppressed excitement, gave a perfunctory knock at the door, and dashed in. Only then did I realize he had company. Seated in a chair near him was a figure which, at first glance, I decided must be George's brother, for he also wore a beard. He was, however, in contrast to George, immaculately dressed in a grey flannel suit with waistcoat, a spotless white shirt, a tasteful but sombre tie, and large, solid, highly polished boots. I paused on the threshold, embarrassed, while George surveyed me sardonically.

'Good evening,' he greeted me. 'From the joyful speed of your entry I take it that you have not come for a little extra tuition.'

I apologized for the intrusion, and then told George about the curious nests I had found.

'Thank heavens you're here, Theodore,' he said to his bearded companion. 'I shall now be able to hand the problem over to expert hands.'

'Hardly an expert . . .' mumbled the man called Theodore, deprecatingly.

'Gerry, this is Doctor Theodore Stephanides,' said George. 'He is an expert on practically everything you care to mention. And what you don't mention, he does. He, like you, is an eccentric nature-lover. Theodore, this is Gerry Durrell.'

I said how do you do, politely, but to my surprise the bearded man rose to his feet, stepped briskly across the room, and held out a large white hand.

'Very pleased to meet you,' he said, apparently addressing his beard, and gave me a quick, shy glance from twinkling blue eyes.

I shook his hand and said I was very pleased to meet him, too. Then we stood in awkward silence, while George watched us, grinning.

'Well, Theodore,' he said at last, 'and what d'you think produced these strange secret passages?'

Theodore clasped his hands behind his back, lifted himself on to his toes several times, his boots squeaking protestingly, and gravely considered the floor.

'Well . . . er . . .' he said, his words coming slowly and meticulously, 'it sounds to me as though they might be the burrows of the trapdoor spider . . . er . . . it is a species which is quite common here in Corfu . . . that is to say, when I say common, I suppose I have found some thirty or . . . er . . . forty specimens during the time I have been here.'

'Ah,' said George, 'trapdoor spiders, eh?'

'Yes,' said Theodore. 'I feel that it's more than probable that that is what they are. However, I may be mistaken.'

He rose and fell on his toes, squeaking gently, and then he shot me a keen glance.

'Perhaps, if they are not too far away, we could go and verify it,' he suggested tentatively. 'I mean to say, if you have nothing better to do, and it's not too far . . .'

His voice trailed away on a faintly interrogative note. I said that they were only just up the hill, not really far.

'Um,' said Theodore.

'Don't let him drag you about all over the place, Theodore,' said George. 'You don't want to be galloped about the countryside.'

'No, no, not at all,' said Theodore; 'I was just about to leave, and I can easily walk that way back. It is quite a simple matter for me to ... er ... cut down through the olive-groves and reach Canoni.'

He picked up a neat grey homburg and placed it squarely on his head. At the door he held out his hand and shook George's briefly.

'Thank you for a delightful tea,' he said, and stumped gravely off along the path by my side.

As we walked along I studied him covertly. He had a straight, well-shaped nose; a humorous mouth lurking in the ash-blond beard: straight, rather bushy eyebrows under which his eyes, keen but with a twinkle in them and laughter-wrinkles at the corners, surveyed the world. He strode along energetically, humming to himself. When we came to a ditch full of stagnant water he stopped for a moment and stared down into it, his beard bristling.

'Um,' he said conversationally, '*Daphnia magna*.'

He rasped at his beard with his thumb, and then set off down the path again.

'Unfortunately,' he said to me, 'I was coming out to see some people ... er ... *friends* of mine, and so I did not bring my collecting bag with me. It is a pity, for that ditch might have contained something.'

When we branched off the fairly smooth path we had been travelling along and started up the stony goat-track, I expected some sort of protest, but Theodore strode behind me with unabated vigour, still humming. At length we came to the gloomy olive-grove, and I led Theodore to the bank and pointed out the mysterious trapdoor.

He peered down at it, his eyes narrowed.

'Ah ha,' he said, 'yes ... um ... yes.'

He produced from his waistcoat pocket a tiny penknife, opened it, inserted the point of the blade delicately under the little door and flipped it back.

'Um, yes,' he repeated; '*Cteniza*.'

He peered down the tunnel, blew down it, and then let the trapdoor fall into place again.

'Yes, they are the burrows of the trapdoor spiders,' he said, 'but this one does not appear to be inhabited. Generally, the creature will hold on to the ... er ... *trapdoor*... with her legs, or rather, her *claws*, and she holds on with such tenacity that you have to be careful or you will damage the door, trying to force it open. Um ... yes ... these are the burrows of the females, of course. The male makes a similar burrow, but it is only about half the size.'

I remarked that it was the most curious structure I had seen.

'Ah ha! yes,' said Theodore, 'they are certainly very curious. A thing that always puzzles me is how the female knows when the male is approaching.'

I must have looked blank, for he teetered on his toes, shot me a quick look, and went on:

'The spider, of course, waits inside its burrow until some insect – a fly or a grasshopper, or something similar – chances to walk past. They can judge, it seems, whether the insect is close enough to be caught. If it is, the spider ... er ... pops out of its hole and catches the creature. Now when the male comes in search of the female he must walk over the moss to the trapdoor, and I have often wondered why it is that he is not ... er ... devoured by the female in mistake. It is possible, of course, that his footsteps sound different. Or he may make some sort of ... you know ... some sort of *sound* which the female recognizes.'

We walked down the hill in silence. When we reached the place where the paths forked I said that I must leave him.

'Ah, well, I'll say goodbye,' he said, staring at his boots. 'I have enjoyed meeting you.'

We stood in silence for a moment. Theodore was afflicted with the acute embarrassment that always seemed to overwhelm him when greeting or saying goodbye to someone. He stared hard at his boots for a moment longer, and then he held out his hand and shook mine gravely.

'Goodbye,' he said. 'I ... er ... I expect we shall meet again.'

He turned and stumped off down the hill, swinging his stick, staring about him with observant eyes. I watched him out of sight and then walked slowly in the direction of the villa. I was at once confused and amazed by Theodore. First, since he was obviously a scientist of considerable repute (and I could have told this by his beard), he was to me a person of great importance. In fact he was the only person I had met until now who seemed to share my enthusiasm for zoology. Secondly, I was extremely flattered to find that he treated me and talked to me exactly as though I was his own age. I liked him for this, as I was not talked down to by my family, and I took rather a poor view of any outsider trying to do so. But Theodore not only talked to me as though I was grown up, but also as though I was as knowledgeable as he.

The facts he told me about the trapdoor spider haunted me: the idea of the creature crouching in its silken tunnel, holding the door closed with its hooked claws, listening to the movement of the insects on the moss above. What, I wondered, did things sound like to a trapdoor spider? I could imagine that a snail would trail over the door with a noise like sticking-plaster being slowly torn off. A centipede would sound like a troop of cavalry. A fly would patter in brisk spurts, followed by a pause while it washed its hands – a dull rasping sound like a knife-grinder at work. The larger beetles, I decided, would sound like steamrollers, while the smaller ones, the lady-birds and others, would probably purr over the moss like clockwork motor-cars. Fascinated by this thought, I made my way back home through the darkening fields, to tell the family of my new discovery and of my meeting with Theodore. I hoped to see him again, for there were many things I wanted to ask him, but I felt it would be unlikely that he would have very much time to spare for me. I was mistaken, however, for two days later Leslie came back from an excursion into the town, and handed me a small parcel.

'Met that bearded johnny,' he said laconically; 'you know, that scientist bloke. Said this was for you.'

Incredulously I stared at the parcel. Surely it couldn't be for me? There must be some mistake, for a great scientist would hardly bother to send me parcels. I turned it over, and there, written on it in neat, spidery writing, was my name. I tore off the paper as quickly as I could. Inside was a small box and a letter.

My dear Gerry Durrell,
I wondered, after our conversation the other day, if it might not assist your investigations of the local natural history to have some form of magnifying instrument. I am therefore sending you this pocket microscope, in the hope that it will be of some use to you. It is, of course, not of very high magnification, but you will find it sufficient for *field* work.

> With best wishes
> Yours sincerely,
> Theo. Stephanides

P. S. If you have nothing better to do on Thursday, perhaps you would care to come to tea, and I could then show you some of my microscope slides.

*   *   *

During the last days of the dying summer, and throughout the warm, wet winter that followed, tea with Theodore became a weekly affair. Every Thursday I would set out, my pockets bulging with matchboxes and test-tubes full of specimens, to be driven into the town by Spiro. It was an appointment that I would not have missed for anything.

Theodore would welcome me in his study, a room that met with my full approval. It was, in my opinion, just what a room should be. The walls were lined with tall bookshelves filled with volumes on freshwater biology, botany, astronomy, medicine, folk-lore, and similar fascinating and sensible subjects. Interspersed with these were selections of ghost and crime stories. Thus Sherlock Holmes rubbed shoulders with Darwin, and Le Fanu with Fabre, in what I considered to be a thoroughly well-balanced library. At one window of the room stood Theodore's telescope, its nose to the sky like a howling dog, while the sills of every window bore a parade of jars and bottles containing minute freshwater fauna, whirling and twitching among the delicate fronds of green weed. On one side of the room was a massive desk, piled high with scrapbooks, micro-photographs, X-ray plates, diaries, and note-books. On the opposite side of the room was the micro-scope table, with its powerful lamp on the jointed stem leaning like a lily over the flat boxes that housed Theodore's collection of slides. The microscopes themselves, gleaming like magpies, were housed under a series of beehive-like domes of glass.

'How are you?' Theodore would inquire, as if I were a complete stranger, and give me his characteristic handshake – a sharp downward tug, like a man testing a knot in a rope. The formalities being over, we could then turn our minds to more important topics.

'I was ... er ... you know ... looking through my slides just before your arrival, and I came across one which may interest you. It is a slide of the mouth-parts of the rat flea ... *Ceratophyllus fasciatus*, you know. Now, I'll just adjust the microscope ... There! ... you see? Very curious. I mean to say, you could almost imagine it was a human face, couldn't you? Now I had another ... er ... slide here ... That's funny. Ah! got it. Now this one is of the spinnerets of the garden or cross spider ... er ... *Epeira fasciata* ...'

So, absorbed and happy, we would pore over the microscope. Filled with enthusiasm, we would tack from subject to subject, and if Theodore could not answer my ceaseless flow of questions himself, he had books that could. Gaps would appear in the bookcase as volume after volume was extracted to be consulted, and by our side would be an ever-growing pile of volumes.

'Now this one is a cyclops . . . *Cyclops viridis.* . . which I caught out near Govino the other day. It is a female with egg-sacs . . . Now, I'll just adjust . . . you'll be able to see the eggs quite clearly . . . I'll just put her in the live box . . . er . . . hum . . . there are several species of cyclops found here in Corfu . . .'

Into the brilliant circle of white light a weird creature would appear, a pear-shaped body, long antennae that twitched indignantly, a tail like sprigs of heather, and on each side of it (slung like sacks of onions on a donkey) the two large sacs bulging with pink beads.

'. . . called cyclops because, as you can see, it has a single eye situated in the centre of its forehead. That's to say, in the centre of what *would* be its forehead if a cyclops had one. In Ancient Greek mythology, as you know, a cyclops was one of a group of giants . . . er . . . each of whom had one eye. Their task was to forge iron for Hephaestus.'

Outside, the warm wind would shoulder the shutters, making them creak, and the rain-drops would chase each other down the window-pane like transparent tadpoles.

'Ah ha! It is curious that you should mention that. The peasants in Salonika have a very similar . . . er . . . superstition . . . No, no, merely a superstition. I have a book here that gives a most *interesting* account of vampires in . . . um . . . Bosnia. It seems that the local people there . . .'

Tea would arrive, the cakes squatting on cushions of cream, toast in a melting shawl of butter, cups a-gleam, and a faint wisp of steam rising from the teapot spout.

'. . . but, on the other hand, it is impossible to say that there is *no* life on Mars. It is, in my opinion, quite possible that some form of life will be found . . . er . . . *discovered* there, should we ever succeed in *getting* there. But there is no reason to suppose that any form of life found there would be identical . . .'

Sitting there, neat and correct in his tweed suit, Theodore would chew his toast slowly and methodically, his beard bristling his eyes kindling with enthusiasm at each new subject that swam into our conversation. To me his knowledge seemed inexhaustible. He was a rich vein of information, and I mined him assiduously. No matter what the subject, Theodore could contribute something interesting to it. At last I would hear Spiro honking his horn in the street below, and I would rise reluctantly to go.

*   *   *

The crumbling wall that surrounded the sunken garden alongside the house was a rich hunting ground for me. It was an ancient brick wall that had been plastered over, but now this outer skin was green with moss, bulging and sagging with the damp of many winters. The whole surface was an intricate map of cracks, some several inches wide, others as fine as hairs. Here and there large pieces had dropped off and revealed the rows of rose-pink bricks lying beneath like ribs. There was a whole landscape on this wall if you peered closely enough to see it: the roofs of a hundred tiny toadstools, red, yellow, and brown, showed in patches like villages on the damper portions; mountains of bottle-green moss grew in tuffets so symmetrical that they might have been planted and trimmed; forests of small ferns sprouted from cracks in the shady places, drooping languidly like little green fountains. The top of the wall was a desert land, too dry for anything except a few rust-red mosses to live in it, too hot for anything except sun-bathing by the dragon-flies. At the base of the wall grew a mass of plants, cyclamen, crocus, asphodel, thrusting their leaves among the piles of broken and chipped roof-tiles that lay there. This whole strip was guarded by a labyrinth of blackberry hung, in season, with fruit that was plump and juicy and black as ebony.

The inhabitants of the wall were a mixed lot, and they were divided into day and night workers, the hunters and the hunted. At night the hunters were the toads that lived among the brambles, and the geckos, pale, translucent with bulging eyes, that lived in the cracks higher up the wall. Their prey was the population of stupid, absent-minded crane-flies that zoomed and barged their way among the leaves; moths of all sizes and shapes, moths striped, tessellated, checked, spotted, and blotched, that fluttered in soft clouds along the withered plaster; the beetles, rotund and neatly clad as business men, hurrying with portly efficiency about their night's work. When the last glow-worm had dragged his frosty emerald lantern to bed over the hills of moss, and the sun rose, the wall was taken over by the next set of inhabitants. Here it was more difficult to differentiate between the prey and the predators, for everything seemed to feed indiscriminately

off everything else. Thus the hunting wasps searched out caterpillars and
spiders; the spiders hunted for flies; the dragon-flies, big, brittle, and
hunting-pink, fed off the spiders and the flies; and the swift, lithe,
and multi-coloured wall lizards fed off everything.

But the shyest and most self-effacing of the wall community were the
most dangerous; you hardly ever saw one unless you looked for it, and yet
there must have been several hundred living in the cracks of the wall. Slide
a knife-blade carefully under a piece of the loose plaster and lever it gently
away from the brick, and there, crouching beneath it, would be a little black
scorpion an inch long, looking as though he were made out of polished
chocolate. They were weird-looking things, with their flattened, oval bodies,
their neat, crooked legs, the enormous crab-like claws, bulbous and neatly
jointed as armour, and the tail like a string of brown beads ending in a
sting like a rose-thorn. The scorpion would lie there quite quietly as you
examined him, only raising his tail in an almost apologetic gesture of warning if you breathed too hard on him. If you kept him in the sun too long
he would simply turn his back on you and walk away, and then slide slowly
but firmly under another section of plaster.

I grew very fond of these scorpions. I found them to be pleasant, unassum-
ing creatures with, on the whole, the most charming habits. Provided you
did nothing silly or clumsy (like putting your hand on one) the scorpions
treated you with respect, their one desire being to get away and hide as
quickly as possible. They must have found me rather a trial, for I was always
ripping sections of the plaster away so that I could watch them, or capturing
them and making them walk about in jam-jars so that I could see the way
their feet moved. By means of my sudden and unexpected assaults on the
wall I discovered quite a bit about the scorpions. I found that they would
eat bluebottles (though how they caught them was a mystery I never solved),
grasshoppers, moths, and lacewing-flies. Several times I found them eating
each other, a habit I found most distressing in a creature otherwise so
impeccable.

By crouching under the wall at night with a torch, I managed to catch
some brief glimpses of the scorpions' wonderful courtship dances. I saw
them standing, claws clasped, their bodies raised to the skies, their tails
lovingly entwined; I saw them waltzing slowly in circles among the moss
cushions, claw in claw. But my view of these performances was all too short,
for almost as soon as I switched on the torch the partners would stop,

pause for moment, and then, seeing that I was not going to extinguish the light, they would turn round and walk firmly away, claw in claw, side by side. They were definitely beasts that believed in keeping themselves *to* themselves. If I could have kept a colony in captivity I would probably have been able to see the whole of the courtship, but the family had forbidden scorpions in the house, despite my arguments in favour of them.

Then one day I found a fat female scorpion in the wall, wearing what at first glance appeared to be a pale fawn fur coat. Closer inspection proved that this strange garment was made up of a mass of tiny babies clinging to the mother's back. I was enraptured by this family, and I made up my mind to smuggle them into the house and up to my bedroom so that I might keep them and watch them grow up. With infinite care I manoeuvred the mother and family into a matchbox, and then hurried to the villa. It was rather unfortunate that just as I entered the door lunch should be served; however, I placed the matchbox carefully on the mantelpiece in the drawing-room, so that the scorpions should get plenty of air, and made my way to the dining-room and joined the family for the meal. Dawdling over my food, feeding Roger surreptitiously under the table and listening to the family arguing, I completely forgot about my exciting new captures. At last Larry, having finished, fetched the cigarettes from the drawing-room, and lying back in his chair he put one in his mouth and picked up the match-box he had brought. Oblivious of my impending doom I watched him interestedly as, still talking glibly, he opened the matchbox.

Now I maintain to this day that the female scorpion meant no harm. She was agitated and a trifle annoyed at being shut up in a matchbox for so long, and so she seized the first opportunity to escape. She hoisted herself out of the box with great rapidity, her babies clinging on desperately, and scuttled on to the back of Larry's hand. There, not quite certain what to do next, she paused, her sting curved up at the ready. Larry, feeling the movement of her claws, glanced down to see what it was, and from that moment things got increasingly confused.

He uttered a roar of fright that made Lugaretzia drop a plate and brought Roger out from beneath the table, barking wildly. With a flick of his hand he sent the unfortunate scorpion flying down the table, and she landed midway between Margo and Leslie, scattering babies like confetti as she thumped on the cloth. Thoroughly enraged at this treatment, the creature sped towards Leslie, her sting quivering with emotion. Leslie leapt to his feet, overturning his chair, and flicked out desperately with his napkin, sending the scorpion rolling across the cloth towards Margo, who promptly let out a scream that any railway engine would have been proud to produce. Mother, completely bewildered by this sudden and rapid change from peace to chaos, put on her glasses and peered down the table to see what was causing the pandemonium, and at that moment Margo, in a vain attempt to stop the scorpion's advance, hurled a glass of water at it. The shower missed the animal completely, but successfully drenched Mother, who, not being able to stand cold water, promptly lost her breath and sat gasping at the end of the table, unable even to protest. The scorpion had now gone to ground under Leslie's plate, while her babies swarmed wildly all over the table. Roger, mystified by the panic, but determined to do his share, ran round and round the room, barking hysterically.

'It's that bloody boy again . . .' bellowed Larry.

'Look out! Look out! They're coming!' screamed Margo.

'All we need is a book,' roared Leslie; 'don't panic, hit 'em with a book.'

'What on earth's the *matter* with you all?' Mother kept imploring, mopping her glasses.

'It's that bloody boy . . . he'll kill the lot of us . . . Look at the table . . . knee-deep in scorpions . . .'

'Quick . . . quick . . . do something . . . Look out, look out!'

'Stop screeching and get a book, for God's sake . . . You're worse than the dog . . . Shut *up*, Roger . . .'

'By the Grace of God I wasn't bitten . . .'

'Look out . . . there's another one . . . Quick . . . quick . . .'

'Oh, shut up and get me a book or something . . .'

'But *how* did the scorpions get on the table, dear?'

'That bloody boy . . . Every matchbox in the house is a deathtrap . . .'

'Look out, it's coming towards me . . . Quick, quick, do something . . .'

'Hit it with your knife . . . *your knife*. . . Go on, hit it . . .'

Since no one had bothered to explain things to him, Roger was under the mistaken impression that the family were being attacked, and that it was his duty to defend them. As Lugaretzia was the only stranger in the room, he came to the logical conclusion that she must be the responsible party, so he bit her in the ankle. This did not help matters very much.

By the time a certain amount of order had been restored, all the baby scorpions had hidden themselves under various plates and bits of cutlery.

Eventually, after impassioned pleas on my part, backed up by Mother, Leslie's suggestion that the whole lot be slaughtered was quashed. While the family, still simmering with rage and fright, retired to the drawing-room. I spent half an hour rounding up the babies, picking them up in a teaspoon, and returning them to their mother's back. Then I carried them outside on a saucer and, with the utmost reluctance, released them on the garden wall. Roger and I went and spent the afternoon on the hillside, for I felt it would be prudent to allow the family to have a siesta before seeing them again.

The results of this incident were numerous. Larry developed a phobia about matchboxes and opened them with the utmost caution, a handkerchief wrapped round his hand. Lugaretzia limped round the house, her ankle enveloped in yards of bandage, for weeks after the bite had healed, and came round every morning, with the tea, to show us how the scabs were getting on. But, from my point of view, the worst repercussion of the whole affair was that Mother decided I was running wild again, and that it was high time I received a little more education.

*   *   *

As the summer drew to a close I found myself, to my delight, once more without a tutor. Mother had discovered that, as she so delicately put it, Margo and Peter were becoming 'too fond of one another'. As the family was unanimous in its disapproval of Peter as a prospective relation by marriage, something obviously had to be done. Leslie's only contribution to the problem was to suggest shooting Peter, a plan that was, for some reason, greeted derisively. I thought it was a splendid idea, but I was in the minority. Larry's suggestion that the happy couple should be sent to live in Athens for a month, in order, as he explained, to get it out of their systems, was quashed by Mother on the grounds of immorality. Eventually Mother dispensed with Peter's services, he left hurriedly and furtively and we had to cope with a tragic, tearful, and wildly indignant Margo, who, dressed in her most flowing and gloomy clothing for the event, played her part magnificently. Mother soothed and uttered gentle platitudes, Larry gave Margo lectures on free love, and Leslie, for reasons best known to himself, decided to play the part of the outraged brother and kept appearing at intervals, brandishing a revolver and threatening to shoot Peter down like a dog if he set foot in the house again. In the midst of all this Margo, tears trickling effectively down her face, made tragic gestures and told us her life was blighted. Spiro, who loved a good dramatic situation as well as anyone, spent his time weeping in sympathy with Margo, and posting various friends of his along the docks to make sure that Peter did not attempt to get back on to the island. We all enjoyed ourselves very much. Just as the thing seemed to be dying a natural death, and Margo was able to eat a whole meal without bursting into tears, she got a note from Peter saying he would return for her. Margo, rather panic-stricken by the idea, showed the note to Mother, and once more the family leapt with enthusiasm into the farce. Spiro doubled his guard on the docks, Leslie oiled his guns and practised on a large cardboard figure pinned to the front of the house, Larry went about alternately urging Margo to disguise herself as a peasant and fly to Peter's arms, or to stop behaving like Camille. Margo, insulted, locked herself in the attic and refused to see anyone except me, as I was the only member of the family who had not taken sides. She lay there, weeping copiously, and reading a volume of Tennyson: occasionally she would break off to consume a large meal – which I carried up on a tray – with undiminished appetite.

Margo stayed closeted in the attic for a week. She was eventually brought down from there by a situation which made a fitting climax to the whole affair. Leslie had discovered that several small items had been vanishing from the Sea Cow, and he suspected the fishermen who rowed past the jetty at night. He decided that he would give the thieves something to think about, so he attached to his bedroom window three long-barrelled shotguns aiming down the hill at the jetty. By an ingenious arrangements of strings he could fire one barrel after the other without even getting out of bed. The range was, of course, too far to do any damage, but the whistling of shot through the olive-leaves and the splashing as it pattered into the sea would, he felt, act as a fairly good deterrent. So carried away was he by his own brilliance that he omitted to mention to anyone that he had constructed his burglar trap.

We had all retired to our rooms and were variously occupied. The house was silent. Outside came the gentle whispering of crickets in the hot night air. Suddenly there came a rapid series of colossal explosions that rocked the house and set all the dogs barking downstairs. I rushed out on to the landing, where pandemonium reigned: the dogs had rushed upstairs in a body to join in the fun, and were leaping about, yelping excitedly. Mother, looking wild and distraught, had rushed out of her bedroom in her voluminous nightie, under the impression that Margo had committed suicide. Larry burst angrily from his room to find out what the row was about, and Margo, under the impression that Peter had returned to claim her and was being slaughtered by Leslie, was fumbling at the lock on the attic door and screaming at the top of her voice.

'She's done something silly . . . she's done something silly . . .' wailed Mother, making frantic endeavours to get herself free from Widdle and Puke, who, thinking this was all a jolly nocturnal romp, had seized the end of her nightie and were tugging at it, growling ferociously.

'It's the limit . . . You can't even sleep in peace . . . This family's driving me mad . . .' bellowed Larry.

'Don't hurt him . . . leave him alone . . . you cowards,' came Margo's voice, shrill and tearful, as she scrabbled wildly in an attempt to get the attic door opened.

'Burglars . . . Keep calm . . . it's only burglars,' yelled Leslie, opening his bedroom door.

'She's still alive . . . she's still alive . . . Get these dogs away . . .'

'You brutes . . . how dare you shoot him? . . . Let me out, *let* me out . . .'

'Stop fussing; it's only burglars . . .'

'Animals and explosions all day, and then bloody great twelve-gun salutes in the middle of the night . . . It's carrying eccentricity too far . . .'

Eventually Mother struggled up to the attic, trailing Widdle and Puke from the hem of her night attire, and, white and shaking, threw open the door to find an equally white and shaking Margo. After a lot of confusion we discovered what had happened, and what each of us had thought. Mother, trembling with shock, reprimanded Leslie severely.

'You mustn't do things like that, dear,' she pointed out. 'It's really stupid. If you fire your guns off do at least let us *know*.'

'Yes,' said Larry bitterly, 'just give us a bit of warning, will you? Shout "Timber", or something of the sort.'

'I don't see how I can be expected to take burglars by surprise if I've got to shout out warnings to you all,' said Leslie aggrievedly.

'I'm damned if I see why we should be taken by surprise too,' said Larry.

'Well, ring a bell or something, dear. Only please don't do that again . . . it's made me feel quite queer.'

But the episode got Margo out of the attic, which, as Mother said, was one mercy.

Gerry wrote two more books about Corfu. The first one began with the family complaining about being lampooned in My Family and Other Animals. *He doesn't spare them, however, but later provides a glimpse of the affection that bonded this extraordinary family in the story of a birthday present. The final piece from the Corfu trilogy was written fully forty years later, but its imagery is as crisp as one of Mother Durrell's brandy snaps, and it tells us that, early on, Gerry's animal collector's instinct never prevented him from letting his furry acquisitions go and rejoicing in their liberty.*

FROM BIRDS, BEASTS, AND RELATIVES:

'I do wish you'd stop harping on Greece,' said Leslie. 'It reminds me of that bloody book of Gerry's. It took me ages to live that down.'

'Took *you* ages?' said Larry caustically. 'What about me? You've no idea what damage that Dickens-like caricature did to my literary image.'

'But the way he wrote about me, you would think I never thought about anything but guns and boats,' said Leslie.

'Well, you never do think about anything but guns and boats.'

'I was the one that suffered most,' said Margo. 'He did nothing but talk about my acne.'

'I thought it was quite an accurate picture of you all,' said Mother, 'but he made me out to be a *positive imbecile.*'

'I wouldn't mind being lampooned in decent prose,' Larry pointed out, blowing his nose vigorously, 'but to be lampooned in bad English is unbearable.'

'The title alone is insulting,' said Margo. '*My Family and Other Animals*! I get sick of people saying, "And which other animal are you?"'

'I thought the title was rather funny, dear,' said Mother. 'The only thing I thought was that he hadn't used all the best stories.'

'Yes, I agree,' said Leslie.

'What best stories?' Larry demanded suspiciously.

'Well, what about the time you sailed Max's yacht round the island? That was damned funny.'

'If that story had appeared in print I would have sued him.'

'I don't see why, it was very funny,' said Margo.

'And what about the time you took up spiritualism – supposing he'd written about that? I suppose you'd enjoy *that*?' inquired Larry caustically.

'No, I would not – he couldn't write that,' said Margo in horror.

'Well, there you are,' said Larry in triumph. 'And what about Leslie's court case?'

'I don't see why you have to bring me into it,' said Leslie.

'You were the one who was going on about him not using the best incidents,' Larry pointed out.

'Yes, I'd forgotten about those stories,' said Mother, chuckling. 'I think they were funnier than the ones you used, Gerry.'

'I'm glad you think that,' I said thoughtfully.

'Why?' asked Larry, glaring at me.

'Because I've decided to write another book on Corfu and use all those stories,' I explained innocently.

The uproar was immediate.

'I forbid it,' roared Larry, sneezing violently. 'I absolutely forbid it.'

*　　*　　*

As I rowed along, I noticed on the smooth waters of the bay what I took to be a large patch of yellow seaweed. Seaweed was always worth investigating, as it invariably contained a host of small life and sometimes, if you were lucky, quite large creatures; so I rowed towards it. But as I got closer, I saw that it was not seaweed, but what appeared to be a yellowish-coloured rock. But what sort of rock could it be that floated in some twenty feet of water? As I looked closer, I saw, to my incredulous delight, that it was a fairly large turtle. Shipping the oars and urging the dogs to silence, I poised myself in the bows and waited, tense with excitement as the *Bootle-bumtrinket* drifted closer and closer. The turtle, outspread, appeared to be floating on the surface of the sea, sound asleep. My problem was to capture him before he woke up. The nets and various other equipment I had in the boat had not been designed for the capture of a turtle measuring some three feet in length, so the only way I felt I could achieve success was by diving in on him, grabbing him, and somehow getting him into the boat before he woke up. In my excitement it never occurred to me that the strength possessed by a turtle of this size was considerable and that it was unlikely he was going to give up without a struggle. When the boat was some six feet away I held my breath and dived. I decided to dive under him so as to cut off his retreat, as it were, and as I plunged into the lukewarm water I uttered a brief prayer that the splash I made would not awaken him and that, even if it did, he would still be too dozy to execute a rapid retreat. I had dived deep and now I turned on my back and there, suspended above me like an enormous golden guinea, was the turtle. I shot up under him and grabbed him firmly by his front flippers, which curved like horny sickles from out of his shell. To my surprise even this action did not wake him, and when I rose, gasping, to the surface, still retaining my grasp on his flippers, and shook the water from my eyes, I discovered the reason. The turtle had been dead for a fair length of time, as my nose and the host of tiny fish nibbling at his scaly limbs told me.

Disappointing though this was, a dead turtle was better than no turtle at all, and so I laboriously towed his body alongside the *Bootle-bumtrinket* and made it fast by one flipper to the side of the boat. The dogs were greatly intrigued, under the impression that this was some exotic and edible delicacy I had procured for their special benefit. The *Bootle-bumtrinket*, owing to her shape, had never been the easiest of craft to steer, and now, with the dead weight of the turtle lashed to one side of her, she showed a tendency to revolve in circles. However, after an hour's strenuous rowing, we arrived safely at the jetty, and having tied up the boat, I then hauled the turtle's carcass on to the shore where I could examine it. It was a hawks-bill turtle, the kind whose shell is used for the manufacture of spectacle frames and whose stuffed carcass you occasionally see in opticians' windows. His head was massive, with a great wrinkled jowl of yellow skin and a swooping beak of a nose that did give him an extraordinarily hawk-like look. The shell was battered in places, presumably by ocean storms or by the snap of a passing shark, and here and there it was decorated with little snow-white clusters of baby barnacles. His underside of pale daffodil-yellow was soft and pliable like thick, damp cardboard.

I had recently conducted a long and fascinating dissection of a dead terrapin that I had found and I felt this would be an ideal opportunity to compare the turtle's internal anatomy with that of his fresh-water brother, so I went up the hill, borrowed the gardener's wheelbarrow, and in it transported my prize up to the house and laid him out in state on the front veranda.

I knew there would be repercussions if I endeavoured to perform my dissection of the turtle inside the house, but I felt that nobody in his right mind would object to the dissection of the turtle on the front veranda. With my notebook at the ready and my row of saws, scalpels, and razor blades neatly laid out as though in an operating theatre, I set to work.

I found that the soft yellow plastern came away quite easily, compared with the underside of the terrapin, which had taken me three quarters of an hour to saw through. When the plastern was free, I lifted it off like a cover off a dish and there, underneath, were all the delicious mysteries of the turtle's internal organs displayed, multi-coloured and odoriferous to a degree. So consumed with curiosity was I that I did not even notice the smell. The dogs, however, who normally considered fresh cow dung to be the ideal scent to add piquancy to their love life, disappeared in a disapproving body, sneezing violently. I discovered, to my delight, that the turtle was a female and had a large quantity of half-formed eggs in her. They were about the size of ping-pong balls, soft, round, and as orange as a nasturtium. There were fourteen of them, and I removed them carefully and laid them in a gleaming, glutinous row on the flagstones. The turtle appeared to have a prodigious quantity of gut, and I decided that I should enter the exact length of this astonishing apparatus in my already blood-stained notebook. With the aid of a scalpel I detached the gut from the rear exit of the turtle and then proceeded to pull it out. It seemed never-ending, but before long I had it all laid out carefully across the veranda in a series of loops and twists, like a rather drunken railway line. One section of it was composed of the stomach, a rather hideous greyish bag like a water-filled balloon. This obviously was full of the turtle's last meal and I felt, in the interests of science, that I ought to check on what it had been eating just prior to its demise. I stuck a scalpel in the great wobbling mound and slashed experimentally. Immediately the whole stomach bag deflated with a ghastly sighing noise and a stench arose from its interior which made all the other smells pale into insignificance. Even I, fascinated as I was by my investigations, reeled back and had to retreat coughing to wait for the smell to subside.

I knew I could get the veranda cleaned up before the family got back from town, but in my excitement with my new acquisition, I had completely overlooked the fact that Leslie was convalescing in the drawing-room. The scent of the turtle's interior, so pungent that it seemed almost solid, floated

in through the french windows and enveloped the couch on which he lay.
My first intimation of this catastrophe was a blood-curdling roar from inside
the drawing-room. Before I could do anything sensible, Leslie, swathed in
blankets, appeared in the french windows.

'What's that bloody awful stink?' he inquired throatily. Then, as his glance
fell upon the dismembered turtle and its prettily arranged internal organs
spread across the flagstones, his eyes bulged and his face took on a heliotrope
tinge. 'What the hell's *that*?'

I explained, somewhat diffidently, that it was a turtle that I was dissecting.
It was a female, I went on hurriedly, hoping to distract Leslie by detail.
Here he could see the fascinating eggs that I had extracted from her interior.

'Damn her eggs,' shouted Leslie, making it sound like some strange medieval oath. 'Get the bloody thing away from here. It's stinking the place out.'

I said that I had almost reached the end of my dissection and that I had
then planned to bury all the soft parts and merely keep the skeleton and
shell to add to my collection.

'You're doing nothing of the sort,' shouted Leslie. 'You're to take the
whole bloody thing and bury it. Then you can come back and scrub the
veranda.'

Lucretia, our cook, attracted by the uproar, appeared in the french
window next to Leslie. She opened her mouth to inquire into the nature
of this family quarrel when she was struck amidships by the smell of the
turtle. Lucretia always had fifteen or sixteen ailments worrying her at any
given moment, which she cherished with the same loving care that other
people devote to window-boxes or Pekinese. At this particular time it was
her stomach that was causing her the most trouble. In consequence she
gasped two or three times, feebly, like a fish, uttered a strangled 'Saint
Spiridion!' and fell into Leslie's arms in a well-simulated faint.

Just at that moment, to my horror, the car containing the rest of the
family swept up the drive and came to a halt below the veranda.

'Hello, dear,' said Mother, getting out of the car and coming up to the
steps. 'Did you have a nice morning?'

Before I could say anything, the turtle, as it were, got in before me. Mother
uttered a couple of strange hiccuping cries, pulled out her handkerchief and
clapped it to her nose.

'What,' she demanded indistinctly, 'is that terrible smell?'

'It's that bloody boy,' roared Leslie from the french windows, making ineffectual attempts to prop the moaning Lucretia against the door jamb.

Larry and Margo had now followed Mother up the steps and caught sight of the butchered turtle.

'What . . . ?' began Larry and then he too was seized with a convulsive fit of coughing.

'It's that damned boy,' he said, gasping.

'Yes, dear,' said Mother through her handkerchief. 'Leslie's just told me.'

'It's disgusting,' wailed Margo, fanning herself with her handkerchief. 'It looks like a railway accident.'

'What *is* it, dear?' Mother asked me.

I explained that it was an exceedingly interesting hawks-bill turtle, female, containing eggs.

'Surely you don't have to chop it up on the veranda?' said Mother.

'The boy's mad,' said Larry with conviction. 'The whole place smells like a bloody whaling ship.'

'I really think you'll have to take it somewhere else, dear,' said Mother. 'We can't have this smell on the front veranda.'

'Tell him to bury the damned thing,' said Leslie, clasping his blankets more firmly about him.

'Why don't you get him adopted by a family of Eskimos?' inquired Larry. 'They like eating blubber and maggots and things.'

'Larry, don't be disgusting,' said Margo. 'They can't eat anything like this. The very thought of it makes me feel sick.'

'I think we ought to go inside,' said Mother faintly. 'Perhaps it won't smell as much in there.'

'If anything, it smells worse in here,' shouted Leslie from the french windows.

'Gerry dear, you must clean this up,' said Mother as she picked her way delicately over the turtle's entrails, 'and disinfect the flagstones.'

The family went inside and I set about the task of clearing up the turtle from the front veranda. Their voices arguing ferociously drifted out to me.

'Bloody menace,' said Leslie. 'Lying here peacefully reading, and I was suddenly seized by the throat.'

'Disgusting,' said Margo. 'I don't wonder Lucretia fainted.'

'High time he had another tutor,' said Larry. 'You leave the house for five minutes and come back and find him disembowelling Moby Dick on the front porch.'

'I'm sure he didn't mean any harm,' said Mother, 'but it was rather silly of him to do it on the veranda.'

'Silly!' said Larry caustically. 'We'll be blundering round the house with gas-masks for the next six months.'

I piled the remains of the turtle into the wheelbarrow and took it up to the top of the hill behind the villa. Here I dug a hole and buried all the soft parts and then placed the shell and the bone structure near a nest of friendly ants, who had, on previous occasions, helped me considerably by picking skeletons clean. But the most they had ever tackled had been a very large green lizard, so I was interested to see whether they would tackle the turtle. They ran towards it, their antennae waving eagerly, and then stopped, thought about it for a bit, held a little consultation and then retreated in a body; apparently even the ants were against me, so I returned despiritedly to the villa.

*   *   *

Although, ever since we arrived in Corfu, I had been aware that there were vast quantities of donkeys there – indeed the entire agricultural economy of the island depended on them – I had not really concentrated on them until we had gone to Katerina's wedding. Here a great number of the donkeys had brought with them their babies, many of them only a few days old. I was enchanted by their bulbous knees, their great ears, and their wobbling, uncertain walk and I had determined then, come what might, that I would possess a donkey of my own.

As I explained to Mother, while trying to argue her into agreeing to this, if I had a donkey to carry me and my equipment, I could go so much farther afield. Why couldn't I have it for Christmas, I asked? Because, Mother replied, firstly, they were too expensive, and secondly, there were not any babies available at that precise time. But if they were too expensive, I argued, why couldn't I have one as a Christmas *and* birthday present? I would willingly forgo all other presents in lieu of a donkey. Mother said she would see, which I knew from bitter experience generally meant that she would forget about the matter as rapidly and as comprehensively as possible. As it got near to my birthday, I once again reiterated all the arguments in favour of having a donkey. Mother just repeated that we would see.

Then one day, Costas, the brother of our maid, made his appearance in the olive grove just outside our little garden carrying on his shoulders a great bundle of tall bamboos. Whistling happily to himself he proceeded to dig holes in the ground and to set the bamboos upright so that they formed a small square. Peering at him through the fuchsia hedge, I wondered what on earth he was doing, so, whistling Roger, I went round to see.

'I am building,' said Costas, 'a house for your mother.'

I was astonished. What on earth could Mother want a bamboo house for? Had she, perhaps, decided to sleep out of doors? I felt this was unlikely. What, I inquired of Costas, did Mother want with a bamboo house?

He gazed at me wall-eyed.

'Who knows?' he said shrugging. 'Perhaps she wants to keep plants in it or store sweet potatoes for the winter.'

I thought this was extremely unlikely as well, but having watched Costas for half an hour I grew bored and went off for a walk with Roger.

By the next day the framework of the bamboo hut had been finished and Costas was now busy twining bundles of reeds between the bamboos to form solid walls and the roof. By the next day it was completed and looked exactly like one of Robinson Crusoe's earlier attempts at house-building. When I inquired of Mother what she intended to use the house for, she said that she was not quite sure, but she felt it would come in useful. With that vague information I had to be content.

The day before my birthday, everybody started acting in a slightly more eccentric manner than usual. Larry, for some reason best known to himself, went about the house shouting 'Tantivy!' and 'Tally-ho' and similar hunting slogans. As he was fairly frequently afflicted in this way, I did not take much notice.

Margo kept dodging about the house carrying mysterious bundles under her arms, and at one point I came face to face with her in the hall and noted, with astonishment, that her arms were full of multi-coloured decorations left over from Christmas. On seeing me she uttered a squeak of dismay and rushed into her bedroom in such a guilty and furtive manner that I was left staring after her with open mouth.

Even Leslie and Spiro were afflicted, it seemed, and they kept going into mysterious huddles in the garden. From the snippets of their conversation that I heard, I could not make head or tail of what they were planning.

'In the backs seats,' Spiro said, scowling. 'Honest to Gods, Masters Leslies, I have dones it befores.'

'Well, if you're sure, Spiro,' Leslie replied doubtfully, 'but we don't want any broken legs or anything.'

Then Leslie saw me undisguisedly eavesdropping and asked me truculently what the hell I thought I was doing, eavesdropping on people's private conversations? Why didn't I go down to the nearest cliff and jump off? Feeling that the family were in no mood to be amicable, I took Roger off into the olive groves and for the rest of the day we ineffectually chased green lizards.

That night I had just turned down the lamp and snuggled down in bed when I heard sounds of raucous singing, accompanied by gales of laughter, coming through the olive groves. As the uproar got closer, I could recognize Leslie's and Larry's voices, combined with Spiro's, each of them appearing to be singing a different song. It seemed as though they had been somewhere and celebrated too well. From the indignant whispering and shuffling going on in the corridor, I could tell that Margo and Mother had reached the same conclusion.

They burst into the villa, laughing hysterically at some witticism that Larry had produced, and were shushed fiercely by Margo and Mother.

'Do be quiet,' said Mother. 'You'll wake Gerry. What have you been drinking?'

'Wine,' said Larry in a dignified voice. He hiccuped.

'Wine,' said Leslie. 'And then we danced, and Spiro danced, and I danced, and Larry danced. And Spiro danced and then Larry danced and then I danced.'

'I think you had better go to bed,' said Mother.

'And then Spiro danced again,' said Leslie, 'and then Larry danced.'

'All right, dear, all right,' said Mother. 'Go to *bed*, for heaven's sake. Really, Spiro, I do feel that you shouldn't have let them drink so much.'

'Spiro danced,' said Leslie, driving the point home.

'I'll take him to bed,' said Larry. 'I'm the only sober member of the party.'

There was the sound of lurching feet on the tiles as Leslie and Larry, clasped in each other's arms, staggered down the corridor.

'I'm now dancing with *you*,' came Leslie's voice as Larry dragged him into his bedroom and put him to bed.

'I'm sorrys, Mrs Durrells,' said Spiro, his deep voice thickened with wine, 'but I couldn't stops thems.'

'Did you get it?' said Margo.

'Yes, Missy Margos. Don'ts you worrys,' said Spiro. 'It's down with Costas.'

Eventually Spiro left and I heard Mother and Margaret going to bed. It made a fittingly mysterious end to what had been a highly confusing day as far as I was concerned. But I soon forgot about the family's behaviour, as, lying in the dark wondering what my presents were going to be the following day, I drifted off to sleep.

The following morning I woke and lay for a moment wondering what was so special about that day, and then I remembered. It was my birthday. I lay there savouring the feeling of having a whole day to myself when people would give me presents and the family would be forced to accede to any reasonable requests. I was just about to get out of bed and go and see what my presents were, when a curious uproar broke out in the hall.

'Hold its head. Hold its *head*,' came Leslie's voice.

'Look out, you're spoiling the decorations,' wailed Margo.

'Damn the bloody decorations,' said Leslie. 'Hold its *head*.'

'Now, now, dears,' said Mother, 'don't quarrel.'

'Dear God,' said Larry in disgust, 'dung all over the floor.'

The whole of this mysterious conversation was accompanied by a strange pitter-pattering noise, as though someone were bouncing ping-pong balls on the tile floor of the hall. What on earth, I wondered, was the family up to now? Normally at this time they were still lying, semi-conscious, groping bleary-eyed for their early morning cups of tea. I sat up in bed, preparatory to going into the hall to join in whatever fun was afoot, when my bedroom door burst open and a donkey, clad in festoons of coloured crêpe paper, Christmas decorations, and with three enormous feathers attached skilfully between its large ears, came galloping into the bedroom, Leslie hanging grimly on to its tail, shouting, 'Woa, you bastard!'

'Language, dear,' said Mother, looking flustered in the doorway.

'You're spoiling the decorations,' screamed Margo.

'The sooner that animal gets out of here,' said Larry, 'the better. There's dung all over the hall now.'

'You frightened it,' said Margo.

'I didn't do anything,' said Larry indignantly. 'I just gave it a little push.'

The donkey skidded to a halt by my bedside and gazed at me out of enormous brown eyes. It seemed rather surprised. It shook itself vigorously so that the feathers between its ears fell off and then very dexterously it hacked Leslie on the shin with its hind leg.

'Jesus!' roared Leslie, hopping around on one leg. 'It's broken my bloody leg.'

'Leslie, dear, there is no need to swear so much,' said Mother. 'Remember Gerry.'

'The sooner you get it out of that bedroom the better,' said Larry. 'Otherwise the whole place will smell like a midden.'

'You've simply *ruined* its decorations,' said Margo, 'and it took me hours to put them on.'

But I was taking no notice of the family. The donkey had approached the edge of my bed and stared at me inquisitively for a moment and then had given a little throaty chuckle and thrust in my outstretched hands a grey muzzle as soft as everything soft I could think of – silkworm cocoons, newly born puppies, sea pebbles, or the velvety feel of a tree frog. Leslie had now removed his trousers and was examining the bruise on his shin, cursing fluently.

'Do you like it dear?' asked Mother.

Like it! I was speechless.

The donkey was a rich dark brown, almost a plum colour, with enormous ears like arum lilies, white socks over tiny polished hooves as neat as a tap-dancer's shoes. Running along her back was the broad black cross that denotes so proudly that her race carried Christ into Jerusalem (and has since continued to be one of the most maligned domestic animals ever), and round each great shining eye she had a neat white circle which denoted that she came from the village of Gastouri.

'You remember Katerina's donkey that you liked so much?' said Margo. 'Well, this is her baby.'

This, of course, made the donkey even more special. The donkey stood there looking like a refugee from a circus, chewing a piece of tinsel meditatively, while I scrambled out of bed and flung on my clothes. Where, I inquired breathlessly of Mother, was I to keep her? Obviously I couldn't keep her in the villa in view of the fact that Larry had just pointed out to Mother that she could, if she so wished, grow a good crop of potatoes in the hall.

'That's what that house Costas built is for,' said Mother.

I was beside myself with delight. What a noble, kindly, benevolent family

I had! How cunningly they had kept the secret from me! How hard they had worked to deck the donkey out in its finery! Slowly and gently, as though she were some fragile piece of china, I led my steed out through the garden and round into the olive grove, opened the door of the little bamboo hut, and took her inside. I thought I ought to just try her for size, because Costas was a notoriously bad workman. The little house was splendid. Just big enough for her. I took her out again and tethered her to an olive tree on a long length of rope, then I stayed for half an hour in a dream-like trance admiring her from every angle while she grazed placidly. Eventually I heard Mother calling me in to breakfast and I sighed with satisfaction. I had decided that, without any doubt whatsoever, and without wishing in any way to be partisan, this donkey was the finest donkey in the whole of the island of Corfu. For no reason that I could think of, I decided to call her Sally. I gave her a quick kiss on her silken muzzle and then went in to breakfast.

After breakfast, to my astonishment, Larry, with a magnanimous air, said that if I liked he would teach me to ride. I said that I didn't know he could ride.

'Of course,' said Larry airily. 'When we were in India I was always galloping about on ponies and things. I used to groom them and feed them and so forth. Have to know what you're doing, of course.'

So, armed with a blanket and a large piece of webbing, we went out into the olive grove, placed the blanket on Sally's back, and tied it in position. She viewed these preparations with interest but a lack of enthusiasm. With a certain amount of difficulty, for Sally would persist in walking round and round in a tight circle, Larry succeeded in getting me on to her back. He then exchanged her tether for a rope halter and rope reins.

'Now,' he said, 'you just steer her as though she's a boat. When you want her to go faster, just simply kick her in the ribs with your heels.'

If that was all there was to riding, I felt, it was going to be simplicity itself. I jerked on the reins and dug my heels into Sally's ribs. It was unfortunate that my fall was broken by a large and exceptionally luxuriant bramble bush. Sally peered at me as I extricated myself, with a look of astonishment on her face.

'Perhaps,' said Larry, 'you ought to have a stick so then you can use your legs for gripping on to her and you won't fall off.'

He cut me a short stick and once again I mounted Sally. This time I wrapped my legs tightly round her barrel body and gave her a sharp tap with my switch. She bucked several times, indignantly, but I clung on like a limpet, and to my delight, within half an hour, I had her trotting to and fro between the olive trees, responding neatly to tugs on the rein. Larry had been lying under the olives smoking and watching my progress. Now, as I appeared to have mastered the equestrian art, he rose to his feet and took a penknife out of his pocket.

'Now,' he said, as I dismounted, 'I'll show you how to look after her. First of all, you must brush her down every morning. We'll get a brush for you in town. Then you must make sure her hooves are clean. You must do that every day.'

I inquired, puzzled, how did one clean donkeys' hooves?

'I'll show you,' said Larry nonchalantly.

He walked up to Sally, bent down, and picked up her hind leg.

'In here,' he said, pointing with the blade of the knife at Sally's hoof, 'an awful lot of muck gets trapped. This can lead to all sorts of things. Foot-rot and so forth, and it's very important to keep them clean.'

So saying, he dug his penknife blade into Sally's hoof. What Larry had not realized was that donkeys in Corfu were unshod and that a baby donkey's hoof is still, comparatively speaking, soft and very delicate. So, not unnaturally, Sally reacted as though Larry had jabbed her with a red-hot skewer. She wrenched her hoof out of his hands and as he straightened up and turned in astonishment, she did a pretty pirouette and kicked him neatly in the pit of the stomach with both hind legs. Larry sat down heavily, his face went white, and he doubled up, clasping his stomach and making strange rattling noises. The alarm I felt was not for Larry but for Sally, for I was quite sure that he would extract the most terrible retribution when he recovered. Hastily I undid Sally's rope and flicked her on the rump with the stick and watched her canter off into the olives. Then I ran into the house and informed Mother that Larry had had an accident. The entire family, including Spiro, who had just arrived, came running out into the olive grove where Larry was still writhing about uttering great sobbing, wheezing noises.

'Larry, dear,' said Mother distraught, 'what *have* you been doing?'

'Attacked,' gasped Larry between wheezes. 'Unprovoked . . . Creature mad . . . Probably rabies . . . Ruptured appendix.'

With Leslie on one side of him and Spiro on the other they carted Larry slowly back to the villa, with Mother and Margo fluttering commiseratingly and ineffectually around him. In a crisis of this magnitude, involving my family, one had to keep one's wits about one or all was lost. I ran swiftly round to the kitchen door where, panting but innocent, I informed our maid that I was going to spend the day out and could she give me some food to eat. She put half a loaf of bread, some onions, some olives, and a hunk of cold meat into a paper bag and gave it to me. Fruit I knew I could obtain from any of my peasant friends. Then I raced through the olive groves, carrying this provender, in search of Sally.

I eventually found her half a mile away, grazing on a succulent patch of grass. After several ineffectual attempts, I managed to scramble up on to her back and then, belabouring her behind with a stick, I urged her to a brisk trot as far away from the villa as possible.

FROM THE GARDEN OF THE GODS:

That summer was a particularly rich one; it seemed as if the sun had drawn up a special bounty from the island for never had we had such an abundance of fruit and flowers, never had the sea been so warm and filled with fish, never had so many birds reared their young, or butterflies and other insects hatched and shimmered across the countryside. Watermelons, their flesh as crisp and cool as pink snow, were formidable botanical cannonballs, each one big enough and heavy enough to obliterate a city; peaches, as orange or pink as a harvest moon, loomed huge in the trees, their thick, velvety pelts swollen with sweet juice; the green and black figs burst with the pressure of their sap, and in the pink splits the gold-green rose beetles sat dazed by the rich, never-ending largesse. Trees had been groaning with the weight of cherries, so that the orchards looked as though some great dragon had been slain among the trees, bespattering the leaves with scarlet and wine-red drops of blood. The maize cobs were as long as your arm and as you bit into the canary-yellow mosaic of seeds, the white milky juice burst into your mouth; and in the trees, swelling and fattening themselves for autumn, were the jade-green almonds and walnuts, and olives, smoothly shaped, bright and shining as birds' eggs strung among the leaves.

Naturally, with the island thus a-burst with life, my collecting activities redoubled. As well as my regular weekly afternoon spent with Theodore, I now undertook much more daring and comprehensive expeditions than I had been able to before, for now I had acquired a donkey. This beast, Sally by name, had been a birthday present; and as a means of covering long distances and carrying a lot of equipment I found her an invaluable, if stubborn, companion. To offset her stubbornness she had one great virtue; she was, like all donkeys, endlessly patient. She would gaze happily into space while I watched some creature or other or else would simply fall into a donkey doze, that happy, trance-like state that donkeys can attain when, with half-closed eyes, they appear to be dreaming of some nirvana and become impervious to shouts, threats, or even whacks with sticks. The dogs, after a short period of patience, would start to yawn and sigh and scratch and show by many small signs that they felt we had devoted enough time to a spider or whatever it was and moved on. Sally, however, once she was in her doze, gave the impression that she would happily stay there for several days if the necessity arose.

One day a peasant friend of mine, a man who had obtained a number of my specimens for me and who was a careful observer, informed me that there were two huge birds hanging about in a rocky valley some five miles north of the villa. He thought that they must be nesting there. From his description they could only be eagles or vultures and I was most anxious to try to get some young of either of these birds. My birds of prey collection now numbered three species of owl, a sparrowhawk, a merlin and a kestrel, so I felt the addition of an eagle or vulture would round it off. Needless to say I did not vouchsafe my ambition to the family, as already the meat bill for my animals was astronomical. Apart from this I could imagine Larry's reaction to the suggestion of a vulture being inserted into the house. When acquiring new pets I always found it wiser to face him with a *fait accompli*, for once the animals were introduced to the villa I could generally count on getting Mother and Margo on my side.

I prepared for my expedition with great care, making up loads of food for myself and the dogs, a good supply of *gasoza* as well as the normal complement of collecting tins and boxes, my butterfly net and a large bag to put my eagle or vulture in. I also took Leslie's binoculars; they were of a higher magnification than my own. He, luckily, was not around for me to ask, but I felt sure he would happily have lent them to me had he been at home. Having checked my equipment for the last time to make sure nothing was missing I proceeded to festoon Sally with the various items.

She was in a singularly sullen and recalcitrant mood, even by donkey standards, and annoyed me by deliberately treading on my foot and then giving me a sharp nip on the buttock when I bent down to pick up my fallen butterfly net. She took grave offence at the clout I gave her for this misbehaviour, so we started this expedition barely on speaking terms. Coldly, I fixed her straw hat over her furry lily-shaped ears, whistled to the dogs and set off.

Although it was still early the sun was hot and the sky clear, burning blue, like the blue you get by scattering salt on a fire, blurred at the edges with heat haze. To begin with we made our way along the road thick with white dust, as clinging as pollen, and we passed many of my peasant friends on their donkeys, going to market or down to their fields to work. This inevitably held up the progress of the expedition, for good manners required that I passed the time of day with each one. In Corfu one must always gossip for the right length of time and perhaps accept a crust of bread, some dry watermelon seeds or a bunch of grapes as a sign of love and affection. So when it was time to turn off the hot, dusty road and start climbing through the cool olive groves I was laden with a variety of edible commodities, the largest of which was a watermelon, a generous present pressed upon me by Mama Agathi, a friend of mine whom I had not seen for a week, an unconscionable length of time, during which she presumed I had been without food.

The olive groves were dark with shadows and as cool as a well after the glare of the road. The dogs went ahead as usual, foraging around the great pitted olive boles and occasionally, maddened by their audacity, chasing skimming swallows, barking vociferously. Failing, as always, to catch one, they would then attempt to vent their wrath on some innocent sheep or vacant-faced chicken, and would have to be sternly reprimanded. Sally, her previous sulkiness forgotten, stepped out at a good pace, one ear pricked forward and the other one backward, so that she could listen to my singing and comments on the passing scene.

Presently we left the shade of the olives and climbed upwards through the heat-shimmered hills, making our way through thickets of myrtle bushes, small copses of holm oak and great wigs of broom. Here Sally's hooves crushed the herb underfoot and the warm air became redolent with the scent of sage and thyme. By midday, the dogs panting, Sally and I sweating profusely, we were high up among the gold and rust red rocks of the central range, while far below us lay the sea, blue as flax. By half past two, pausing to rest in the shade of a massive outcrop of stone, I was feeling throughly frustrated. We had followed the instructions of my friend and had indeed found a nest, which to my excitement proved to be that of a Griffin vulture; moreover, the nest, perched on a rocky ledge, contained two fat and almost fully fledged youngsters at just the right age for adoption. The snag was that I could not reach the nest, either from above or below. After having spent a fruitless hour trying to kidnap the babies I was forced, albeit reluctantly, to give up the idea of adding vultures to my birds of prey collection. We moved down the mountainside and stopped to rest and eat in the shade. While I ate my sandwiches and hard-boiled eggs, Sally had a light lunch of dry maize cobs and watermelon, and the dogs assuaged their thirst with a mixture of watermelon and grapes, gobbling the juicy fruit eagerly and occasionally choking and coughing as a melon seed got stuck. Because of their voraciousness and total lack of table manners, they had finished their lunch long before Sally or I, and having reluctantly come to the conclusion that I did not intend to give them any more to eat they left us and slouched down the mountainside to indulge in a little private hunting.

I lay on my tummy eating crisp, cool watermelon, pink as coral, and examined the hillside. Fifty feet or so below where I lay were the ruins of a small peasant house. Here and there on the hillside I could just discern the crescent-shaped, flattened areas which had once been the tiny fields of the farm. Eventually, it must have become obvious that the impoverished soil would no longer support maize or vegetables on the pocket handkerchief fields, and so the owner had moved away. The house had tumbled down and the fields become overrun with weeds and myrtle. I was staring at the remains of the cottage, wondering who had lived there, when I saw something reddish moving through the thyme at the base of one of the walls.

Slowly I reached out for the field-glasses and put them to my eyes. The tumbled mass of rocks at the base of the wall sprang into clear view, but for a moment I could not see what it was that had attracted my attention. Then, to my astonishment, from behind a clump of thyme appeared a lithe, tiny animal, as red as an autumn leaf. It was a weasel, and to judge by its behaviour, a young and rather innocent one. It was the first weasel I had seen on Corfu and I was enchanted by it. It peered about with a slightly bemused air and then stood up on its hind legs and sniffed the air vigorously. Apparently not smelling anything edible, it sat down and had an intensive and, from the look of it, very satisfying scratch. Then it suddenly broke off from its toilet and carefully stalked and attempted to capture a vivid canary-yellow Brimstone butterfly. The insect, however, slipped out from under its jaws and flipped away, leaving the weasel snapping at thin air and looking slightly foolish. It sat up on its hind legs once more, to see where its quarry had gone and, over-balancing, almost fell off the stone on which it was sitting.

I watched it, entranced by its diminutive size, its rich colouring and its air of innocence. I wanted above all things to catch it and take it home with me to add to my menagerie but I knew this would be difficult. While I was musing on the best method of achieving this result a drama unfolded in the ruined cottage below. I saw a shadow, like a Maltese cross, slide over the low scrub, and a sparrowhawk appeared, flying low and fast towards the weasel who was sitting up on his stone sniffing the air and apparently unaware of his danger. I was just wondering whether to shout or clap my hands to warn him when he saw the hawk. With an incredible turn of speed he turned, leapt gracefully on to the ruined wall and disappeared into a crack between two stones that I would have thought would not have allowed the passage of a slow-worm, let alone a mammal the size of the weasel. It was like a conjuring trick; one minute he had been sitting on his rock, the next he vanished into the wall like a drop of rain water. The sparrowhawk checked with fanned tail and hovered briefly, obviously hoping the weasel would reappear. After a moment or so it got bored and slid off down the mountainside in search of less wary game. After a short time the weasel poked his little face out of the crack. Seeing the coast was clear he emerged cautiously. Then he made his way along the wall and, as though his recent escape into the crack had given him the idea, he proceeded to investigate and disappear into every nook and cranny that existed between the stones. As I watched him I was wondering how to make my way down the hill so as to throw my shirt over him before he was aware of my presence. In view of his expert vanishing trick when faced with the hawk, it was obviously not going to be easy.

At that moment he slid, sinuous as a snake, into a hole in the base of the wall. From another hole a little higher up there emerged a second animal in a great state of alarm, which made its way along the top of the wall and disappeared into a crevice. I was greatly excited, for even with the brief glimpse I had got of it, I recognized it as a creature that I had tried for many months to track down and capture, a Garden dormouse, probably one of the most attractive of the European rodents. It was about half the size of a full-grown rat, with cinnamon-coloured fur, brilliant white underpants, a long furry tail ending in a brush of black and white hair and a black mask of fur beneath the ears, running across the eyes and making it look ridiculously as though it was wearing an old-fashioned mask of the sort that burgars were reputed to indulge in.

I was now in something of a quandary, for there below me were two animals I dearly wanted to possess, one hotly pursuing the other, and both of them exceedingly wary. If my attack was not well planned I stood a good chance of losing both animals. I decided to tackle the weasel first, as he was the more mobile of the two, and I felt that the dormouse would not move from its new hole if undisturbed. On reflection I decided that my butterfly net was a more suitable instrument than my shirt, so armed with it I made my way down the hillside with the utmost caution, freezing immobile every time the weasel appeared out of the hole and looked around. Eventually I got to within a few feet of the wall without being detected. I tightened my grip on the long handle of my net and waited for the weasel to come out from the depths of the hole he was now investigating. When he did emerge he did so with such suddenness that I was unprepared. He sat up on his hind legs and stared at me with interest untinged by alarm. I was just about to take a swipe at him with my net when, crashing through the bushes, tongues lolling, tails wagging, came the three dogs, as vociferously pleased to see me as if we had been separated for months. The weasel vanished. One minute he was sitting there, frozen with horror at this avalanche of dogs, the next he was gone. Bitterly I cursed the dogs and banished them to the higher reaches of the mountain, where they went to lie in the shade, hurt and puzzled at my bad temper. Then I set about trying to capture the dormouse.

Over the years the mortar between the stones had grown frail and heavy winter rains had washed it away so that now, to all intents and purposes, the remains of the house was a series of dry-stone walls. With its maze of intercommunicating tunnels and caves, it formed the ideal hideout for any small animal. There was only one way to hunt for an animal in this sort of terrain and that was to take the wall to pieces, so rather laboriously this was what I started to do. After having dismantled a good section of it I had unearthed nothing more exciting than a couple of indignant scorpions, a few woodlice and a young gecko who fled, leaving his writhing tail behind him. It was hot and thirsty work and after an hour or so I sat down in the shade of the, as yet, undismantled wall to have a rest.

I was just wondering how long it would take me to demolish the rest of the wall when from a hole some three feet from me, the dormouse appeared. It scrambled up like a somewhat overweight mountain climber and then, having reached the top, sat down on its fat bottom and began to wash its face with great thoroughness, totally ignoring my presence. I could hardly believe my luck. Slowly and with great caution I manoeuvred my butterfly net towards him, got it into position and then clapped it down suddenly. This would have worked perfectly if the top of the wall had been flat, but it was not. I could not press the rim of the net down hard enough to avoid leaving a gap. To my intense annoyance and frustration, the dormouse, recovering from its momentary panic, squeezed out from under the net, galloped along the wall and disappeared into another crevice. However this proved to be its undoing, for it had chosen a 'cul de sac' and before it had discovered its mistake I had clamped the net over the entrance.

The next thing was to get it out and into the bag without getting bitten. This was not easy and before I had finished it had sunk its exceedingly sharp teeth into the ball of my thumb, so that I, the handkerchief and the dormouse were liberally bespattered with gore. Finally, however, I got it into the bag. Delighted with my success, I mounted Sally and rode home in triumph with my new acquisition.

On arrival at the villa I carried the dormouse up to my room and housed it in a cage which had, until recently been the home of a baby black rat. This rat had met an unfortunate end in the claws of my scops owl, Ulysses, who was of the opinion that all rodents had been created by a beneficent providence in order to fill his stomach. I therefore made quite sure that my precious dormouse could not escape and meet a similar fate. Once it was in the cage I was able to examine it more closely. I discovered it was a female with a suspiciously large tummy, which led me to believe that she might be pregnant. After some consideration I called her Esmerelda (I had just been reading *The Hunchback of Notre Dame* and had fallen deeply in love with the heroine), and provided her with a cardboard box full of cotton waste and dried grass in which to have her family.

For the first few days Esmerelda would leap at my hand like a bulldog when I went to clean her cage or feed her, but within a week she had grown tame and tolerated me, though still viewing me with a certain reserve. Every evening Ulysses, on his special perch above the window, would wake up and I would open the shutters so that he could fly off into the moonlit olive groves and hunt, only returning for his plate of mincemeat at about two in the morning. Once he was safely out of the way I could let Esmerelda out of her cage for a couple of hours' exercise. She proved to be an enchanting creature with enormous grace in spite of her rotundity, and would take prodigious and breathtaking leaps from the cupboard on to the bed (where she bounced as if it was a trampoline), and from the bed to the bookcase or table, using her long tail with its bushy end as a balancing rod. She was vastly inquisitive and nightly would subject the room and its contents to a minute scrutiny, scowling through her black mask with whiskers quivering. I discovered that she had a consuming passion for large brown grasshoppers and she would often come and sit on my bare chest, as I lay in bed, and scrunch these delicacies. The result was that my bed always seemed to contain a prickly layer of wing cases, bits of leg and chunks of horny thorax, for she was a greedy and not particularly well-mannered feeder.

Then came the exciting evening when, after Ulysses had floated on silent wings into the olive groves and commenced to call 'toink toink' after the manner of his kind, I opened the cage door to find that she would not come out but lurked inside the cardboard box and made angry chittering noises at me. When I tried to investigate her bedroom she fastened on to my forefinger like a tiger and I had great difficulty in getting her to let go. Eventually I managed to get her off and, holding her firmly by the scruff of the neck, investigated the box. I found there, to my infinite delight, eight babies, each the size of a hazelnut and as pink as a cyclamen bud. Delighted with Esmerelda's happy event I showered her with grasshoppers, melon seeds, grapes and other delicacies of which I knew she was particularly fond, and followed the progress of the babies with breathless interest.

Gradually the babies developed. Their eyes opened and their fur grew. Within a short time the more powerful and adventurous of them would climb laboriously out of their cardboard nursery and wobble about on the floor of the cage when Esmerelda was not looking. This filled her with alarm, and she would pick the errant baby up in her mouth, and uttering peevish growling noises, transfer it to the safety of the bedroom. This was all very well with one or two, but as soon as all eight babies reached the inquisitive stage, it was impossible for her to control them and so she had to let them wander at will. They started to follow her out of the cage and it was then that I discovered that dormice, like shrews, have a habit of caravanning. That is to say that Esmerelda would go first; hanging on to her tail would be baby number one, hanging on to his or hers would be baby number two, on to his baby number three, and so on. It was a magical sight to see these nine diminutive creatures, each wearing his little black mask, wending their way around the room like an animated furry scarf, flying over the bed or shillying up the table leg. A scattering of grasshoppers on the bed or floor, and the babies, squeaking excitedly, would gather round to feed, looking ridiculously like a convention of bandits.

Eventually, when the babies were fully adult, I was forced to take them into the olive grove and let them go. The task of providing sufficient food for nine rapacious dormice was proving too time-consuming. I released them at the edge of the olive grove, near a thicket of holm oak, and these they colonized successfully. In the evenings, when the sun was setting and the sky was getting as green as a leaf, striped with sunset clouds, I used to go down to watch the little masked dormice flitting through the branches with a ballerina-like grace, chittering and squeaking to each other as they pursued moths, or fireflies or other delicacies through the shadowy branches.

It was a wrench for Gerry, at the outbreak of war, to leave Corfu – the gaiety, freedom and colour, the wide circle of friends from peasants to poets. He told me he took up smoking cigarettes to ease his awkwardness at dealing with the new social set he was thrust into. But his single-minded purpose in life – to be close to and study animals – was undiminished, and he took jobs in a London pet shop and at Whipsnade Zoo. He read widely, a habit fostered by Larry in Corfu, from the ancients to the moderns, and by the end of this period he was clearly pursuing the lines of later conservation thinking. He even devised a youthful equivalent of The Red Data Books, *the conservation community's register of species threatened with extinction, first published more than twenty years after Gerry worked on his.*

FROM FILLETS OF PLAICE:

Towards the end of 1939, when it looked as though war was inevitable, my family uprooted itself from Corfu and came back to England. We settled for a time in a flat in London while my mother made repeated forays into different parts of the English countryside in search of a house. And while she was doing this I was free to explore London. Although I have never been a lover of big cities I found London, at that time, fascinating. After all, the biggest metropolis I was used to was the town of Corfu, which was about the size of a small English market town, and so the great sprawling mass of London had hundreds of exciting secrets for me to discover. There was, of course, the Natural History Museum, and the inevitable visits to the Zoo, where I got on quite intimate terms with some of the keepers. This only strengthened my belief that working in a zoo was the only real vocation for anyone, and confirmed me in my desire to possess a zoo of my own.

Quite close to the flat where we were staying was a shop which always had my undivided attention. It was a place called 'The Aquarium', and its window was full of great tanks full of brightly coloured fish and, what was even more interesting, rows of glass-fronted boxes that contained grass snakes, pine snakes, great green lizards and bulbous-eyed toads. I used to gaze longingly in the window at these beautiful creatures and I had a great desire to possess them. But as I already had a whole host of birds, two magpies and a marmoset in the flat, I felt that the introduction of any other livestock of any shape or form would bring down the wrath of the family upon me and so I could only gaze longingly at these lovely reptiles.

Then, one morning, when I happened to pass the shop, my attention was riveted by a notice that was leaning up against an aquarium. It said, 'Wanted: Young, reliable assistant'. I went back to the flat and thought about it for some time.

'They've got a job going in that pet shop down the road,' I said to my mother.

'Have they, dear?' she said, not really taking any notice.

'Yes. They say they want a young, reliable assistant. I . . . I thought of applying for it,' I said carelessly.

'What a good idea,' said Larry. 'Then, perhaps, you could take all your animals there.'

'I don't think they'd let him do that, dear,' said my mother.

'How much do you think they'd pay for a job like that?' I asked.

'Not very much, I shouldn't think,' said Larry. 'I doubt that you are what they mean by reliable.'

'Anyway, they'd have to pay me something, wouldn't they?' I said.

'Are you old enough to be employed?' inquired Larry.

'Well, I'm almost sixteen,' I said.

'Well, go and have a shot at it,' he suggested.

So the following morning I went down to the pet shop and opened the door and went in. A short, slender, dark man with very large horn-rimmed spectacles danced across the floor towards me.

'Good morning! Good morning! Good morning, sir!' he said. 'What can I do for you?'

'You, um . . . you want an assistant . . .' I said.

He cocked his head on one side and his eyes grew large behind his spectacles.

'An assistant,' he said. 'Do you mean to say you want the job?'

'Er . . . yes,' I said.

'Have you had any experience?' he inquired doubtfully.

'Oh, I've had plenty of experience,' I said. 'I've always kept reptiles and fish and thing like that. I've got a whole flatful of things now.'

The little man looked at me.

'How old are you?' he asked.

'Sixteen . . . nearly seventeen,' I lied.

'Well,' he said, 'we can't afford to pay very much, you know. The overheads on this shop are something extraordinary. But I could start you off at one pound ten.'

'That's all right,' I said. 'When do I start?'

'You'd better start on Monday,' he said. 'I think on Monday because then I can get all your cards stamped up and straight. Otherwise we get in such a muddle, don't we? Now, my name's Mr Romilly.'

I told him my name and we shook hands rather formally, and then we stood looking at each other. It was obvious that Mr Romilly had never employed anybody before and did not know quite what the form was. I thought perhaps I ought to help him out.

'Perhaps you could just show me round,' I suggested, 'and tell me a few things that you will want me to do.'

'Oh, what an excellent idea,' said Mr Romilly. 'An excellent idea!'

He danced round the shop waving his hands like butterfly wings and showed me how to clean out a fish tank, how to drop the mealworms into the cages of frogs and toads, and where the brush and broom were kept that we swept the floor with. Under the shop was a large cellar where various fish foods, nets and other things were kept, and it included a constantly running tap that dripped into a large bowl containing what at first glance appeared to be a raw sheep's heart. This, on close inspection, turned out to be a closely knitted ball of threadlike tubifex worms. These bright red worms were a favourite food of all the fish and some of the amphibians and reptiles as well. I discovered that as well as the delightful things in the window there were hosts of other creatures in the shop besides – cases full of lizards, toads, tortoises and treacle-shiny snakes, tanks full of moist, gulping frogs, and newts with frilled tails like pennants. After having spent so many months in dry, dusty and desiccated London, the shop was, as far as I was concerned, a Garden of Eden.

'Now,' said Mr Romilly, when he had shown me everything, 'you start on Monday, hm? Nine o'clock sharp. Don't be late, will you?'

I did not tell Mr Romilly that nothing short of death would have prevented me from being there at nine o'clock on Monday.

So at ten to nine on Monday morning I paced the pavement outside the shop and eventually Mr Romilly appeared, clad in a long black coat and a black Homburg hat, waving his bunch of keys musically.

'Good morning, good morning,' he trilled. 'I'm glad to see you're on time. What a good start.'

So we went into the shop and I started on the first chores of the day, which were to sweep the comparatively spotless floor clean and then to go round feeding little knots of wriggling tubifex to the fishes.

I very soon discovered that Mr Romilly, though a kindly man, had little or no knowledge of the creatures in his care. Most of the cages were most unsuitably decorated for the occupants' comfort and, indeed, so were the fish tanks. Also, Mr Romilly worked on the theory that if you got an animal to eat one thing, you then went on feeding it with that thing incessantly. I decided that I would have to take a hand both in the cage decoration and also in brightening up the lives of our charges, but I knew I would have to move cautiously for Mr Romilly was nothing if not conservative.

'Don't you think the lizards and toads and things would like a change from mealworms, Mr Romilly?' I said one day.

'A change?' said Mr Romilly, his eyes widening behind his spectacles. 'What sort of a change?'

'Well,' I said, 'how about woodlice? I always used to feed my reptiles on woodlice.'

'Are you sure?' said Mr Romilly.

'Quite sure,' I said.

'It won't do them any harm, will it?' he asked anxiously.

'No,' I said, 'they love woodlice. It gives them a bit of variety in their diet.'

'But where are we going to get them?' asked Mr Romilly despondently.

'Well, I expect there are plenty in the parks,' I said. 'I'll see if I can get some, shall I?'

'Very well,' said Mr Romilly reluctantly, 'if you're quite sure they won't do them any harm.'

So I spent one afternoon in the park and collected a very large tin full of woodlice, which I kept in decaying leaves down in the cellar, and when I thought that the frogs and the toads and the lizards had got a bit bored with the mealworms, I would try them on some mealworm beetles, and then, when they had had a surfeit of those, I would give them some woodlice. At first, Mr Romilly used to peer into the cages with a fearful look on his face, as though he expected to see all the reptiles and amphibians dead. But when he found that they not only thrived on this new mixture but even started to croak in their cages, his enthusiasm knew no bounds.

My next little effort concerned two very large and benign Leopard toads which came from North Africa. Now, Mr Romilly's idea of North Africa was an endless desert where the sun shone day and night and where the temperature was never anything less than about a hundred and ninety in the shade, if indeed any shade was to be found. So in consequence he had incarcerated these two poor toads in a small, glass-fronted cage with a couple of brilliant electric light bulbs above them. They sat on a pile of plain white sand, they had no rocks to hide under to get away from the glare, and the only time the temperature dropped at all was at night when we switched off the light in the shop. In consequence, their eyes had become milky and looked almost as though they were suffering from cataract, their skins had become dry and flaky, and the soles of their feet were raw.

I knew that suggesting to Mr Romilly anything so drastic as putting them into a new cage with some damp moss would horrify him beyond all bounds, so I started surreptitiously to try and give the toads a slightly happier existence. I pinched some olive oil from my mother's kitchen for a start, and when Mr Romilly went out to have his lunch hour, I massaged the oil into the skin of both toads. This improved the flakiness. I then got some ointment from the chemist, having explained – to his amusement – why I wanted it, and anointed their feet with it. This helped, but it did not clear up the foot condition completely. I also got some Golden Eye Ointment, which one normally used for dogs, and applied it to their eyes with miraculous results. Then, every time Mr Romilly had his lunch hour I would give them a warm spray and this they loved. They would sit there, gulping benignly, blinking their eyes and, if I moved the spray a little, they would shuffle across the floor of their cage to get under it again. One day I put a small section of moss in the cage and both toads immediately burrowed under it.

'Oh, look, Mr Romilly,' I said with well-simulated surprise, 'I put a bit of moss in the toads' cage by mistake, and they seem to like it.'

'Moss?' said Mr Romilly. 'Moss? But they live in the desert.'

'Well, I think some parts of the desert have got a *little* bit of vegetation,' I said.

'I thought it was all sand,' said Mr Romilly. 'All sand. As far as the eye could see.'

'No, er . . . I think they've got some small cactuses and things,' I said. 'Anyway, they seem to like it, don't they?'

'They certainly do,' said Mr Romilly. 'Do you think we ought to leave it in?'

'Yes,' I said. 'Shall we put a little more in, too?'

'I don't suppose it could do any harm. They can't eat it and strangle themselves with it, can they?' he asked anxiously.

'I don't think they will,' I said reassuringly.

So from then onwards my two lovely toads had a bit of moss to hide under and, what was more important, a bed of moss to sit on, and their feet soon cleared up.

I next turned my attention to the fish, for although they loved tubifex dearly I felt that they, too, should have a little variety in their diet.

'Wouldn't it be possible,' I suggested to Mr Romilly in a tentative sort of way, 'to give the fish some daphnia?'

Now, daphnia were the little water fleas that we used to get sent up from the farm that supplied the shop with all its produce, like waterweed and water snails and the freshwater fish that we sold. And the daphnia we used to sell in little pots to fish lovers to feed their fish with.

'Daphnia?' said Mr Romilly. 'Feed them on daphnia? But they wouldn't eat it, would they?'

'Well, if they won't eat it, why do we sell it to people to feed their fish?' I inquired.

Mr Romilly was powerfully struck by this piece of logic.

'You're right, you know,' he said. 'You're right. There's a little left over down in the cellar now. The new supply comes tomorrow. Try some on them and see.'

So I dropped about a tablespoonful of daphnia into each tank and the fish went as mad over them as the toads and frogs had gone over the woodlice.

The next thing I wanted to do, but I had to do it more cautiously, was to try and decorate the cages and tanks to make them look more attractive. Now, this was a task that Mr Romilly always undertook himself, and he did it with a dogged persistence. I do not think he really enjoyed it, but he felt that, as the senior member of the firm, as it were, it was his duty to do.

'Mr Romilly,' I said one day. 'I've got nothing to do at the moment, and there are no customers. You wouldn't let me decorate a fish tank, would you? I'd love to learn how to do them as well as you do.'

'Well, now,' said Mr Romilly, blushing. 'Well, now. I wouldn't say I was all that good . . .'

'Oh, I think you do it beautifully,' I said. 'And I'd like to learn.'

'Well, perhaps just a small one,' said Mr Romilly. 'And I can give you some tips as you go along. Now, let's see . . . let's see . . . Yes, now, that mollies' tank over there. They need clearing out. Now, if you can move them to the spare tank, and then empty it and give it a good scrub, and then we'll start from scratch, shall we?'

And so, with the aid of a little net, I moved all the black mollies, as dark and glistening as little olives, out of their tank and into the spare one. Then I emptied their tank and scrubbed it out and called Mr Romilly.

'Now,' he said. 'You put some sand at the bottom and . . . um . . . a couple of stones, and then perhaps er . . . Vallisneria, I would say, probably in that corner there, wouldn't you?'

'Could I just try it on my own?' I asked. 'I, er . . . I think I'd learn better that way – if I could do it on my own. And then, when I'm finished you could criticize it and tell me where I've gone wrong.'

'Very good idea,' said Mr Romilly. And so he pottered off to do his petty cash and left me in peace.

It was only a small tank but I worked hard on it. I piled up the silver sand in great dunes. I built little cliffs. I planted forests of Vallisneria through which the mollies could drift in shoals. Then I filled it carefully with water, and when it was the right temperature I put the mollies back in it and called Mr Romilly to see my handiwork.

'By Jove!' he said, looking at it. 'By Jove!'

He glanced at me and it was almost as though he was disappointed that I had done so well. I could see that I was on dangerous ground.

'Do . . . do you like it?' I inquired.

'It . . . it's remarkable! Remarkable! I can't think how you . . . how you managed it.'

'Well, I only managed it by watching *you*, Mr Romilly,' I said. 'If it hadn't been for you teaching me how to do it I could never have done it.'

'Well, now. Well, now,' said Mr Romilly, going pink. 'But I see you've added one or two little touches of your own.'

'Well, they were just ideas I'd picked up from watching you,' I said.

'Hmmm . . . Most commendable. Most commendable,' said Mr Romilly.

The next day he asked me whether I would like to decorate another fish tank and I knew that I had won the battle without hurting his feelings.

The tank that I really desperately wanted to do was the enormous one that we had in the window. It was some four and a half feet long and about two foot six deep, and in it we had a great colourful mixed collection of fish. But I knew that I must not overstep the bounds of propriety at this stage. So I did several small fish tanks first, and when Mr Romilly had got thoroughly used to the idea of my doing them, I broached the subject of our big show tank in the window.

'Could I try my hand at that, Mr Romilly?' I asked.

'What? Our show piece?' he said.

'Yes,' I said. 'It's . . . it's in need of . . . of a clean, anyway. So I thought, perhaps, I could try my hand at redecorating it.'

'Well, I don't know . . .' said Mr Romilly doubtfully. 'I don't know. It's a most important piece that, you know. It's the centrepiece of the window. It's the one that attracts all the customers.'

He was quite right, but the customers were attracted by the flickering shoals of multi-coloured fish. They certainly were not attracted by Mr

Romilly's attempts at decoration, which made it look rather like a blasted heath.

'Well, could I just try?' I said. 'And if it's no good, I'll do it all over again. I'll even ... I'll even spend my half day doing it.'

'Oh, I'm sure that won't be necessary,' said Mr Romilly, shocked. 'You don't want to spend all your days shut up in the shop, you know. A young boy like you ... you want to be out and about ... Well, all right, you try your hand at it, and see what happens.'

It took me the better part of a day to do, because in between times I had to attend to the various customers who came to buy tubifex or daphnia or buy a tree frog for their garden pond or something similar. I worked on that giant tank with all the dedication of a marine Capability Brown. I built rolling sand dunes and great towering cliffs of lovely granite. And then, through the valleys between the granite mountains, I planted forests of Vallisneria and other, more delicate, weedy ferns. And on the surface of the water I floated the tiny little white flowers that look so like miniature water-lilies. With the aid of sand and rocks I concealed the heater and thermostat and also the aerator, none of which were attractive to look at. When I had finally finished it and replaced the brilliant scarlet sword-tails, the shiny black mollies, the silver hatchet fish, and the brilliant Piccadilly-like neon-tetras, and stepped back to observe my handiwork, I found myself deeply impressed by my own genius. Mr Romilly, to my delight, was ecstatic about the whole thing.

'Exquisite! Exquisite!' he exclaimed. 'Simply exquisite.'

'Well, you know what they say, Mr Romilly,' I said. 'That a good pupil needs a good master.'

'Oh, you flatter me, you flatter me,' he said, wagging his finger at me playfully. 'This is a case where the pupil has surpassed the master.'

'Oh, I don't think that,' I said. 'But I do think that I'm getting almost as good as you.'

After that, I was allowed to decorate all the tanks and all the cages.

FROM BEASTS IN MY BELFRY:

It was in the mid-nineteenth century that the great German animal dealer Karl Hagenbeck created an entirely new form of zoological garden. Up until then animals had been stuffed into ill-designed, unsanitary, heavily-barred cages that made it difficult for the public to see the animals and even more so for the animals to survive these appalling concentration-camp-like conditions. Hagenbeck had an absolutely new conception of how animals should be displayed. Instead of grim, iron-barred dungeons, he gave his animals light and space, with huge artificial mountains of rocks to climb on, and he separated them from the public with either dry moats or moats filled with water. To the pundits of zoo keeping this was heresy. To begin with, they said it was unsafe, for animals were sure to get out of moats, and even if this did not happen, all the animals would die for it was well known that unless you kept tropical animals in fuggy, germ-infested steam heat, they would die instantly. The fact that tropical animals frequently languished and died in these Turkish-bath conditions anyway was neither here nor there. But, to the pundits' surprise, Hagenbeck's animals flourished. They not only improved their condition in their outdoor quarters but even bred successfully. Once Hagenbeck had proved his contention that keeping animals under these conditions made them not only happier and healthier but a better and more spectacular show from the public's point of view, then all zoological gardens in the world started to turn over to this new method of keeping and displaying their collections.

Whipsnade, then, was really London Zoo's attempt to out-Hagenbeck Hagenbeck. This huge farm estate perched up on the Dunstable Downs had been purchased by the society and laid out at considerable expense. Here animals were to be displayed in as close to natural surroundings as possible; that is, surroundings that to the zoo-going public *seemed* natural. Lions were to have forests to live in; wolves to have woods; and for the antelopes and other hoofed animals, great rolling paddocks. From my point of view Whipsnade then was the nearest approach to going on safari that one could attempt at that time. For this was in the days before the aristocrats of England were forced by crippling death duties to become a collection of zoo keepers.

Whipsnade, I found, was an extremely small village consisting of one pub and just a handful of cottages scattered lazily among valleys full of hazel copses. I went to the pay-box to explain my presence and then, leaving my suitcases there, went along to the administration building. Peacocks gleamed and shimmered as they dragged their tails across the green lawns, and in the pine trees along the main drive there hung a gigantic nest –

like a haystack of twigs – around which Quaker parakeets chittered and screamed.

I went into the administration building and was then ushered into the office of Captain Beale, the superintendent. He was sitting there, in his shirt sleeves, sporting some very handsome striped braces. The large desk in front of him was piled high with a great assortment of papers, most of which looked terribly official and scientific, and a mound of them partially covered the telephone. As the captain stood up I saw that he was a man of immense height and girth and he looked, with his bald head, steel-rimmed spectacles and mouth drawn down into what was almost a sneer, exactly like one of the drawings of Billy Bunter. He came lumbering round the desk and stared at me, breathing heavily through his nose.

'Durrell?' he boomed interrogatively. 'Durrell?'

He had a very deep voice and he spoke in a sort of muted roar which some people get into the habit of doing after many years on the West Coast of Africa.

'Yes, sir,' I said.

'Glad to meet you. Sit down,' said the captain. He shook my hand and retired behind his desk.

He threw his bulk back in the chair and it creaked alarmingly. He stuck his thumbs under his braces and played a tattoo on them with his fingers, staring at me. The silence seemed interminable. I sat timidly on the edge of my chair; I desperately wanted to make a good impression to begin with.

'Think you'll like it here?' asked Captain Beale so suddenly and so loudly that I jumped.

'Er . . . yes, sir, I'm sure I shall,' I said.

'You've never done any of this sort of work before?' he inquired.

'No, sir,' I replied, 'but I've kept a lot of animals at one time or another.'

'Ha!' he said, almost sneeringly. 'Guinea pigs, rabbits, goldfish – that sort of thing. Well, you'll find it a bit different here.'

I was longing to tell him that I had kept considerably more exotic pets than rabbits, guinea pigs and goldfish but I did not feel that this was the right moment.

*   *   *

My first few days were fully occupied with the learning process, memorizing the routine work of feeding, cleaning and other daily chores, but this routine work was fairly basic and once I had mastered it I had more opportunity for watching the animals in our care and trying to learn something about them. Both Jesse and Joe were vastly amused at the fact that I carried an enormous notebook in my pocket and would – at the slightest provocation – whip it out and make an entry.

'Bloody Sherlock Holmes,' was Jesse's description of me, 'always writing frigging things down.'

Joe would attempt to pull my leg by describing long and complicated actions that he had just seen the animal performing but he would always let his imagination get the better of him and I could soon spot the deception.

Naturally enough, I started my researches on the lions. Being for the first time in my life on an intimate footing with these beasts I decided to read up all I could about them and see how it tallied with my own observations. I discovered, not altogether to my surprise, that there is probably no other animal (except some purely mythological creatures) that has been endowed with so many imaginary virtues. Ever since someone in a moment of unzoological enthusiasm named it the King of Beasts, writers have vied with each other to produce proof of the lion's right to this title. This particularly applied, I found, to the ancient writers who were unanimous in praising *Felix leo* for its sweetness of character, sagacity, courage and sportsmanship; thus, I suppose, it was a foregone conclusion that it should be adopted as a national emblem by that modest and retiring race, the English. I had not been working with Albert and his wives for any length of time before I discovered that lions were not all that the old writers cracked them up to be.

In Pliny's *Natural History*, published round about 1674, I found the following delightful account of the King of Beasts:

> The Lion alone of all wild beasts is gentle to those who humble themselves unto him, and will not touch any such upon their submission, but spareth what creatures soever lieth prostrate before him.
>   As fell and furious as hee is otherwhiles, yet hee dischargeth his rage upon man, before that hee setteth upon women, and never preyeth upon babes unless it be for extreme hunger.

After knowing Albert for only three days I realized that this description did not fit him. He was, to be sure, as fell and furious as he could possibly be, but I do not think he had an ounce of mercy in his makeup. Anyone who had attempted to 'lie prostrate' in front of him would have received a bite in the back of the neck for his pains.

Another ancient writer I perused was Purchase, and he informed me, with all the assurance of one who has never seen a lion, that 'the Lyons in cold places are more gentle, and hotter more fierce.' When I first read this it gave me a certain hope that I would be able to get on friendly terms with Albert for, just after my arrival at Whipsnade, the weather had turned cold and an icy wind roared across the downs, making the misshapen elder bushes creak and groan and shudder against each other. In this type of weather, according to Purchase, Albert and his wives should be gambolling around like friendly kittens.

On my second morning my faith in Purchase was rudely shattered. I was walking past the lions' cage, bent double against the wind and blue with cold, on my way back to the shelter and warmth of 'The Haven'. Albert had concealed himself in a thick bed of grass and nettles in the curve of the cage near the path. He had, I am sure, seen me pass earlier and had decided that he would surprise me on my return journey. He waited until I was opposite and then he suddenly jumped out against the bars with a hair-raising cough of wrath. Then he squatted on his haunches and glared at me, his yellow eyes full of ferocious amusement at my sudden panic. He decided that this was a good joke and repeated it later the same day. Again he had the pleasure of watching me leap in the air like a startled stag, but this time he was gratified to observe me drop the bucket I was carrying, trip over it, and fall heavily into a bed of particularly luxuriant nettles. I discovered afterwards that cold weather, instead of making Albert gentle, infected him with a dreadful skittishness, and he would spend his time hiding behind bushes and leaping out at unsuspecting old ladies as they passed. I presume that this exercise improved his circulation when there was a nip in the air . . .

Once a week we had to trap up Albert and his wives so that we could enter the cage and clean up the bones and other signs of their tenancy. Built into the side of the enclosure was a large, iron-barred trap with a sliding door, and we had to get all three lions securely locked up in this before we could get on with the work. This trapping was a tedious perform- ance, the monotony of which was only relieved by its ridiculousness. To trap Albert and his wives, who were, needless to say, unco-operative in the extreme, you had to be very cunning and combine this with the ability to look innocent and run fast. The first requisite for successful trapping was that Albert should be very hungry; he would then prowl along the bars, his little eyes glinting, his mane shaggy with ferocity. We would arrive at the trap, looking radiantly innocent, and place our various spades, buckets, brushes and forks on the path. Then we would produce a large, gory joint of meat and place it in a position where Albert could both see and smell it. He would greet this manoeuvre with a series of wicked, chuckling snarls, deep in the scarf of his mane. Then we would raise the sliding door at the end of the trap and stand about, all talking loudly, as if there was no thought further from our minds than the trapping of lions. I must explain, in defence of Albert's intelligence, that he was not fooled by all this for one minute, but it had become a sort of ritual which had to be respected or the whole procedure would become disorganized.

When sufficient time had passed and Albert had studied the joint and pondered its possibilities, we would put it inside the trap. Leaning on the barrier rail, we would indulge in autosuggestion. The following remarks would be made with complete lack of tone and interest: 'How about it, Alb? Hungry boy? Come on, then, come on. There's a good lad. Have some meat, then. Come on, then. Come on. Come on . . .' We would repeat this endlessly, like a part song, and the whole performance was made doubly ridiculous by the fact that Albert understood none of it.

Having exhausted our encouraging remarks, we would reach a deadlock; we would glare at Albert and he would glare back at us. All through this Nan and Jill would be prowling in the background, obviously impatient but doing nothing, for tradition demanded that their lord and master should take the lead. Albert would now give the impression of having gone into a trance. During these spells of waiting I would while away the time by attempting to find an answer to that much disputed question of whether or not the human eye has any power over the mere beast. I would stare with intense concentration into Albert's little yellow eyes, and he would stare back unblinkingly. The only effect it ever had was to make me feel a trifle uncomfortable.

Generally, after about ten minutes, Albert would still show no signs of entering the trap and so we would be forced to try another ruse. Leaving the meat in the trap, we would saunter off down the path until Albert thought we were too far away to be dangerous. Then he would make a sudden dash into the trap, grab the meat, and endeavour to escape with it before we had time to rush down the path and slam the door on him. More often than not, the iron door clanged down some two inches behind his retreating tail and we would be left standing there foolishly while he carried his trophy off to some secluded spot to settle down and enjoy it. This, of course, would put an end to our trapping and we would be forced to wait twenty-four hours until Albert felt peckish again. With the other animals on the section we had to go through much the same business to get them trapped up, but they never gave us as much trouble as the lions. Albert had a genius for being annoying.

If, however, we did get the lions safely locked up in the trap, we had to make our way round to a small door in the opposite side of the cage. Once we had entered the enclosure we had to shut and lock this door behind us. It was a feeling I never really relished, for it meant that we were shut in a two-acre cage, surrounded by a barred fence some sixteen feet high, with no means of escape should the lions, by some magical means, get out of the trap. On one occasion Joe and I entered the cage and, as usual, separated and worked our way through the bushes, picking up the gnawed white bones from last week's meals. Soon we lost sight of each other in the thick undergrowth; I could hear Joe whistling and an occasional clang as he dropped a bone into his bucket. I was working my way along a narrow path between great bramble bushes which must have been a favourite haunt of Albert's for I could see his great paw marks in the soft clay of the path and, here and there, a tuft of hair from his mane which had caught on a thorn. I was musing over the big paw marks and thinking what a vicious and sultry character Albert was, when suddenly he roared. Now the traps were some distance away through the trees, on my left, yet I could have sworn that the roar came from directly in front of me. Without waiting to find exactly where Albert was, I made my way with all speed to the exit gate. Joe and I arrived at the gate simultaneously.

'Is he out?' I inquired when we were safely outside the cage.

'I don't know,' said Joe, 'I didn't wait to see.'

We went round to the other side of the enclosure and found the lions still locked up in the trap, but Albert had a humorous glint in his eyes that made me think.

This incident was my first experience of the so-called ventriloquial powers of the lion. Many writers assert that a lion can throw his roar so that it appears to come from two or three different directions at once. This is not quite as impossible as it sounds, for many species of birds and insects have the most astonishing ventriloquial powers. In some cases you can actually watch the creature making the sound and yet the sound itself appears to come from several feet, or even yards, away. Obviously, if the lion possessed this power it would be immensely useful to him; he would be able to panic herds of game at night so that, in their terror they might run towards their hunter instead of away from him. Judging by that morning's experience it certainly seemed as though Albert could throw his roar; he had been about the same distance away from Joe as from me, yet both of us were sure that the roar had come from close by.

Some time after this experience I had another and equally startling example of Albert's voice throwing. I was coming back from some village festivities late one night and I decided to take a short-cut through the park. My path took me along the side of the lion cage and as I hurried along through the rustling elders Albert gave a sudden snarling grunt that brought me to a standstill. The sound was difficult to place, although I knew the direction from which it must have come. It had a certain earth-trembling quality that made it seem as though it was vibrating up through the soles of my feet. To judge by the sound, Albert might have been inside or outside his cage. It was not very pleasant, and only my devotion to natural history prevented me from running like a hare. With considerable temerity, I walked up to the barrier rail and peered into the gloom, but I could not see anything and there was no moon to help me. The bushes were black and still. As I moved along the side of the cage I knew that I was being followed; I could almost feel the eager eyes fixed on me, but the tawny bodies made no sound and the great paws did not snap a single twig as a guide to their whereabouts. As I started up the hillside, away from the cage, there came a great sniff, full of scorn and derision.

Some people refuse to believe that a lion can throw his voice deliberately. They maintain that all he does is to hold his mouth close to the ground when roaring, so that the sound is blurred and it is impossible to tell from which direction it is coming. Now, in order to find out if this was true I tried very hard to be present when Albert was roaring, but with little success. Time after time I would walk hopefully past his cage thinking that he might roar while I was there to see, but every time he remained stubbornly silent.

Sometimes, when I heard him start up, I would treat the visitors to the sight of a keeper running madly along the path through the trees as though some escaped beast were at my heels. But every time, when I arrived panting at the barrier rail. I would find that Albert had either finished or else had thought better of it and had relapsed into silence after two or three coughs. However, I was more than compensated for this by the magnificent sounds he would produce when I could hear, but not see, him.

He always seemed to choose the late afternoon to burst into song. He would start, quite suddenly, with two or three preliminary 'Aroom' noises, with long pauses in between, as if he were making sure of the right note. Then he would launch into the full song: the 'Arooms' would become throaty and rich and the pause between each shorter and shorter, until they ran together in a terrific crescendo of sound. It would rasp out, faster and faster, then start to slow down: then, just as suddenly as it began, it would stop. It is difficult to describe the frightening possibilities that were snarled at you when the sound reached its zenith. Considered dispassionately, the song resembled, more than anything else, someone sawing wood on a gigantic echoing barrel. First there would be the slow strokes of the saw; then they would get faster and faster as the steel bit into the wood; then the strokes would get slow again, as an indication that the sawing was nearly done; then, silence. And at that moment I always waited to hear the thud of the piece of wood hitting the ground.

After some weeks' association with Albert I decided that he did not in any way measure up to the popular estimation of what a lion should be. He was sulky, blustery and devoid of any finer feelings whatsoever. His small, golden eyes always had in them an expression of baffled rage; it seemed that he was trying to uphold his race's reputation for fierceness but could not remember why. There was always a faintly puzzled look about him, as though he were wondering whether it was necessary to behave in this way. When he was not prowling about in a filthy temper he was indulging in his 'joke' of jumping out suddenly at unsuspecting passers-by and getting a sardonic pleasure out of their panic. At mealtimes he would behave in a reprehensible manner and then, gorged with his own meat and his ill-gotten gains, he would sprawl in the long grass and belch. I tried very hard, but I could not find a single endearing quality in Albert.

*   *   *

To the north of the section lay a large, green, velvety paddock surrounded by a crisp crinoline of oak trees. Here lived what were undoubtedly the rarest animals in our care, a pair of young Père David deer. To look at, they were not nearly so graceful as, say, the red deer or fallow deer that lived not far away from them. By deer standards one would almost have called them ungainly. They stood some four foot high at the shoulder and they had long, earnest faces with curiously slanted, almond-shaped eyes. Under each eye there was a curious vent; a little pocket of pink skin which could open and close at will, which led nowhere and seemed to fulfil no useful purpose. They had stocky, rather donkey-like bodies; their colour was a peculiar acorn-brown, with white bellies and a heart-shaped patch on their bottoms. The shape and slant of the eyes, the curious body, the long black hooves, and – unique in the deer family – a long tufted tail like a donkey, all went to make them look as though they had wandered out of a rather uncertain Chinese print.

Their movements were clumsy, lacking in the grace that is usually displayed by their family. Occasionally when I passed their paddock my sudden appearance would startle them and they would wheel round to face me, legs spread out, ears pricked; then they would set off in panic-stricken flight to the other end of their domain with a gait reminiscent of a drunken donkey. The legs seemed to be held very stiffly and the abnormal length of the body made the whole deer roll from side to side. When you compared it to the beautiful movements of the other deer you realized just how donkey-like the Père David was. The only part of it that had any of the normal beauty of line and movement of the deer family was the head and neck.

The story of the discovery and subsequent survival of this odd-looking deer is as curious as any in the annals of natural history. In the middle 1800s Père David, a Franciscan missionary, worked and travelled in China and, like so many men of the Church in those days, took a deep interest in natural history. I suspect, in fact, that the number of unique natural history specimens he obtained greatly outnumbered the souls he saved during his sojourn in China. It was he, in fact, who first obtained specimens of the new and famous giant panda. While in Peking he heard a rumour to the effect that in the Royal Gardens of the Emperor's Palace there existed a herd of deer – a type of deer, it was said, unknown anywhere else in China. This naturally intrigued Father David, but the problem was how to get a chance of seeing these animals. They were in a walled garden carefully guarded by Tartars. At that time, of course, foreigners were scarcely tolerated in China so Père David had to move with great caution. It shows the depth of the interest that the man had in natural history that he was prepared to take risks that could well have led to imprisonment or even death. His first step was to bribe a Tartar guard on the gate of the Royal Palace to allow him to climb up on top of the wall and survey the garden. From this vantage point he could see eventually a herd of deer feeding among the trees. It must have been a thrilling moment for him as he found himself looking at a herd of deer grazing about a hundred yards away, and realized that he was seeing a new and particularly unusual species.

He at once wrote home to Paris, to Professor Milne-Edwards at the Museum of Natural History, describing his discovery:

> Three miles to the south of Peking there is a vast Imperial Park about thirty-six miles perhaps all round. There it is that since time immemorial deer and antelopes have lived in peace. No European can get into this park, but this spring, from the top of the surrounding wall, I had the good fortune to see, rather far off, a herd of more than a hundred of these animals, which looked to me like elks. Unfortunately, they had no antlers at this time: what characterizes the animal that I saw is the length of the tail, which struck me as being comparatively as long as the tail of the donkey, a feature not to be found in any of the cervides that I know. It is also smaller than the northern elk. I have made fruitless attempts to get the skin of this species. It is quite impossible to have even portions and the French Legation feel incapable of managing to procure this curious animal by unofficial approaches to the Chinese Government. Luckily I know some Tartar soldiers who are going to do guard duty in this park and I am sure, by means of a bribe, that I shall get hold of a few skins which I shall hasten to send you. The Chinese give to this animal the name of Mi-Lou, which means the four odd features, because they consider that this deer takes after the stag by its antler, the cow by its hooves, the camel by its neck and the mule or even the donkey by its tail.

Père David was now determined to obtain specimens, but this was not so easily done. He knew that, in spite of the penalty for such an action being death, sometimes the Tartar guards fed on poached venison, so with the aid of more bribes he succeeded in getting them to agree to save for him the skins and the skulls of the next ones they ate. In due course this was done and Père David shipped the skins and skulls back to the Museum of Natural History in Paris where it was discovered that they were indeed a species new to science. In recognition of Father David's great contribution to oriental natural history they were named *Elaphurus davidianus* in his honour.

Naturally, zoological gardens and private collections in Europe wanted to obtain specimens of this rare deer and, indeed, if any deer could be called rare, Père David's could, for the only known living herd was in the Imperial Palace Gardens, and there is still a certain amount of doubt as to where they came from in the first place. It is almost as though they had evolved within the grounds of the Emperor's summer palace. As a wild animal, it is now believed to have been extinct two or three thousand years ago. Semi-fossil remains show that before this time it apparently roamed wild about the Honan district of China. The Chinese authorities, however, were not anxious for any of their national treasures to be exported, but at length, after prolonged negotiations, several pairs of the deer were sent to various zoos in Europe and a pair was sent to the then Duke of Bedford's extraordinary private menagerie at Woburn.

Not long after this the Yangtze River flooded its banks and the flood waters breached the wall round the Emperor's Palace Gardens in several places. Most of the deer escaped into the surrounding countryside where of course they were immediately slaughtered by the starving peasantry. There still remained a tiny nucleus in the gardens; but it seemed that the Père David deer was dogged by bad luck for next came the Boxer Rebellion and during this time the Tartar guards seized the opportunity of eating the remaining deer. So now the species was extinct in its home of origin and the total world population consisted of animals scattered about Europe.

The Duke of Bedford, one of the earliest and most intelligent conservationists, decided that he must add to his tiny herd at Woburn if the species was to be saved, so he negotiated with the zoological gardens that had specimens of the deer and eventually managed to establish a herd of eighteen. This was the total world population. Gradually, living under ideal conditions at Woburn, the animals increased in number until, at the time I was at Whipsnade, the Woburn herd numbered nearly five hundred. Now, the duke felt, was the time when the animals should be distributed because to have every living representative of the species congregated in one spot was risky in the extreme. An outbreak of foot-and-mouth disease, for example, could have exterminated the Père David very successfully. Therefore, the duke started by giving a pair to Whipsnade as the nucleus of a breeding herd.

While I was on the bear section came the news that the duke was going to let several other zoos have pairs of this deer and was going to donate yet another pair to Whipsnade. We were going to have the task of collecting all the baby animals as soon as they were born at Woburn and hand-rearing them until they were of a suitable age to be transported to their new homes. The reason for this rather laborious method was the extreme nervousness of the deer. They would quite easily, if frightened – and they seemed more apt to be frightened by practically anything than any other animal I have met – display a stupidity that was unbelievable, such as charging a stone wall time and time again in an effort to break through. It was felt that if the baby deer were hand-reared by us they would at least be used to human beings, in which case perhaps unusual sights and sounds would not panic them to the same extent as if they had been caught as semi-adults.

When I discovered that I and another boy, called Bill, had been chosen to assist Phil Bates in the task of hand-rearing these deer I was overwhelmed. The babies were to be kept in two big stables and as they had to be fed during the night as well as very early in the morning Bill and I would take turns to sleep in the small shed up in the woods near the stables so that we could be on hand to help Phil both at night and during the day. The great day came and we went to Woburn in the lorry.

The parkland at Woburn was one of the most beautiful I had ever seen. This, of course, was in the days before merry-go-rounds and enormous parties of sightseers had turned the place into a sort of three-ring circus. The massive and beautifully-spaced trees, rolling green sward, and the gently moving herds of deer made a picture that was unforgettable, one that would have made Edward Landseer burst into tears of frustration. The babies, all wide-eyed and startled-looking, were each inside a sack with only their heads poking out. This was a precautionary measure so that they could not stand up or try to run and break a leg while travelling in the lorry. We loaded them on to a thick layer of straw and surrounded them with bales of straw as a cushioning. Then Bill and I took up our stations in the back amongst this forest of tiny heads and the lorry proceeded to Whipsnade at a gentle thirty miles an hour while we watched the babies closely to see what effect the journey was having on them. When the lorry first started to move, one or two of them kicked and bucked a bit inside their sacks but they soon settled down, and by the time we reached Whipsnade several of them had fallen asleep with the bored expression of professional railway travellers.

We carried them into the stables and cut away the sacking; then, in that incredibly wobbly and pathetic manner of young deer, they all staggered inebriatedly to their feet and weaved about the stable. It was only at this point that they seemed to realize that something was missing and so they started revolving in circles, bleating like goats – an astonishingly long, harsh 'baaaa'. Hastily, Bill and I milked the herd of goats that had been carefully installed against the babies' arrival, poured the still-warm, frothing milk into bottles, added the necessary vitamin drops and cod liver oil, and then, holding a bottle apiece, we entered the stable. Père David deer are just as stupid when babies as any other form of life and at that first feed I think Bill and Phil and I got at night more goat's milk in our trouser turn-ups, in our pockets, and squirted into our eyes and ears than the babies consumed. They very soon got the hang of the idea that they should suck on the teat and thus obtain milk, but the co-ordination between their mouths and their brains left a lot to be desired and we had to be constantly on the alert, for they would mumble the teat around in their mouths until eventually the end was poking out of the side of their mouths, then, scrunching it between their teeth they would send a jet of goat's milk straight into your eye. However, within two days they had mastered this and had decided that Phil, Bill and I constituted a joint mother-figure. There were eight of them and so we divided them up and put four in each stable, but as they grew bigger it became more and more difficult, for their exuberance at mealtimes was such that the moment they saw us they would deafen us with their harsh bleats and as soon as the stable door was open there would be a cascade of deer. On several occasions both Bill and I were knocked down by the fawns and we had to roll quickly out of their way, for they would stamp all over us with complete lack of discrimination and their very long hooves were exceedingly sharp.

I think it was at this time that I suddenly realized the full meaning of the term 'rare'. Hitherto, when people talked of a rare animal, I had always been under the impression that this simply meant that it was rare in museum collections or in zoological gardens, but actual rarity in numbers had not really impinged on me. This, I think, was because people tended to say an animal was rare rather as though this were an accolade, as though it were something the animal should be proud of. But with the advent of the Père David deer and working so closely with them, it suddenly occurred to me that an astonishing number of animals were rare in quite a different sense. I started my researches on the subject and kept a massive file of the results. I did not know it at the time but I was producing a rather shaky and amateurish version of the Red Data Book now published by the International Union for the Conservation of Nature. The results of my researches horrified me: figures like 'total population of Indian rhinos left – 250; Sumatran rhinos – 150; Bornean rhinos – 20; world population of Flightless Rail – 72 pairs; Arabian Oryx shot and machine-gunned to a possible total population of 30,' and so on. The list, it seemed, was unending. It was then that I realized what the true function of a zoological garden should be; for, while trying to protect these animals in the wild state, it was obviously of urgent necessity that breeding groups should be set up in captivity as widely spread all over the world as possible. It was then that I conceived the idea that, should I ever acquire a zoo of my own, its main function would be this one work: to act as a reservoir and sanctuary for those harried creatures.

When it was my turn on duty with the deer I gave a lot of thought to these problems. At midnight, with the deer's great, liquid eyes glittering in the light of the storm lantern as they butted and sucked greedily at the bottles of warm milk, it seemed to me that by any standards these animals had as much right to existence as I did. Getting up at five in the morning to give them their bottle feed was no penance. The oak woods in the first pale spears of sunlight would be as gold-green as a quetzal's tail, leaves blurred with a gossamer coating of dew, and as one walked through the great trunks towards the stable where the deer were kept the birdsong was like an enormous chorus of thanksgiving in a green cathedral. Then one would open the stable door and be knocked down by one's loving charges and they would nuzzle, bleating at one, slapping one with their long, wet, warm tongues. Though the precarious state of so many animal species all over the world still filled me with despondency, at least by helping to rear Père David deer I felt I was doing something concrete, however infinitesimal the gesture was.

PART TWO

1945–1965

'The man is mad, wanting to have a zoo!'

LAWRENCE DURRELL, C. 1945

Gerry left Whipsnade just before his twenty-first birthday, when he was to inherit £3,000 – a fortune in those days. He had planned to pay his way on animal-collecting expeditions for zoos, so that he could observe wild animals in their natural habitats, but because of his lack of experience none of the professional collectors would take on this young, eager volunteer. He decided to finance his own expeditions and, in the late forties and early fifties, made several trips to Africa and South America. As in Corfu, his observations of animals and people are equally enchanting.

A most poignant story from Gerry's very first trip is that of Cholmondely, a chimpanzee he was looking after on behalf of London Zoo. While his references to natives and cigarette smoking may not be 'politically correct' today, do remember that the tale was written more than forty years ago. I particularly wanted to include it here because it foreshadows his unease over zoos of the day and their attitude towards the animals in their care.

Throughout the writings of 1945 to 1965 Gerry sharpens his appreciation for the 'big picture' in the natural world, which, of course, for him has moved beyond the historically human-dominated habitats of Corfu. He begins to describe the ensemble of animals, plants and landscapes and how these parts relate to the whole of a wild ecosystem. And yet he always becomes personally involved in the panorama, as when he saves a family of lily-trotters from a hungry cayman.

FROM THE BAFUT BEAGLES:

Now I have always like toads, for I have found them to be quiet, well-behaved creatures with a charm of their own; they have not the wildly excitable and rather oafish character of the frog, nor his gulping and moist appearance. But, until I met these two, I had always imagined that all toads were pretty much the same, and that having met one you had met them all as far as personality was concerned, though they might differ much in colour and appearance. But I very soon found out that these two amphibians had personalities so striking that they might almost have been mammals.

These creatures are called Brow-leaf Toads, because the curious cream-coloured marking on the back is, in shape and colour, exactly like a dead and withered leaf. If the toad crouches down on the floor of the forest it merges into its background perfectly. Hence its English title; its scientific title is 'Eyebrow Toad', which in Latin sounds even more apt: *Bufo supercili-arus*, for the Brow-leaf, on first acquaintance, gives the impression of being overwhelmingly supercilious. Above its large eyes the skin is hitched up into two little points, so that the creature has its eyebrows raised at the world in a markedly sardonic manner. The immensely wide mouth adds to this impression of aristocratic conceit by drooping gently at the corners, thus giving the toad a faintly sneering expression that can only be achieved by one other animal that I know of, the camel. Add to this the slow, swaggering walk, and the fact that the creature squats down every two or three steps and gazes at you with a sort of pitying disdain, and you begin to feel that superciliousness could not go much farther.

My two Brow-leafs squatted side by side on a bed of fresh grass in the bottom of the basket and gazed up at me with expressions of withering scorn. I tipped the basket on its side and they waddled out on to the floor with all the indignation and dignity of a couple of Lord Mayors who had been accidentally locked in a public lavatory. They walked about three feet across the floor and then, apparently exhausted by this effort, squatted down, gulping gently. They surveyed me very fixedly for some ten minutes with what appeared to be ever-increasing disgust. Then one of them wandered away and eventually crouched down by the leg of the table, evidently under the mistaken impression that it was the trunk of a tree. The other continued stare at me, and after mature reflection he summed up his opinion of my worth by being sick, bringing up the semi-digested corpses of a grasshopper and two moths. Then he gave me a pained and reproachful look and joined his friend under the table.

As I had no suitable cage ready for them, the Brow-leafs spent the first few days locked in my bedroom, wandering slowly and meditatively about the floor, or squatting in a trance-like state under my bed, and affording me untold amusement by their actions. I discovered, after a few hours' acquaintance with my plump room-mates, that I had sadly misjudged them, for they were not the arrogant, conceited creatures they pretended to be.

They were actually shy and easily embarrassed beasts, completely lacking in self-confidence; I suspect that they suffered from deep and ineradicable inferiority complexes and that their insufferable air of superiority was merely a pose to hide from the world the hideous truth, that they had no faith in their fat selves. I discovered this quite by accident the night of their arrival. I was making notes on their coloration, while the toads squatted on the floor at my feet, looking as though they were composing their own entries for Burke's *Peerage*. Wanting to examine their hindquarters more closely, I bent down and picked up one of them between finger and thumb, holding him under the arm-pits, so that he dangled in the air in a most undignified manner. He uttered a loud indignant belch at this treatment and kicked out with his fat hind legs, but my grip was too strong for him and he just had to dangle there until I had finished my examination of his lower regions. Eventually, when I replaced him on the ground next to his companion, he was a different toad altogether. Gone was his aristocratic expression: he was a deflated and humble amphibian. He crouched down, blinking his great eyes nervously, while a sad and timid expression spread over his face. He looked almost as if he was going to cry. This transformation was so sudden and complete that it was astonishing, and I felt absurdly guilty at having been the cause of his ignominy. In order to even things up a bit, I picked up the other one and let him dangle for a while, and he, too, lost his self-confidence and became timid and embarrassed when I replaced him on the floor. They sat there looking so dejected and miserable that it was ludicrous, and my unmannerly laughter proved too much for their sensitive natures, for they waddled rapidly away and hid under the table for the next half-hour. But now that I had learnt their secret I could deflate them at will when they became too haughty: all I had to do was to rap them gently on the nose with my finger, and they would crouch down guiltily, look-ing as though they were about to blush, and gaze at me with pleading eyes.

I built a nice large cage for my Brow-leafs, and they settled down in it quite happily; however, to keep them healthy, I allowed them to have a walk in the garden every day. When the collection increased, I found that there was too much work to be done for me to be able to stand around patiently while my two blue-blooded aristocrats took the air; I had to cut down on their walks, much to their annoyance. Then, one day, I found a guardian for them in whose hands I could safely leave them while I got on with my work. This guardian was none other than Pavlova the Patas monkey.

Pavlova was extremely tame and gentle, and she took an intense interest in everything that went on around her. The first time I put the Brow-leafs out for a walk near her she was quite captivated by them and stood up on her hind legs, craning her neck to get a better view as they walked sedately across the compound. Going back ten minutes later to see how the toads were getting on, I found that they had both wandered close to the spot where Pavlova was tied. She was squatting between them, stroking them gently with her hands, and uttering loud purring cries of astonishment and pleasure. The toads had the most ridiculously, self-satisfied expressions on their faces, and they were sitting there unmoving, apparently flattered and soothed by her caresses.

Every day after that I would put the toads out near to the place where Pavlova was tied, and she would watch them wandering about. She would give occasional cries of amazement at the sight of them, or else stroke them gently until they lay there in a semi-hypnotized condition. If ever they wandered too far away and were in danger of disappearing into the thick undergrowth at the edge of the compound, Pavlova would get very excited and call me with shrill screams to let me know that her charges were escaping, and I would hurry down and bring them back to her. One day she called me when the toads had wandered too far afield, but I did not hear her, and when I went down some time later Pavlova was dancing hysterically at the end of her string, screaming furiously, and the Brow-leafs were nowhere to be seen. I undid the monkey's leash, and she at once led me towards the thick bushes at the edge of the compound, and within a very short time she had found the runaways and had fallen on them with loud purring cries of joy.

Pavlova really got terribly fond of these fat toads, and it was quite touching to see how eagerly she greeted them in the morning, gently stroking and patting them, and how worried she got when they wandered too far away. A thing that she found very difficult to understand was why the toads were not clad in fur, as another monkey would be. She would touch their smooth skins with her fingers, endeavouring to part the non-existent fur, a worried expression on her little black face; occasionally she would bend down and lick their backs in a thoughtful sort of way. Eventually she ceased to worry over their baldness, and treated them with the same gentleness and affection she would have displayed towards offspring of her own. The toads, in their own curious way, seemed to become quite fond of her as well, though she sometimes upset their dignity, which annoyed them. I remember one morning I had just given them both a bath, which they thoroughly enjoyed, and on walking across the compound they got various bits of stick and dirt stuck to their wet tummies. This worried Pavlova, for she liked her protégés to be clean and neat. I found her sitting in the sunshine, her feet resting on the back of one Brow-leaf as though he were a footstool, while the other one dangled in the most undignified fashion from her hand. As he slowly revolved in mid-air, Pavlova solemnly picked all the bits of rubbish from his tummy, talking to him all the time in a series of squeaks and trills. When she had finished with him she put him on the ground, where he sat looking very crestfallen, while his partner was hoisted up into the air and forced to undergo the same indignity. The poor Brow-leafs had no chance of being superior and pompous when Pavlova was around.

*   *   *

The great day of the grass-gathering ceremony arrived at last. Before dawn, when the stars had only just started to fade and dwindle, before even the youngest and most enthusiastic village cockerel had tried his voice, I was awakened by the gentle throb of small drums, laughter and chatter of shrill voices, and the soft scuff of bare feet on the dusty road below the house. I lay and listened to these sounds until the sky outside the window was faintly tinged with the green of the coming day, then I went out on to the veranda to see what was happening.

The mountains that clustered around Bafut were mauve and grey in the dim morning light, striped and patterned with deep purple and black in the valleys, where it was still night. The sky was magnificent, black in the West where the last stars quivered, jade green above me, fading to the palest kingfisher blue at the eastern rim of hills. I leant on the wall of the veranda where a great web of bougainvillaea had grown, like a carelessly flung cloak of brick-red flowers, and looked down the long flight of steps to the road below, and beyond it to the Fon's courtyard. Down the road, from both directions, came a steady stream of people, laughing and talking and beating on small drums when the mood took them. Over their shoulders were long wooden poles, and tied to these with creepers were big conical bundles of dried grass. The children trotted along carrying smaller bundles on thin saplings. They made their way down past the arched opening into the Fon's courtyard and deposited their grass in heaps under the trees by the side of the road. Then they went through the arch into the courtyard, and there they stood about in chattering groups; occasionally a flute and a drum would strike up a brief melody, and then some of the crowd would break into a shuffling dance, amid handclaps and cries of delight from the onlookers. They were a happy, excited, and eager throng.

By the time I had finished breakfast the piles of grass bundles by the roadside were towering skywards, and threatening to overbalance as each new lot was added; the courtyard was now black with people, and they overflowed through the arched door and out into the road. The air was full of noise as the first arrivals greeted the late-comers and chaffed them for their laziness. Children chased each other in and out of the crowd, shrieking with laughter, and hordes of thin and scruffy dogs galloped joyfully at their heels, yelping enthusiastically. I walked down the seventy-five steps to the road to join the crowd, and I was pleased and flattered to find that they did not seem to resent my presence among them, but greeted me with quick, welcoming smiles that swiftly turned to broad grins of delight when I exchanged salutations in pidgin English. I eventually took up a suitable position by the roadside, in the shade of a huge hibiscus bush, scarlet with flowers and filled with the drone of insects. I soon had round me an absorbed circle of youths and children, who watched me silently as I sat and smoked and gazed at the gay crowd that surged past us. Eventually I was run to earth by a panting Ben, who pointed out reproachfully that it was long past lunch-time, and that the delicacy the cook had prepared would undoubtedly be ruined. Reluctantly I left my circle of disciples (who all stood up politely and shook my hand) and followed the grumbling Ben back to the house.

Having eaten, I descended once more to my vantage point beneath the hibiscus, and continued my anthropological survey of the Bafut people as they streamed steadily past. Apparently during the morning I had been witnessing the arrival of the common or working man. He was, as a rule, dressed in a gaudy sarong twisted tightly round the hips; the women wore the same, though some of the very old ones wore nothing but a dirty scrap of leather at the loins. This, I gathered, was the old style of costume: the bright sarong was a modern idea. Most of the older women smoked pipes – not the short, stubby pipes of the lowland tribes, but ones with long, slender stems, like old-fashioned clay pipes; and they were black with use. This was how the lower orders of Bafut dressed. In the afternoon the council members, the petty chiefs, and other men of substance and importance started to arrive, and there was no mistaking them for just ordinary creatures of the soil. They all wore long, loose-fitting robes of splendid colours, which swished and sparkled as they walked, and on their heads were perched the little flat skull-caps I had noticed before, each embroidered with an intricate and colourful design. Some of them carried long, slender staves of a dark brown wood, covered with a surprisingly delicate tracery of carving. They were all middle-aged or elderly, obviously very conscious of their high office, and each greeted me with great solemnity, shaking me by the hand and saying 'Welcome' several times very earnestly. There were many of these aristocrats and they added a wonderful touch of colour to the proceedings. When I went back to the house for tea I paused at the top of the steps and looked down at the great courtyard: it was a solid block of humanity, packed so tightly together that the red earth was invisible, except in places where some happy dancers cleared a small circle by their antics. Dotted among the crowd I could see the colourful robes of the elders like flowers scattered across a bed of black earth.

Towards evening I was in the midst of the thickest part of the throng, endeavouring to take photographs before the light got too bad, when a resplendent figure made his appearance at my side. His robe glowed with magenta, gold, and green, and in one hand he held a long leather switch. He was the Fon's messenger, he informed me, and, if I was quite ready, he would take me to the Fon for the grass ceremony. Hastily cramming another film into the camera, I followed him through the crowd, watching with admiration as he cut a way through the thickest part by the simple but effective method of slicing with his switch across the bare buttocks that presented themselves so plentifully on all sides. To my surprise the crowd did not seem to take exception to this treatment but yelped and screamed in mock fear, and pushed and stumbled out of our way, all laughing with delight. The messenger led me across the great courtyard, through the arched doorway, along a narrow passage, and then through another arched doorway that brought us out into a honeycomb of tiny courtyards and passages. It was as complicated as a maze, but the messenger knew his way about, and ducked and twisted along passages, through courtyards, and up and down small flights of steps until at length we went through a crumbling brick archway and came out into an oblong courtyard about a quarter of an acre in extent, surrounded by a high red brick wall. At one end of this courtyard grew a large mango tree, and around its smooth trunk had been built a circular raised dais; on this was a big heavily carved chair, and in it sat the Fon of Bafut.

His clothing was so gloriously bright that, for the moment, I did not recognize him. His robe was a beautiful shade of sky blue, with a wonderful design embroidered on it in red, yellow, and white. On his head was a conical red felt hat, to which had been stitched vast numbers of hairs from elephants' tails. From a distance it made him look as though he were wearing a cone-shaped haystack on his head. In one hand he held a fly-whisk, the handle of delicately carved wood and the switch made from the long, black-and-white tail of a colobus monkey – a thick silky plume of hair. The whole very impressive effect was somewhat marred by the Fon's feet: they were resting on a huge elephant tusk – freckled yellow and black with age – that lay before him, and they were clad in a pair of very pointed piebald shoes, topped off by jade-green socks.

After he had shaken me by the hand and asked earnestly after my health, a chair was brought for me and I sat down beside him. The courtyard was lined with various councillors, petty chiefs, and their half-naked wives, all of them squatting along the walls on their haunches, drinking out of carved cow-horn flasks. The men's multi-coloured robes made a wonderful tapestry along the red stone wall. To the left of the Fon's throne was a great pile of black calabashes, their necks stuffed with bunches of green leaves, containing mimbo or palm wine, the most common drink in the Cameroons. One of the Fon's wives brought a glass for me, and then lifted a calabash, removed the plug of leaves, and poured a drop of mimbo into the Fon's extended hand. He rolled the liquid round his mouth thoughtfully, and then spat it out and shook his head. Another flask was broached with the same result, and then two more. At last a calabash was found that contained mimbo the Fon considered fine enough to share with me, and the girl filled my glass. Mimbo looks like well-watered milk, and has a mild, faintly sour, lemonade taste which is most deceptive. A really good mimbo tastes innocuous, and thus lures you on to drink more and more, until suddenly you discover that it is not so harmless as you had thought. I tasted my glass of wine, smacked my lips, and complimented the Fon on the vintage. I noticed that all the councillors and petty chiefs were drinking out of flasks made

Gerry, about age ten, with a favourite treasure – a stuffed barn owl.

INSET: In Corfu, about age nine, with two young friends.

With Claudius, a tapir, in Buenos Aires in 1959. Claudius was one of the lovable characters in *The Whispering Land*. (© *La Nacion Taller Fotografice*)

Signing his sixth book, *My Family and Other Animals*, in 1956. It became a classic and inspired countless young naturalists, many of whom have become leading figures in the conservation movement today.

ABOVE: A popular talk at a school in Jersey in 1961, with two Zoo favourites, N'Pongo, the gorilla, and Lulu, the chimpanzee, as youngsters. N'Pongo is still with us, a venerable old lady at thirty-eight, mother and grandmother several times over.
(© *Jersey Evening Post*)

ABOVE LEFT: With koalas in Australia on the 1961-2 trip which resulted in the book *Two in the Bush*.

LEFT: With David Attenborough at Jersey Zoo, shortly after it opened in 1959. David has been an avid supporter of Gerry's work.
(© *Jersey Evening Post*)

ABOVE RIGHT:
Offering a treat to
a young chimp in
Sierra Leone in the
mid-1960s.
(© *George Baker*)

RIGHT:
Publication day in
1977 of *Golden
Bats and Pink
Pigeons*, Gerry's
account of his first
visit to Mauritius,
land of the dodo,
and the beginning
of our conserva-
tion programme
there. (© *Bristol
United Press*)

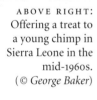

RIGHT: Signing the government agreement to launch our conservation programme in Madagascar in 1983.

Seated:
Me and Mme Berthe Rakotosamimanina of the Ministry of Higher Education.

Standing, l to r:
Dr Voara Randrianasolo of the Ministry of Higher Education, Gerry, Barthélémi Vaohita of the WWF. (© *Phillip Coffey*)

ABOVE: The arrival of Jambo the gorilla in 1972. He was welcomed by Professor Ernst Lang, Director of Basle Zoo, where Jambo was born, and Brian and Olive Park, who funded the building of Jambo's new home at Jersey Zoo.
(© *Jersey Evening Post*)

RIGHT: A long-time patriarch of Jersey Zoo, Jambo was famed for his gentle behaviour towards a child who fell into our gorilla enclosure in 1988.
(© *Phillip Coffey*)

ABOVE: Princess Anne officially opening our International Training Centre for the Breeding and Conservation of Endangered Species during the 1984 celebrations of the 25th anniversary of Jersey Zoo and the 21st anniversary of the Jersey Wildlife Preservation Trust. (© *Gary Grimshaw/ Jersey Evening Post*)

Princess Anne returned to Jersey in 1988 to break ground for our conservation education pavilion and bury a time capsule with a message from Gerry to future generations. Jeremy Mallinson, Zoogical Director, is in the foreground, with John Hartley behind. (© *Reg Cridland/Jersey Evening Post*)

Warm greeting for a new friend during a lecture tour
in the USA in the mid-1970s.

from cow's horn, whereas the Fon imbibed his mimbo from a beautifully carved and polished buffalo horn. We sat there until it was almost dark, talking and gradually emptying the calabashes of mimbo.

Eventually the Fon decided that the great moment for feeding the masses had arrived. We rose and walked down the courtyard between the double ranks of bowing subjects, the men clapping their hands rhythmically, while the women held their hands over their mouths, patting their lips and hooting, producing a noise that I, in my ignorance, had thought to be the prerogative of the Red Indian. We made our way through the doors, passages, and tiny courtyards, the concourse filing behind, still clapping and hooting. As we came out of the archway into the main courtyard there arose from the multitude a deafening roar of approval, accompanied by clapping and drumming. Amid this tumultuous reception the Fon and I walked along the wall to where the Fon's throne had been placed on a leopard skin. We took our seats, the Fon waved his hand, and the feast began.

Through the archway came an apparently endless stream of young men, naked except for small loin-cloths, carrying on their shining and muscular shoulders the various foods for the people. There were calabashes of palm wine and corn beer, huge bunches of plantain and bananas, both green and golden yellow; there was meat in the shape of giant Cane Rats, mongooses, bats and antelope, monkeys and great hunks of python, all carefully smoked and spitted on bamboo poles. Then there were dried fish, dried shrimp and fresh crabs, scarlet and green peppers, mangoes, oranges, pawpaws, pineapples, coconuts, cassava, and sweet potatoes. While this enormous quantity of food was being distributed, the Fon greeted all the headmen, councillors, and chiefs. They would each approach him, then bend double before him and clap their hands three times. The Fon would give a brief and regal nod, and the man would retire backwards. If anyone wanted to address the Fon they had to do so through their cupped hands.

I had by now absorbed quite a quantity of mimbo and was feeling more than ordinarily benign; it seemed to have much the same effect on the Fon. He barked a sudden order, and, to my horror, a table was produced on which reposed two glasses and a bottle of gin, a French brand that I had never heard of, and whose acquaintance I am not eager to renew. The Fon poured out about three inches of gin into a glass and handed it to me; I smiled and tried to look as though gin, neat and in large quantities, was just what I had been wanting. I smelt it gingerly, and found that it was not unlike one of the finer brands of paraffin. Deciding that I really could not face such a large amount undiluted, I asked for some water. The Fon barked out another order, and one of his wives came running, clutching a bottle of Angostura bitters in her hand.

'Beeters!' said the Fon proudly, shaking about two teaspoonfuls into my gin; 'you like gin wit beeters?'

'Yes,' I said with a sickly smile, 'I love gin with bitters.'

The first sip of the liquid nearly burnt my throat out: it was quite the most filthy raw spirits I have ever tasted. Even the Fon, who did not appear to worry unduly about such things, blinked a bit after his first gulp. He coughed vigorously and turned to me, wiping his streaming eyes.

'Very strong,' he pointed out.

Presently, when all the food had been brought out and arranged in huge piles in front of us, the Fon called for silence and made a short speech to the assembled Bafutians, telling them who I was, why I was there, and what I wanted. He ended by explaining to them that they had to procure plenty of animals for me. The crowd listened to the speech in complete silence, and when it had ended a chorus of loud 'Arhhh's!' broke loose, and much hand-clapping. The Fon sat down looking rather pleased with himself, and, carried away by his enthusiasm, he took a long swig at his gin. The result was an anxious five minutes for us all as he coughed and writhed on his throne, tears streaming down his face. He recovered eventually and sat there glaring at the gin in his glass with red and angry eyes. He took another very small sip of it, and rolled it round his mouth, musing. Then he leant over to confide in me.

'Dis gin strong too much,' he said in a hoarse whisper; 'we go give dis strong drink to all dis small-small men, den we go for my house and we drink, eh?'

I agreed that the idea of distributing the gin among the petty chiefs and councillors – the small-small men as the Fon called them – was an excellent one.

The Fon looked cautiously around to make sure we were not overheard; as there were only some five thousand people wedged around us he felt that he could tell me a secret in complete safety. He leant over and lowered his voice to a whisper once more.

'Soon we go for my house,' he said, gleefully; 'we go drink White Horshe.'

He sat back to watch the effect of his words on me. I rolled my eyes and tried to appear overcome with joy at the thought of this treat, while wondering what effect whisky would have on top of mimbo and gin. The Fon, however, seemed satisfied, and presently he called over the small-small men, one by one, and poured the remains of the gin into their cow-horn drinking cups, which were already half filled with mimbo. Never have I given up a drink so gladly. I wondered at the cast-iron stomachs that could face with equanimity, and even pleasure, a cocktail composed of that gin and mimbo. I felt quite sick at the mere thought of it.

Having distributed this rather doubtful largesse among his following, the Fon rose to his feet, amid handclaps, drumbeats, and Red Indian hootings, and led the way back through the intricate web of passages and courts, until we came to his own small villa, almost hidden among his wives' many grass huts, like a matchbox in an apiary. We went inside, and I found myself in a large, low room furnished with easy-chairs and a big table, the wooden floor covered with fine leopard skins and highly coloured, locally made grass mats. The Fon, having done his duty to his people, relaxed in a long chair, and the White Horse was produced; my host smacked his lips as the virginal bottle was uncorked, and gave me to understand that, now the boring duties of state were over, we could start to drink in earnest. For the next two hours we drank steadily, and discussed at great length and in the most complicated detail such fascinating topics as the best type of gun to use on an elephant, what White Horse was made of, why I didn't attend dinners at Buckingham Palace, the Russian question, and so on. After this neither the Fon's questions nor my answers had the skill and delicate construction that we would have liked, so the Fon called for his band, being under the misguided impression that the ravages of strong drink could be dissipated by sweet music. The band came into the courtyard outside and played and danced for a long time, while the Fon insisted that another bottle of White Horse be broached to celebrate the arrival of the musicians. Presently the band formed a half-circle, and a woman did a swaying, shuffling dance and sang a song in a shrill and doleful voice. I could not understand the words, but the song was strangely mournful, and both the Fon and I were deeply affected by it. Eventually the Fon, wiping his eyes, sharply informed the band that they had better play something else. They had a long discussion among themselves and finally broke into a tune which was the most perfect Conga rhythm imaginable. It was so bright and gay that it quickly revived our spirits, and very soon I was tapping the rhythm out with my feet, while the Fon conducted the band with a glass of White Horse clutched in one hand. Flushed with the Fon's hospitality, and carried away by the tune, an idea came to me.

'The other night you done show me native dance, no be so?' I asked the Fon.

'Na so,' he agreed, stifling a hiccup.

'All right. Tonight you like I go teach you European dance?'

'Ah! my friend,' said the Fon, beaming and embracing me; 'yes, yes, foine, you go teach me. Come, we go for dancing house.'

We rose unsteadily to our feet and made our way to the dance-hall. When we reached it, however, I found that the effort of walking fifty yards had told on my companion; he sank on to his ornate throne with a gasp.

'You go teach all dis small-small men first,' he said, gesturing wildly at the throng of chiefs and councillors, 'den I go dance.'

I surveyed the shuffling, embarrassed crowd of council members that I was supposed to teach, and decided that the more intricate parts of the Conga – which was the jig I proposed to tutor them in – would be beyond them. Indeed, I was beginning to feel that they might even be beyond me. So I decided that I would content myself with showing them the latter part of the dance only, the part where everyone joins into a line and does a sort of follow-my-leader around the place. The whole dance-hall was hushed as I beckoned the two-and-twenty council members to join me on the floor, and in the silence you could hear their robes swishing as they walked. I made them tag on behind me, each holding on to his predecessor's waist; then I gave a nod to the band, who, with great gusto, threw themselves into the conga rhythm, and we were off. I had carefully instructed the pupils to follow my every movement, and this they did. I soon discovered, however, that everything I knew about the Conga had been swamped by the Fon cellars: all I could remember was that somewhere; some time, one gave a kick. So off we went, with the band playing frenziedly, round and round the dance-hall; one, two, three, kick; one, two, three, kick. My pupils had no difficulty in following this simple movement, and we went round the floor in great style, all their robes swishing in unison. I was counting the beats and shouting 'Kick' at the appropriate moment, in order to make the thing simpler for them to follow; apparently they took this to be part of the dance, a sort of religious chant that went with it, for they all started shouting in unison. The effect on our very considerable audience was terrific: screeching with delight, various other members of the Fon's retinue, about forty of his wives, and several of his older offspring, all rushed to join on to the column of dancing councillors, and as each new dancer joined on to the tail he or she also joined the chant.

'One, two three, keek!' yelled the councillors.

'One, two, three, YARR!' yelled the wives.

'On, doo, ree, YARR!' screeched the children.

The Fon was not going to be left out of this dance. He struggled up from his throne and, supported by a man on each side, he tagged on behind; his kicks did not altogether coincide with the rhythmic movement of the rest of us, but he enjoyed himself none the less. I led them round and round the dance-hall until I grew giddy and the whole structure seemed to vibrate with the kicks and yells. Then, feeling that a little fresh air was indicated, I led them out of the door and into the open. Off we went in a tremendous, swaying line, up and down steps, in and out of courtyards, through strange huts – in fact everywhere that offered a free passage. The band, not to be outdone, followed us as we danced, running behind, sweating profusely, but never for one moment losing the tune. At last, more by luck than a sense of direction, I led my followers back into the dance-hall, where we collapsed in a panting, laughing heap. The Fon, who had fallen down two or three times during our tour, was escorted back to his chair, beaming and gasping. 'Na foine dance, dis,' he proclaimed; 'foine, foine!'

'You like?' I asked, gulping for air.

'I like too much,' said the Fon firmly; 'you get plenty power; I never see European dance like dis.'

I was not surprised; few Europeans in West Africa spend their spare time teaching the Conga to native chieftains and their courts. I have no doubt that, if they could have seen me doing that dance, they would have informed me that I had done more damage to the White Man's prestige in half an hour than anyone else had done in the whole history of the West Coast. However, my Conga appeared to have increased my prestige with the Fon and his court. 'One, two, three, keek!' murmured the Fon reminiscently; 'na fine song dis.'

'Na very special song,' said I.

'Na so?' said the Fon, nodding his head; 'na foine one.'

He sat on his throne and brooded for a while; the band struck up again and the dancers took the floor; I regained my breath and was beginning to feel rather proud of myself, when my companion woke up suddenly and gave an order. A young girl of about fifteen left the dancers and approached the dais where we sat. She was plump and shining with oil, and clad in a minute loin-cloth which left few of her charms to the imagination. She sidled up to us, smiling shyly, and the Fon leant forward and seized her by the wrist. With a quick pull and a twist he catapulted her into my lap, where she sat convulsed with giggles.

'Na for you, dis woman,' said the Fon, with a lordly wave of one enormous hand, 'na fine one. Na my daughter. You go marry her.'

To say that I was startled means nothing; I was horror-stricken. My host was by now in that happy state that precedes belligerency, and I knew that my refusal would have to be most tactfully put so that I should not undo the good work of the evening. I glanced around helplessly and noticed for the first time what a very large number of the crowd had spears with them. By now the band had stopped playing, and everyone was watching me expectantly. My host was regarding me glassy-eyed. I had no means of telling whether he was really offering me the girl as a wife, or whether this term was used as an euphemism for a more indelicate suggestion. Whichever it was, I had to refuse: quite apart from anything else, the girl was not my type. I licked my lips, cleared my throat, and did the best I could. First, I thanked the Fon graciously for the kind offer of his well-oiled daughter, whose eleven odd stone were at that moment making my knees ache. However, I knew that he was well versed in the stupid customs of my countrymen, and that being so, he knew it was impossible (however desirable) for a man in England to have more than one wife. The Fon nodded wisely at this. Therefore, I went on, I would be forced to refuse his extremely generous offer, for I already had one wife in England, and it would be unlawful, as well as unsafe, to take a second one back with me. If I had not already been married, I went on fluently, there would have been nothing I could have liked better than to accept his gift, marry the girl, and settle down in Bafut for the rest of my life.

To my great relief a loud round of applause greeted my speech, and the Fon wept a bit that this lovely dream could never be realized. During the uproar I eased my dusky girl friend off my lap, gave her a slap on the rump and sent her giggling back to the dance-floor. Feeling that I had undergone quite enough for one night in the cause of diplomatic relations, I suggested

that the party break up. The Fon and his retinue accompanied me to the
great courtyard and here he insisted on clasping me round the waist and
doing the Durrell Conga once more. The crowd fell in behind and we
danced across the square, kicking and yelling, frightening the Fruit Bats out
of the mango trees, and setting all the dogs barking for miles around. At
the bottom of the steps the Fon and I bade each other a maudlin farewell,
and I watched them doing an erratic Conga back across the courtyard. Then
I climbed up the seventy-five steps, thinking longingly of bed.

FROM THE OVERLOADED ARK:

Shortly before we left our hill-top hut at Bakebe [in what was then the
British Cameroons] and travelled down to our last camp at Kumba, we had
to stay with us a most unusual guest in the shape of Cholmondeley, known
to his friends as Chumley.

Chumley was a full-grown chimpanzee; his owner, a District Officer, was
finding the ape's large size rather awkward, and he wanted to send him to
London Zoo as a present, so that he could visit the animal when he was
back in England on leave. He wrote asking us if we would mind taking
Chumley back with us when we left, and depositing him at his new home
in London, and we replied that we would not mind at all. I don't think
that either John or myself had the least idea how big Chumley was: I know
that I visualized an ape of about three years old, standing about three feet
high. I got a rude shock when Chumley moved in.

He arrived in the back of a small van, seated sedately in huge crate. When
the doors of his crate were opened and Chumley stepped out with all the ease
and self-confidence of a film star, I was considerably shaken for, standing
on his bow legs in a normal slouching chimp position, he came up to my
waist, and if he had straightened up, his head would have been on a level
with my chest. He had huge arms, and must have measured at least twice
my measurements round his hairy chest. Owing to bad tooth growth both
sides of his face were swollen out of all proportion, and this gave him a
weird pugilistic look. His eyes were small, deep set and intelligent; the top
of his head was nearly bald owing, I discovered later, to his habit of sitting
and rubbing the palms of his hand backwards across his head, an exercise
which seemed to afford him much pleasure and which he persisted in until

the top of his skull was quite devoid of hair. This was no young chimp as I had expected, but a veteran of about eight or nine years old, fully mature, strong as a powerful man and, to judge by his expression, with considerable experience of life. Although he was not exactly a nice chimp to look at (I had seen more handsome), he certainly had a terrific personality: it hit you as soon as you set eyes on him. His little eyes looked at you with a great intelligence, and there seemed to be a glitter of ironic laughter in their depths that made one feel uncomfortable.

He stood on the ground and surveyed his surroundings with a shrewd glance, and then he turned to me and held out one of his soft, pink-palmed hands to be shaken, with exactly that bored expression that one sees on the faces of professional hand-shakers. Round his neck was a thick chain, and its length drooped over the tailboard of the lorry and disappeared into the depths of his crate. With an animal of less personality than Chumley, this would have been a sign of his subjugation, of his captivity. But Chumley wore the chain with the superb air of a Lord Mayor; after shaking my hand so professionally, he turned and proceeded to pull the chain, which measured some fifteen feet, out of his crate. He gathered it up carefully into loops, hung it over one hand and proceeded to walk into the hut as if he owned it. Thus, in the first few minutes of arrival, Chumley had made us feel inferior, and had moved in not, we felt, because we wanted it, but because he did. I almost felt I ought to apologize for the mess on the table when he walked in.

He seated himself in a chair, dropped his chain on the floor, and then looked hopefully at me. It was quite obvious that he expected some sort of refreshment after his tiring journey. I roared out to the kitchen for them to make a cup of tea, for I had been warned that Chumley had a great liking for the cup that cheers. Leaving him sitting in the chair and surveying our humble abode with ill-concealed disgust, I went out to his crate, and in it I found a tin plate and a battered tin mug of colossal proportions. When I returned to the hut bearing these Chumley brightened considerably, and even went so far as to praise me for my intelligence.

'Ooooooo, umph!' he said, and then crossed his legs and continued his inspection of the hut. I sat down opposite him and produced a packet of cigarettes. As I was selecting one a long black arm was stretched across the table, and Chumley grunted in delight. Wondering what he would do I handed him a cigarette, and to my astonishment he put it carefully in the corner of his mouth. I lit my smoke and handed Chumley the matches thinking that this would fool him. He opened the box, took out a match, struck it, lit his cigarette, threw the matches down on the table, crossed his legs again and lay back in his chair inhaling thankfully, and blowing clouds of smoke out of his nose. Obviously he had vices in his make-up of which I had been kept in ignorance.

Just at that moment Pious entered bearing the tray of tea: the effect on him when he saw me sitting at the table with the chimp, smoking and apparently exchanging gossip, was considerable.

'Eh . . . eahh!' he gasped, backing away.

'Whar . . . hooo,' said Chumley, sighting the tea and waving one hand madly.

'Na whatee that, sah?' asked Pious, from the doorway.

'This is Chumley,' I explained, 'he won't hurt you. Put the tea on the table.'

Pious did as he was told and then retreated to the door again. As I poured tea and milk into Chumley's mug, and added three tablespoons of sugar, he watched me with a glittering eye, and made a soft 'ooing' noises to himself. I handed him the mug and he took it carefully in both hands. There was a moment's confusion when he tried to rid himself of the cigarette, which he found he could not hold as well as the mug; he solved the problem by placing the cigarette on the table. Then he tested the tea carefully with one lip stuck out, to see if it was too hot. As it was, he sat there and blew on it until it was the right temperature, and then he drank it down. When he had finished the liquid there still remained the residue of syrupy sugar at the bottom, and as Chumley's motto was obviously waste not want not, he balanced the mug on his nose and kept it there until the last of the sugar had trickled down into his mouth. Then he held it out for a refill.

Chumley's crate was placed at a convenient point about fifty yards from the hut, next to a great gnarled tree stump to which I attached his chain. From here he could get a good view of everything that went on in and around the hut, and as we were working he would shout comments to me and I would reply. That first day he created an uproar, for no sooner had I left him chained up and gone into the hut to do some work, than a frightful upheaval took place among the monkeys. All these were tethered on ropes under a palm leaf shelter just opposite the hut. Chumley, after I had left him, felt bored, so looking around he perceived some sizeable rocks lying about within easy reach. Arming himself with these he proceeded to have a little underarm bowling practice. The first I knew of this was when I heard shrill screams and chatterings from the Drills and Guenons, and dashing out I was just in time to see a rock the size of a cabbage land in their midst, fortunately missing them all. If one of these rocks had hit a monkey it would have been squashed flat. Seizing a stick I raced down upon Chumley waving it and shouting at him, trying to appear fearsome, while all the time I was wondering what was going to happen if I tried to deal out punishment to an animal almost my own size and with twice my strength, when I was armed with only a short stick that seemed ridiculously flimsy. However, to my surprise, Chumley saw me coming and promptly lay on the ground, covering his face and his head with his long arms, and proceeded to scream at the top of his voice. I gave him two cuts with the stick across his back, and it had about as much effect as if I had tried to demolish St Paul's Cathedral with a toothpick. His back was broad and flat, solid muscle as hard as iron.

'You are a very wicked animal,' I said sternly, and Chumley, realizing that punishment was apparently over, sat up and started to remove bits of leaf from himself.

'Whoooooo . . .' he said, glancing up at me shyly.

'If you do that again I will have to give you a really good beating,' I continued, wondering if anything short of a tree trunk would make any impression on him.

'Arrrrrr . . . oooo,' said Chumley. He shifted forward, squatted down and commenced to roll up my trouser leg, and then search my calf for any spots, bits of dirt, or other microscopic blemishes. While he was thus engaged I called the animal staff and had them remove every rock from the vicinity. Later, after giving the beast yet another talking to, I left him, and shortly afterwards I noticed him digging hopefully in the earth near his crate, presumably in search of more rocks.

That night, when I carried Chumley's food and drink of tea out to him, he greeted me with loud 'hoo hoos' of delight, and jogged up and down beating his knuckles on the ground. Before he touched his dinner, however, he seized one of my hands in his and carried it to his mouth. With some trepidation I watched as he carefully put one of my fingers between his great teeth and very gently bit it. Then I understood: in the chimpanzee world to place your finger between another ape's teeth and to do the same with his, is a greeting and sign of trust, for to place a finger in such a vulnerable position is a sure display of your belief in the other's friendliness. So Chumley was flattering me by treating me as he would another chimp. Then he set to and soon polished off his meal. When he had finished I sat beside him on the ground, and he went carefully through my pockets and examined everything I had on me.

When I decided that it was time he went to bed he refused to give back a handkerchief which he had removed. He held it behind his back and passed it from one hand to the other as I tried to get it. Then, thinking that the action would settle the matter, he stuffed it hurriedly into his mouth. I realized that if I gave in and let him keep the handkerchief he would think that he could get away with anything, so for half an hour I sat there pleading and cajoling with him, until eventually, very reluctantly, he disgorged it, now very sodden and crumpled. After this I had no trouble with him: if he was playing with something that I wanted I would simply hold out my hand and ask him for it, and he would give it to me without any fuss.

Now, I had known a great number of attractive and charming animals from mice to elephants, but I have never seen one to compare with Chumley for force and charm of personality, or for intelligence. After knowing him for a while you ceased to look upon him as an animal; you regarded him more as a wizard, mischievous, courtly old man, who had, for some reason best known to himself, disguised himself as a chimpanzee. His manners were perfect: he would never grab his food and start guzzling, as the other monkeys did, without first giving you a greeting, and thanking you with a series of his most expressive 'hoo hoos'. Then he would eat delicately and slowly, pushing those pieces he did not want to the side of his plate with his fingers. His only breach of table manners came at the end of a meal, for then he would seize his empty mug and plate and hurl them as far away as possible.

He had, of course, many habits which made him seem more human, and his smoking was one. He could light his cigarette with matches or a lighter with equal facility, and then he would lie down on the ground on his back, one arm under his head and his legs bent up and crossed, blowing great clouds of smoke into the sky, and occasionally examining the end of his cigarette professionally to see if the ash needed removing. If it did he would perform the operation carefully with one finger-nail. Give him a bottle of lemonade and a glass, and he would pour himself out a drink with all the care and concentration of a world-famous barman mixing a cocktail. He was the only animal I have met that would think of sharing things with you: on many occasions, if I gave him a bunch of bananas or two or three mangoes, he would choose one and hold it out to me with an inquiring expression on his face, and he would grunt with satisfaction if I accepted it and sat down beside him on the ground to eat it.

Chumley had three aversions in life: coloured people, giant millipedes, and snakes. Natives he would tolerate, and he got a great kick out of attracting them within range and then leaping at them with a ferocious scream. Not that I think he would ever have harmed them; he just liked to watch them run screaming in fear. But the trouble was that the natives would tease him if they got the chance, and Chumley would get more and more excited, his hair would stand on end, he would sway from side to side swinging his powerful arms and baring his great teeth, and then Heaven help the native who came too close.

Giant millipedes fascinated him, but he could never bring himself to trust them whole-heartedly. The giant millipede looks not unlike a thin black pudding, with a fringe of legs (a hundred or so pairs) arranged along the underside, and a pair of short feelers in front. They were completely harmless creatures, that would glide about on their numerous legs, their feelers waving about, and liked nothing so much as a really rotten log of wood to feed on. However, their snake-like motion made them suspect in Chumley's eyes, although he seemed to realize that they were not snakes. If I placed a couple on his box he would sit and watch them for ages, his lips pursed, occasionally scratching himself. If one walked over the edge of the crate and fell to the ground, and then started to walk in his direction he would leap to his feet, retreat to the end of his chain, and scream loudly until I came and rescued him from the monster.

Snakes, of course, worried him a lot and he would get really most upset if he saw me handling one, uttering plaintive cries and wringing his hands until I had put it down. If I showed him my hands after handling a snake he would always examine them carefully, I presume to make sure I had not been bitten. If, of course, the snake slid towards him he would nearly have a fit, his hair would stand on end, he would moan, and as it got closer, throw bits of grass and twig at it in a vain effort to stop its advance. One night he flatly refused to be shut in his box when it grew dark, a thing he had never done before. When I tried to force him in, thinking he was merely playing up, he led me to the door of the crate and, leaving me there, he retreated, pointing with one hand and 'hoo hoooing' loudly and in obvious fear. Investigating his blankets and banana-leaf bed I discovered a small, blind burrowing snake coiled up in the middle. This was a harmless creature, but Chumley was taking no chances.

Not long after Chumley's arrival he suddenly went off his food, lost all his interest in life, and would spend all day crouched in his crate. He would refuse all drink except about half a mug full of water a day. I was away at the time, and John's frantic message brought me hurrying back, for John was not sure what the ape was suffering from, or how ill he really was. On my return I tried everything I knew to tempt Chumley to eat, for he was growing visibly thinner. The staff was sent to search the country-side for ripe mangoes and pawpaws, and delicate fruit salads were concocted with great care by my own hands. But Chumley would not eat. This went on for nearly a week, until I was really beginning to think we should lose him. Every evening I would force him to take a walk with me, but he was so weak that he had to sit down and rest every few yards. But I knew it would be fatal to let him lose all interest in life, for once an ape does that he is doomed. One evening before I went to take Chumley for his walk I opened a tin of Ryvita biscuits and concealed a dozen or so in my pockets. When we had walked some distance Chumley sat down and I sat beside him. As we both examined the view I took a biscuit from my pocket and started to eat it. He watched me; I think he was rather surprised when I did not offer him any, as I usually did, but finished it up and smacked my lips appreciatively. He moved nearer and started to go through my pockets, which was in itself a good sign, for he had not done that since the first day he had been taken ill. He found a biscuit, pulled it out, sniffed it, and then, to my delight, ate it up. He again broached my pocket and got another, which he also ate. Altogether he ate six, and for the next four days he existed on water and Ryvita. Then came the morning when he accepted, first his cup of tea, and then two bananas. I knew he was going to be all right. His appetite came back with a rush, and he ate us out of house and home for about two weeks, and then he returned to normal. I was very glad to have pulled him round, for we were due to leave for Kumba, and he was certainly in no condition to face the journey as thin as he had been.

The day of our departure from Bakebe dawned, and when Chumley saw the lorry arrive to load the collection he realized he was in for one of his favourite sports, a lorry ride. He hooted and yelled and danced on the end of his chain with excitement, and beat a wild tattoo on his crate, making as much noise as possible so that we should not overlook him. When everything else had been loaded his crate was hoisted on board, and then he climbed into it, hooting delightedly. We started off, and we had not gone far before the staff, all clinging to the back and sides of the vehicle, started to sing loudly, as they always did, and presently Chumley joined in with a prolonged and melodious hooting, which convulsed the staff. In fact, the cook-mate found a singing chimpanzee so amusing that he fell off the back of the lorry, and we had to stop and pick him up, covered with dust, but still mirthful. It was a good thing we were not going at any speed.

On arrival at Kumba we had put at our disposal three school-houses belonging to the Basle mission, through the kindness of the Reverend Paul Schibler and his wife. On moving in, as always happened when you made a fresh camp there was complete chaos for a while, and apart from numerous other things that had to be attended to, there was the question of water supply. While a suitable water-carrier was being employed, furnished with tins, and told to do his job at the double, Chumley made it quite clear that he was very thirsty indeed. He was chained outside, and had already attracted a large crowd of natives who had never seen a fully grown chimp before. In desperation I opened a bottle of beer and gave him that, and to my surprise he greeted its arrival with hoots of joy and smacked his lips over the froth. The lower the level fell in the bottle the more Chumley showed off, and the greater the crowd grew around him. Soon he was turning somersaults, and in between dancing a curious sort of side shuffle and clapping his hands. He was covered with beer froth, and enjoying himself hugely. But this drunken jig caused me a lot of trouble, for it took Chumley several hours to sober up and behave properly, and it took three policemen to disperse the crowd of two hundred odd people who were wedged round our houses, making entry and exit impossible. After that Chumley never had anything stronger than tea or lemonade, no matter how thirsty he became . . .

London Zoo's official collector arrived in the Cameroons, and with great regret I handed Chumley over to be transported back to England. I did not see him again for over four months, and then I went to visit him in the sanatorium at Regent's Park. He had a great straw-filled room to live in, and was immensely popular with the sanatorium staff. I did not think that he would recognize me, for when he had last seen me I had been clad in tropical kit and sporting a beard and moustache, and now I was clean-shaven and wearing the garb of a civilized man. But recognize me he did, for he whirled around his room like a dervish when he saw me and then came rushing across to give me his old greeting, gently biting my finger. We sat in the straw and I gave him some sugar I had brought for him, and then we smoked a cigarette together while he removed my shoes and socks and examined my feet and legs to make sure there was nothing wrong with them. Then he took his cigarette butt and carefully put it out in one corner of his room, well away from his straw. When the time came to go, he shook hands with me formally and watched my departure through the crack in the door. Shortly after he was moved to the monkey-house, and so he could receive no more visitors in his private room.

I never saw Chumley again, but I know his history: he became a great television star, going down to Alexandra Palace and doing his act in front of the cameras like an old trouper. Then his teeth started to worry him, and so he was moved from the monkey-house back to the sanatorium to have an operation. One day, feeling bored with life, he broke out and sallied forth across Regent's Park. When he reached the main road he found a bus conveniently at hand, so he swung himself aboard; but his presence caused such horror amongst the occupants of the bus that he got excited and forgot himself so far as to bite someone. If only people would realize that to scream and panic is the best way of provoking an attack from any wild animal. Leaving the bus and its now bloodstained passengers, Chumley walked down the road, made a pass at a lady with a pram (who nearly fainted) and was wandering about to see what else he could do to liven life up for Londoners, when a member of the sanatorium staff arrived on the scene. By now I expect Chumley had realized that civilized people were no decent company for a well-brought-up chimp, so he took his keeper's hand and walked back home. After this he was branded as not safe and sent back to the monkey-house. But he had not finished with publicity yet, for some time later he had to go back to the sanatorium for yet more treatment on his teeth, and he decided to repeat his little escapade.

It was Christmas Eve and Chumley obviously had memories of other and more convivial festivities, probably spent at some club in the depths of Africa. Anyway, he decided that if he had a walk round London on Christmas

Eve, season of goodwill, he might run across someone who would offer him a beer. So he broke open his cage and set off once more across Regent's Park. At Gloucester Gate he looked about hopefully for a bus, but there was not one in sight. But there were some cars parked there and Chumley approached them and beat on the doors vigorously, in the hope that the occupants would open up and offer him a lift. Chumley loved a ride in any sort of conveyance. But the foolish humans misconstrued his actions: there he was full of Christmas spirit, asking for a lift, and all they could do was to wind up their windows and yell for help. This, thought Chumley, was a damn poor way to show a fellow the traditional British hospitality. But before he had time to explain his mission to the car owners, a panting posse of keepers arrived, and he was bundled back to the Zoo. Chumley had escaped twice, and they were not going to risk it happening again: from being a fine, intelligent animal, good enough to be displayed on television, he had suddenly become (by reason of his escapades) a fierce and untrustworthy monster, he might escape yet again and bite some worthy citizen, so rather than risk this Chumley was sentenced to death and shot.

FROM ENCOUNTERS WITH ANIMALS:

British Guiana, lying in the northern part of South America, is probably one of the most beautiful places in the world, with its thick tropical forest, its rolling savannah land, its jagged mountain ranges and giant foaming waterfalls. To me, however, one of the most lovely parts of Guiana is the creek lands. This is a strip of coastal territory than runs from Georgetown to the Venezuelan border; here a thousand forest rivers and streams have made their way down towards the sea, and on reaching the flat land have spread out into a million creeks and tiny waterways that glimmer and glitter like a flood of quicksilver. The lushness and variety of the vegetation is extraordinary, and its beauty has turned the place into an incredible fairyland. In 1950 I was in British Guiana collecting wild animals for zoos in England, and during my six months there I visited the savannah lands to the north, the tropical forest and, of course, the creek lands, in pursuit of the strange creatures living there.

  I had chosen a tiny Amerindian village near a place called Santa Rosa as my headquarters in the creek lands, and to reach it required a two-day journey. First, by launch down the Essequibo River and then through the wider creeks until we reached the place where the launch could go no farther, for the water was too shallow and too choked with vegetation. Here we took to dug-out canoes, paddled by the quiet and charming Indians who were our hosts, and leaving the broad main creek we plunged into a maze of tiny waterways on one of the most beautiful journeys I can remember.

Some of the creeks along which we travelled were only about ten feet wide, and the surface of the water was completely hidden under a thick layer of great creamy water-lilies, their petals delicately tinted pink, and a small fern-like water-plant that raised, just above the surface of the water, on a slender stem, a tiny magenta flower. The banks of the creek were thickly covered with undergrowth and great trees, gnarled and bent, leant over the waters to form a tunnel; their branches were festooned with long streamers of greenish-grey Spanish moss and clumps of bright pink-and-yellow orchids. With the water so thickly covered with vegetation, you had the impression when sitting in the bows of the canoe that you were travelling smoothly and silently over a flower-studded green lawn that undulated gently in the wake of your craft. Great black woodpeckers, with scarlet crests and whitish beaks, cackled loudly as they flipped from tree to tree, hammering away at the rotten bark, and from the reeds and plants along the edges of the creek there would be a sudden explosion of colour as we disturbed a marsh bird which flew vertically into the air, with its hunting-pink breast flashing like a sudden light in the sky.

The village, I discovered, was situated on an area of high ground which was virtually an island, for it was completely surrounded by a chess-board of creeks. The little native hut that was to be my headquarters was some distance away from the village and placed in the most lovely surroundings. On the edge of a tiny valley an acre or so in extent, it was perched amongst some great trees which stood round it like a group of very old men, with long grey beards of Spanish moss. During the winter rains the surrounding creeks had overflowed so that the valley was now drowned under some six feet of water out of which stuck a number of large trees, their reflections shimmering in the sherry-coloured water. The rim of the valley had grown a fringe of reeds and great patches of lilies. Sitting in the doorway of the hut, one had a perfect view of this miniature lake and its surroundings, and it was sitting here quietly in the early morning or evening that I discovered what a wealth of animal life inhabited this tiny patch of water and its surrounding frame of undergrowth.

In the evening, for example, a crab-eating raccoon would come down to drink. They are strange-looking animals, about the size of a small dog, with bushy tails ringed in black and white, large, flat, pink paws, the grey of their body-fur relieved only by a mask of black across the eyes, which gives the creature a rather ludicrous appearance. These animals walk in a curious humpbacked manner with their feet turned out, shuffling along in this awkward fashion like someone afflicted with chilblains. The raccoon came down to the water's edge and, having stared at his reflection dismally for a minute or so, drank a little and then with a pessimistic air shuffled slowly round the outer rim of the valley in search of food. In patches of shallow water he would wade in a little way and, squatting on his haunches, feel about in the dark water with the long fingers of his front paws, patting and touching and running them through the mud, and he would suddenly extract something with a look of pleased surprise and carry it to the bank to be eaten. The trophy was always carried clasped delicately between his front paws and dealt with when he arrived on dry land. If it was a frog, he would hold it down and with one quick snap decapitate it. If, however, as was often the case, it was one of the large freshwater crabs, he would hurry shorewards as quickly as possible, and on reaching land flick the crab away from him. The crab would recover its poise and menace him with open pincers, and the raccoon would then deal with it in a very novel and practical way. A crab is very easily discomfited, and if you keep tapping at it and it finds that every grab it makes at you with its pincers misses the mark, it will eventually fold itself up and sulk, refusing to participate any more in such a one-sided contest. So the raccoon simply followed the crab around, tapping him on his carapace with his long fingers and whipping them out of the way every time the pincers came within grabbing distance. After five minutes or so of this the frustrated crab would fold up and just squat. The raccoon, who till then had resembled a dear old lady playing with a Pekinese, would straighten up and become businesslike, and, leaning forward, with one quick snap would cut the unfortunate crab almost in two.

Along one side of the valley some previous Indian owner of the hut had planted a few mango and guava trees, and while I was there the fruit ripened and attracted a great number of creatures. The tree-porcupines were generally the first on the scene. They lumbered out of the undergrowth, looking like portly and slightly inebriated old men, their great bulbous noses whiffling to and fro, while their tiny and rather sad little eyes, that always seemed full of unshed tears, peered about them hopefully. They climbed up into the mango-trees very skilfully, winding their long, prehensile tails round the branches to prevent themselves from falling, their black-and-white spines rattling among the leaves. They then made their way along to a comfortable spot on a branch, anchored themselves firmly with a couple of twists of the tail, then sat up on their hind legs, and plucked off a fruit. Holding it in their front paws, they turned it round and round while their large buck teeth got to work on the flesh. When they had finished a mango they sometimes began playing a rather odd game with the big seed. Sitting there they looked round in a vague and rather helpless manner while juggling the seed from paw to paw as though not quite certain what to do with it, and occasionally pretending to drop it and recovering it at the last moment. After about five minutes of this they tossed the seed down to the ground below and shuffled about the tree in search of more fruit.

Sometimes when one porcupine met another face to face on a branch, they both anchored themselves with their tails, sat up on their hind legs and indulged in the most ridiculous boxing-match, ducking, and slapping with their front paws, feinting and lunging, giving left hooks, uppercuts and body blows, but never once making contact. Throughout this performance (which lasted perhaps for a quarter of an hour) their expression never changed from one of bewildered and benign interest. Then, as though prompted by an invisible signal, they went down on all fours and scrambled away to different parts of the tree. I could never discover the purpose of these boxing bouts nor identify the winner, but they afforded me an immense amount of amusement.

Another fascinating creature that used to come to the fruit trees was the douroucouli. These curious little monkeys, with long tails, delicate, almost squirrel-like bodies and enormous owl-like eyes, are the only nocturnal species of monkey in the world. They arrived in small troops of seven or eight and, though they made no noise as they jumped into the fruit trees, you could soon tell they were there by the long and complicated conversation they held while they fed. They had the biggest range of noises I have ever heard from a monkey, or for that matter from any animal of similar size. First they could produce a loud purring bark, a very powerful vibrating cry which they used as a warning; when they delivered it their throats would swell up to the size of a small apple with the effort. Then, to converse with one another, they would use shrill squeaks, grunts, a mewing noise not unlike a cat's and a series of liquid, bubbling sounds quite different from anything else I have ever heard. Sometimes one of them in an excess of affection would drape his arm over a companion's shoulder and they would sit side by side, arms round each other, bubbling away, peering earnestly into each other's faces. They were the only monkeys I know that would on the slightest provocation give one another the most passionate human kisses, mouth to mouth, arms round each other, tails entwined.

Naturally these animals made only sporadic appearances; there were, however, two creatures which were in constant evidence in the waters of the drowned valley. One was a young cayman, the South American alligator, about four feet long. He was a very handsome reptile with black-and-white skin as knobbly and convoluted as a walnut, a dragon's fringe on his tail, and large eyes of golden-green flecked with amber. He was the only cayman to live in this little stretch of water. I could never understand why no others had joined him, for the creeks and waterways, only a hundred feet or so away, were alive with them. None the less this little cayman lived in solitary state in the pool outside my hut and spent the day swimming round and round with a rather proprietory air. The other creature always to be seen was a jacana, probably one of the strangest birds in South America. In size and appearance it is not unlike the English moorhen, but its neat body is perched on long slender legs which end in a bunch of enormously elongated toes. It is with the aid of these long toes and the even distribution of weight they give that the jacana manages to walk across water, using the water-lily leaves and other water-plants as its pathways. It has thus earned its name of lily-trotter.

The jacana disliked the cayman, while the cayman had formed the impression that Nature had placed the jacana in his pool to add a little variety to his diet. He was, however, a young and inexperienced reptile, and at first his attempts to stalk and capture the bird were ridiculously obvious. The jacana would come mincing out of the undergrowth, where it used to spend much of its time, and walk out across the water, stepping delicately from one lily leaf to the next, its long toes spreading out like spiders and the leaves dipping gently under its weight. The cayman, on spotting it, immediately submerged until only his eyes showed above water. No ripple disturbed the surface, yet his head seemed to glide along until he got nearer and nearer to the bird. The jacana, always pecking busily among the water-plants in search of worms and snails and tiny fish, rarely noticed the cayman's approach and would probably have fallen an easy victim if it had not been for one thing. As soon as the cayman was within ten or twelve feet he would become so excited that instead of submerging and taking the bird from underneath he would suddenly start to wag his tail vigorously and shoot along the surface of the water like a speedboat, making such large splashes that not even the most dim-witted bird could have been taken unawares; and the jacana would fly up into the air with a shrill cry of alarm, wildly flapping its buttercup-yellow wings.

For a long time it did not occur to me to wonder why the bird should spend a greater part of the day in the reed-bed at one end of the lake. But on investigating this patch of reed I soon discovered the reason, for there on the boggy ground I found a mat neatly made of weed on which lay four round creamy eggs heavily blotched with chocolate and silver. The bird must have been sitting for some time, for only a couple of days later I found the nest empty and a few hours after that saw the jacana leading out her brood for its first walk into the world.

She emerged from the reed-bed, trotted out on to the lily leaves, then paused and looked back. Out of the reeds her four babies appeared, with the look of outsize bumble-bees, in their golden-and-black fluff, while their long slender legs and toes seemed as fragile as spider-webs. They walked in single file behind their mother, always a lily leaf behind, and they waited patiently for their mother to test everything before moving forward. They could all cluster on one of the great plate-like leaves, and they were so tiny and light that it scarcely dipped beneath their weight. Once the cayman had seen them, of course, he redoubled his efforts, but the jacana was a very careful mother. She kept her brood near the edge of the lake, and if the cayman showed any signs of approaching, the babies immediately dived off the lily leaves and vanished into the water, to reappear mysteriously on dry land a moment later.

The cayman tried every method he knew, drifting as close as possible without giving a sign, concealing himself by plunging under a mat of water-weeds and then surfacing so that the weeds almost covered eyes and nose. There he lay patiently, sometimes even moving very close inshore, presumably in the hope of catching the jacanas before they ventured out too far. For a week he tried each of these methods in turn, and only once did he come anywhere near success. On this particular day he had spent the hot noon hours lying, fully visible, in the very centre of the lake, revolving slowly round and round so that he could keep an eye on what was happening on the shore. In the late afternoon he drifted over to the fringe of lilies and weeds and managed to catch a small frog that had been sunning itself in the centre of a lily. Fortified by this, he swam over to a floating raft of green weeds, studded with tiny flowers, and dived right under it. It was only after half an hour of fruitless search in other parts of the little lake that I realized he must be concealed under the weeds. I trained my field-glasses on them, and although the entire patch was no larger than a door, it took me at least ten minutes to spot him. He was almost exactly in the centre and as he had risen to the surface a frond of weed had become draped between his eyes; on the top of this was a small cluster of pink flowers. He looked somewhat roguish with this weed on his head, as though he were wearing a vivid Easter bonnet, but it served to conceal him remarkably well. Another half an hour passed before the jacanas appeared and the drama began.

The mother, as usual, emerged suddenly from the reed-bed, and stepping daintily on to the lily leaves paused and called her brood, who pattered out after her like a row of quaint clockwork toys and then stood patiently clustered on a lily leaf, awaiting instructions. Slowly the mother led them out into the lake, feeding as they went. She would poise herself on one leaf and, bending over, catch another in her beak, which she would pull and twist until it was sufficiently out of the water to expose the underside. A host of tiny worms and leeches, snails and small crustaceans, generally clung to it. The babies clustered round and pecked vigorously, picking off all this small fry until the underside of the leaf was clean, whereupon they all moved off to another.

Quite early in the proceedings I realized that the female was leading her brood straight towards the patch of weeds beneath which the cayman was hiding, and I remembered then that this particular area was one of her favourite hunting-grounds. I had watched her standing on the lily pads, pulling out the delicate, fern-like weed in large tangled pieces and draping it across a convenient lily flower so that her babies could work over it for the mass of microscopic life it contained. I felt sure that, having successfully managed to evade the cayman so far, she would notice him on this occasion, but although she paused frequently to look about her, she continued to lead her brood towards the reptile's hiding-place.

I was now in a predicament. I was determined that the cayman was not going to eat either the female jacana or her brood if I could help it, but I was not quite sure what to do. The bird was quite used to human noises and took no notice of them whatever, so there was no point in clapping my hands. Nor was there any way of getting close to her, for this scene was being enacted on the other side of the lake, and it would have taken me ten minutes to work my way round, by which time it would be too late, for already she was within twenty feet of the cayman. It was useless to shout, too far to throw stones, so I could only sit there with my eyes glued to my field-glasses, swearing that if the cayman so much as touched a feather of my jacana family I would hunt him out and slaughter him. And then I suddenly remembered the shotgun.

It was, of course, too far for me to shoot at the cayman: the shot would have spread out so much by the time it reached the other side of the lake that only a few pellets would hit him, whereas I might easily kill the birds I was trying to protect. It occurred to me, however, that as far as I knew the jacana had never heard a gun, and a shot fired into the air might therefore frighten her into taking her brood to safety. I dashed into the hut and found the gun, and then spent an agonizing minute or two trying to remember where I had put the cartridges. At last I had it loaded and hurried out to my vantage-point again. Holding the gun under my arm, its barrels pointing into the soft earth at my feet, I held the field-glasses up in my other hand and peered across the lake to see if I was in time.

The jacana had just reached the edge of the lilies nearest the weed patch. Her babies were clustered on a leaf just behind and to one side of her. As I looked she bent forward, grabbed a large trailing section of weed and pulled it on to the lily leaves, and at that moment the cayman, only about four feet away, rose suddenly from his nest of flowers and weeds and, still wearing his ridiculous bonnet, charged forward. At the same moment I let off both barrels of the shotgun, and the roar echoed round the lake.

Whether it was my action that saved the jacana or her own quick-wittedness I do not know, but she rose from the leaf with extraordinary speed just as the cayman's jaws closed and cut the leaf in half. She swooped over his head, he leapt half out of the water in an effort to grab her (I could hear the clop of his jaws) and she flew off unhurt but screaming wildly.

The attack had been so sudden that she had apparently given no orders to her brood, who had meanwhile been crouching on the lily leaf. Now, hearing her call, they were galvanized into action, and as they dived overboard the cayman swept towards them. By the time he reached the spot, they were under water, so he dived too and gradually the ripples died away and the surface of the water became calm. I watched anxiously while the female jacana, calling in agitation, flew round and round the lake. Presently she disappeared into the reed-bed and I saw her no more that day. Nor did I see the cayman for that matter. I had a horrible feeling that he had succeeded in catching all those tiny bundles of fluff as they swam desperately under water, and I spent the evening planning revenge.

The next morning I went round to the reed-bed, and there to my delight I found the jacana, and with her three rather subdued-looking babies. I searched for the fourth one, but as he was nowhere to be seen it was obvious that the cayman had been at any rate partially successful. To my consternation the jacana, instead of being frightened off by her experience of the previous day, proceeded once more to lead her brood out to the water-lilies, and for the rest of the day I watched her with my heart in my mouth. Though there was no sign of the cayman, I spent several nerve-wracking hours, and by evening I decided I could stand it no longer. I went to the village and borrowed a tiny canoe which two Indians kindly carried down to the little lake for me. As soon as it was dark I armed myself with a powerful torch and a long stick with a slip-knot of rope on the end, and set off on my search for the cayman. Though the lake was so small, an hour had passed before I spotted him, lying on the surface near some lilies. As the torch-beam caught him, his great eyes gleamed like rubies. With infinite caution I edged closer and close until I could gently lower the noose and pull it carefully over his head, while he lay there quietly, blinded or mesmerized by the light. Then I jerked the noose tight and hauled his thrashing and wriggling body on board, his jaws snapping and his throat swelling as he gave vent to loud harsh barks of rage. I tied him up in a sack and the next day took him five miles deep into the creeks and let him go. He never managed to find his way back, and for the rest of my stay in the little hut by the drowned valley I could sit and enjoy the sight of my lily-trotter family pottering happily over the lake in search of food, without suffering any anxiety every time a breeze ruffled the surface of the rich tawny water.

FROM THE DRUNKEN FOREST:

Shortly after the arrival of Eggbert and his brethren we received a pair of animals which soon became known as the Terrible Twins. They were a pair of large and very corpulent hairy armadillos. Both of them were nearly identical in size and girth and, we soon discovered, in habits. As they were both female, one could quite easily have supposed that they were sisters from the same litter, except for the fact that while one was caught a stone's throw away from Los Ingleses [in Argentina], the other was sent over from a neighbouring *estancia* several miles away. The Twins were housed in a cage with a special sleeping compartment. It had originally been designed to accommodate one large armadillo, but owing to a housing shortage when they arrived, we were forced to put them both in the one cage. As it happened, since they were not quite fully grown, they fitted in very snugly. Their two pleasures in life were food and sleep, neither of which they could apparently get enough of. In their sleeping compartment they would lie on their backs, head to tail, their great pink and wrinkled tummies bulging and deflating as they breathed stertorously, their paws twitching and quivering. Once they were asleep, it seemed that nothing on earth would wake them. You could bang on the box, shout through the bars, open the bedroom door, and, holding your breath (for the Twins had a powerful scent all their own), poke their obese stomachs, pinch their paws, or flick their tails, but still they slumbered as though they were both in a deep hypnotic trance. Then, under the impression that nothing short of a world catastrophe would shake them into consciousness, you would fill a tin tray high with the revolting mixture they liked, and proceed to insert it into the outside portion of the cage. However delicately you performed this operation, however careful you were to make sure the silence was not broken by the slightest sound, no sooner had you got the dish and your hand inside the door than from the bedroom would come a noise like a sea-serpent demolishing a woodshed with its tail. This was the Twins tumbling and struggling to get upright – to get to action stations, as it were. That was the warning to drop the plate and remove your hand with all speed, for within a split second the armadillos would burst from their bedroom door, like cannon-balls, skid wildly across the cage, shoulder to shoulder, in the manner of a couple of Rugby players fighting for the ball, grunting with the effort. They would hit the tin (and your hand if it was still there) amidships, and the armadillos and tin would end in the far corner in a tangled heap, and a tidal wave of chopped banana, milk, raw egg and minced meat would splash against the wall, and then rebound to settle like a glutinous shawl over the Twins' grey backs. They would stand there, giving satisfied squeaks and grunts, licking the food as it trickled down their shells, occasionally going into a scrum in the corner over some choice bit of fruit or meat which had just given up the unequal contest with gravity and descended suddenly from the ceiling. Watching them standing knee-deep in that tide of food, you might think that it was impossible for two animals to get through such a quantity of vitamin and protein. Yet within half an hour the cage would be spotless, licked clean even to the least splashes on the ceiling, which they had to stand on their hind legs to reach. And the Twins themselves would be in their odoriferous boudoir, on their backs, head to tail, deeply and noisily asleep. Eventually, owing to this health-giving diet, the Twins increased their girth to such an extent that they could only just manage to get through the bedroom door, leaving about a millimetre's clearance all round. I was contemplating some drastic structural alterations when I found that one of the Twins had discovered the way to utilize this middle-age spread to her advantage. Instead of sleeping length-wise in the bedroom, as she used to do, she now started to sleep across it, the right way up, with her head pointing towards the door. As soon as the first faint sound or smell of food reached her, she would shoot across the intervening space, before her companion could even get the right way up, and then, when half-way through the door, she would hunch her back and become wedged there as firmly as a cork in a bottle. Then, taking her time, she would reach out a claw, hook the food-pan into position, and proceed to browse dreamily, if not altogether quietly, in the depths, while in the bedroom, her frantic relative squealed and snorted and scrabbled ineffectually at the well-corseted and impervious behind.

The hairy armadillo is the vulture of the Argentine pampa. Low-slung, armoured against most forms of attack, he trots through the moonlit grass like a miniature tank, and nearly everything is grist to his mill. He will eat fruit and vegetables, but failing those he is quite happy with a bird's nest containing eggs or young; a light snack of young mice; or even a snake, should he happen to meet one. But what attracts the armadillo, as a magnet attracts steel-filings, is a nice juicy rotten carcass. In Argentina, where distances and herds are so great, it often happens that a sick or elderly cow will die, and its body will lie out in the grasslands unnoticed, the sun ripening it until its scent is wafted far and wide, and the humming of flies sounds like a swarm of bees. When this smell reaches the nose of a foraging armadillo it is an invitation to a banquet. Leaving his burrow, he scuttles along until he reaches the delectable feast: the vast, maggot-ridden dish lying in the grass. Then, having filled himself on a mixture of rotten meat and maggots, he cannot bring himself to leave the carcass when there is still so much nourishment left on it, so he proceeds to burrow under it. Here he ponders and sleeps his first course off until the pangs of hunger assail him once again. Then all he has to do is to scramble to the top of his burrow, stick out his head and there he is, so to speak, right in the middle of dinner. An armadillo will very rarely leave a carcass until the last shreds of meat have been stripped from the already bleaching bones. Then, sighing the happy sigh of an animal that is replete, he will return home, to wait hopefully for the next fatality among the cattle or sheep. Yet, despite its depraved tastes, the armadillo is considered excellent eating, the flesh tasting mid-way between veal and sucking pig. He is frequently caught by the peons on the *estancia* and kept in a barrelful of mud, being fattened up until he is ready for the pot. Now, it may be considered rather disgusting that anyone should eat a creature with such a low taste in carrion, but, on the other hand, pigs have some pretty revolting feeding habits, while the feeding habits of plaice and dabs would, I've no doubt, leave most ghouls feeling queasy.

In the late fifties Gerry is on the point of realizing his lifelong dream – to have a zoo of his own. It is to be unlike any other zoo in history, for its main purpose will be to save animals threatened with extinction. However, much has to happen before his zoo opens and begins to develop its full potential. He starts by acquiring the animals first and then finding a site, noting at the time that 'I have rarely if ever achieved anything I wanted by tackling it in a logical fashion ... now I am speechless at my audacity ...' But achieve it he did, with great hilarity along the way, aided and abetted by his own chimpanzee, Cholmondely St John, not to be confused with the Cholmondely he knew in 1946.

Gerry is quite fierce about zoo architects, 'the most dangerous animals to let loose unsupervised in a zoo', but he also sternly lectures the zoo-going public about laudable but misguided sentiments on animals' freedom versus confinement. Nearly thirty years before the current vogue of zoo-bashing, he developed guidelines for the proper care of captive wild animals and castigated those zoos that did not follow them.

In the last piece of this section, Gerry charmingly expresses something he has long felt – that the 'creepie crawlies' of the world are as important as the big, cuddly animals and that his zoo is prepared to take on the animals that other zoos prefer to forget. He tries to redress the balance for snakes in particular, which have had an undeservedly bad press.

FROM THE STATIONARY ARK:

One way and another, I have been associated with zoos throughout my life. I was smitten by what can only be called 'zoomania' at the very early age of two, when my family inhabited a town somewhere in the centre of India, a town that boasted a zoo of sorts. Twice a day, when asked by my long-suffering ayah where I wanted to go for my walk, I would drag her round the rows of odoriferous cages with their moth-eaten exhibits. Any attempt on her part to change this ritual, and my screams of rage could be heard as far south as Bombay and as far north as the Nepalese border. In view of this, it was not altogether surprising to learn from my mother that the first word that I could enunciate with any clarity was 'zoo'.

I have been saying it ever since in alternating tones of delight and despair.

Naturally, this early experience created in me a desire to have my own zoo. So, from the age of two to six, I practised assiduously for the day when I would have my own collection by assembling everything from minnows to woodlice, which inhabited my bedroom and my person in ever-increasing quantities. At this point we moved to Greece, where I lived a life of great freedom and could indulge my passion for keeping and studying wild animals. Everything, from eagle owls to scorpions, was grist to my mill. Later, returning to England, I realized that if I was ever to acquire a zoo of my own, I would need some experience in dealing with larger animals such as lions, buffaloes and giraffes, which could not – in spite of my enthusiasm – be conveniently housed in the back garden, my bedroom, nor, indeed, about my person. At this point I applied for, and was lucky enough to get, a job at Whipsnade Zoo, the Zoological Society of London's country estate in Bedfordshire. I was a student keeper, which grandiose title meant that I was an odd-job boy who was shoved on to any section that needed a helping hand with the dirty work. In many ways it was ideal training, for it taught me (if nothing else) that, for the most part, animal work is hard, dirty and very unglamorous, but it gave me contact with a host of lovely creatures, from emus to elephants. On leaving Whipsnade, I spent the next ten years animal collecting – financing and leading ten major expeditions to various parts of the world to acquire animals for zoological gardens.

It was while I was at Whipsnade and during my first four expeditions that I began to have doubts about zoos. Not doubts about the necessity for having them, for I believed (and still believe) that zoos are very important institutions. My doubts were about the way that some zoos were run and the way that the majority of them were orientated. Until I had gone to Whipsnade, zoomaniac that I was, I felt that to criticize any zoo, however lightly, was asking to be struck down by a bolt of lightning straight from heaven. But my experiences at Whipsnade and later, in collecting animals for zoos (thus visiting a great many of them), gave me an ever-growing sense of disquiet. As my experience grew, I came to the conclusion that there was a great deal to be criticized in the average zoo and, indeed, a lot that *needed* to be criticized if zoos, as the valuable institutions that I felt them to be, were to progress out of the stagnant state into which the great majority appeared to have fallen or from which they had never succeeded in emerging since their inception. However, it is simplicity itself to criticize a tightrope walker if you have never been aloft yourself and so I became even more determined to start my own zoo.

The low ebb to which zoos had allowed themselves to fall in public estimation was made apparent by the reactions I got when people found out what I intended to do. If I had informed them that I was going to start a plastic bottle factory, a pop group, a strip club or something else of such obvious benefit to mankind, they would doubtless have been deeply sympathetic. But a *zoo*? A place where you reluctantly took the children to ride on an elephant and get sick on ice cream? A place where animals were imprisoned? Surely I could not be serious? Why a zoo, of all things, they asked?

To a certain extent I understood and even sympathized with their views.

Theirs was a difficult question to answer, for their conception of a zoo and mine were totally different. The core of the problem lay in the fact that in the past – and even today – few people, scientists or laymen, properly appreciate the value of a good zoological garden. As scientific institutions, they are simply not taken seriously and there is too little recognition of the fact that they can provide the opportunity for an enormous amount of valuable work in research, conservation and education. To a large extent, this ignorance has been promoted by the zoos themselves, for far too many of them seem totally unaware of their own potentialities, scientifically speaking, and continue to encourage everyone to look upon them as mere places of amusement. It is therefore not altogether surprising that both the public and the scientific fraternity regard zoos as places of entertainment, something less mobile and transitory than a circus but of much the same level of scientific importance. Zoos have, in the main, encouraged this, for to be considered scientific is, to most people, synonymous with being dull, and this is not box-office.

A zoological garden can offer facilities that no other similar institution can emulate. At its best, it should be a complex laboratory, educational establishment and conservation unit. Our biological knowledge of even some of the commonest animals is embarrassingly slight and it is here that zoos can be of inestimable value in amassing information. That this can only help the ultimate conservation of an animal in the wild state is obvious, for you cannot begin to talk about conservation of a species unless you have some knowledge of how it functions. A well-run zoological garden should provide you with the facilities for just such work.

While it is obviously more desirable to study animals in the wild state, there are many aspects of animal biology that can be more easily studied in zoos and, indeed, there are certain aspects that can only be studied conveniently when the animal is in a controlled environment, such as a zoo. For example, it is almost impossible to work out accurate gestation periods for animals in the wild or follow the day-to-day growth and development of the young and so on. All this can be studied in a zoo. Therefore zoological gardens – properly run zoological gardens – are enormous reservoirs of valuable data, if the animals in them are studied properly and the results recorded accurately.

Educationally, too, zoos have a most important role to play. Now that we have invented the megalopolis, we are spawning a new generation, reared without benefit of dog, cat, goldfish or budgerigar, in the upright coffins of the high-rise flats, a generation that will believe that milk comes from a bottle, without benefit of grass or cow or the intricate process between the two. This generation or its future offspring might have only the zoo to show them that creatures other than their own kind are trying to inhabit the earth as well.

Finally, zoos can be of immense importance in the field of conservation. Firstly, they should endeavour to breed as many of the animals in their care as possible, thus lessening the drain upon wild stocks. More important still, they can build up viable breeding groups of those species whose numbers in the wild state have dropped to an alarmingly low level. Many zoos have done, and are doing, this successfully.

Out of the thousand or so species of animal that are currently in danger of extinction, a great number have populations that have dropped so low in terms of individual specimens that it is imperative a controlled-breeding programme should be set up for them, in addition to the more conventional methods of protection. Over the years, people I have talked to (including zoo directors) seem to have only the vaguest idea as to the scope and importance of controlled breeding as a conservation tool and little idea of the necessity for it. In recent years, however, more progressive zoos and the more realistic conservationists have been talking in terms of zoo banks for certain species. Let us call them low-ebb species. This means that when the numbers of a creature drop to a certain level, all efforts should be made to maintain it in the wild state but, as a precautionary measure, a viable breeding group should be set up in a zoo, or, better still, a breeding centre created specially for the purpose. Thus, whatever happens in the wilds, your species is safe. Moreover, should it become extinct in the wild, you still have a breeding nucleus and from this you can, at some future date, try to reintroduce it into safe areas of its previous range.

This sort of captive breeding has already helped – and in some cases saved – such species as the Père David deer, the European bison, the bontebok, the nene goose and so on, but the zoos undertaking this work were in the minority and the help was given to only a handful of species. The list of animals that needed this sort of assistance for survival was increasing with alarming rapidity. It was apparent to me that unless more attention was paid to this particular form of conservation, a whole host of species was in danger of vanishing.

I felt that this most urgent work was one that the zoos already in existence should be concentrating on to a much greater degree than they were. Any new zoo that came into being should have it as its major objective. What was wanted, in fact, was not more large, comprehensive zoos, but smaller specialist ones, which could concentrate their efforts and devote the time and the trouble to the controlled breeding of species in urgent need of this type of help. Such a place would, moreover, be able to help some of the more obscure and unattractive animals, which generally tended to get neglected because they were not box-office; it would concentrate on building up and maintaining (at least until they were numerically out of danger) viable breeding *groups* of threatened species, and the whole organization would act not only as a sanctuary, but a research station and, most important, as a training ground. Keeping and breeding animals, particularly rare and delicate animals, is an art that has to be taught and learned. Unfortunately, in the past (and even today in many zoos) the people employed to look after the animals would be far better employing their minuscule talents elsewhere.

While the urgent need for the sort of place I wished to create seemed patently obvious to me, one had still, in those days (and to a lesser extent today), considerable opposition from what one could describe as hard-core conservationists. It was difficult to get them to see that controlled breeding was a desirable and necessary second line of defence to the conventional method of conservation, such as the creation of reserves, parks and so on. For many years, if you mentioned the subject in any august body of conservationists, they tended to look at you as if you had confessed to the belief that necrophilia was an ideal form of population control.

So ingrained was the idea that zoos were nothing more than Victorian menageries that it was almost impossible to get anyone to believe that a zoo could have a purpose more serious. The basic argument was that all zoos were badly run and few, if any, had shown any ability or desire to assist in conservation by controlled-breeding programmes. Rather, by their cavalier attitude of 'there's plenty more where that came from', zoos had been a drain on wild stocks, depleting animal populations to replace the ones in their collections, lost through bad luck or carelessness, or both. There were too many zoos (so the conservationists argued) paying vociferous lip service to conservation without doing anything worthwhile; too many zoos who only thought of a rare animal in terms of gate money and publicity and not of its importance from a conservation point of view; too many zoos whose much-publicized 'conservation efforts' bore about as much resemblance to intelligent conservation work as a window box does to a reforestation programme.

It is unfortunate that these criticisms, to a large extent, were, and still are, valid. My plea that what was wanted now was not more normal zoos, but specialist ones with carefully worked out conservation breeding programmes fell on deaf ears. In this atmosphere, it required a certain amount of resolve to start yet another zoo, even if one intended that it should grow into something quite different from most of the others already in existence. I felt, however, that it was useless waiting for the approbation of the conservationists. The only thing to do was to start a specialist zoo of my own and see if it worked.

FROM A ZOO IN MY LUGGAGE:

Yes, bring the animals here. Don't know what the neighbours will say, but never mind. Mother very anxious to see chimps so hope you are bringing them as well. See you all soon. Much love from us all.

Margo

Most people who lived in this suburban road in Bournemouth could look out on their back gardens with pride, for each other resembled its neighbour's. There were minor differences, of course: some preferred pansies to sweet peas, or hyacinths to lupins, but basically they were all the same. But anyone looking out at my sister's back garden would have been forced to admit that it was, to say the least, unconventional. In one corner stood a huge marquee, from inside which came a curious chorus of squeaks, whistles, grunts and growls. Alongside it stretched a line of Dexion cages from which glowered eagles, vultures, owls and hawks. Next to them was a large cage containing Minnie, the Chimp. On the remains of what had once been a lawn, fourteen monkeys rolled and played on long leashes, while in the garage frogs croaked, touracos called throatily, and squirrels gnawed loudly on hazel-nut shells. At all hours of the day the fascinated, horrified neighbours stood trembling behind their lace curtains and watched as my sister, my mother Sophie, Jacquie and I trotted to and fro through the shambles of the garden, carrying little pots of bread and milk, plates of chopped fruit or, what was worse, great hunks of gory meat or dead rats. We had, the neighbours felt, taken an unfair advantage of them. If it had been a matter of a crowing cockerel, or a barking dog, or our cat having kittens in their best flower-bed, they would have been able to cope with the situation. But the action of suddenly planting what amounted to a sizeable zoo in their midst was so unprecedented and unnerving that it took their breath away, and it was some time before they managed to rally their forces and start to complain.

In the meantime I had started on my search for a zoo in which to put my animals. The simplest thing to do, it occurred to me, was to go to the local council, inform them that I had the contents of a fine little zoo and wanted them to let me rent or purchase a suitable site for it. Since I already had the animals, it seemed to me in my innocence that they would be delighted to help. It would cost them nothing, and they would be getting what was, after all, another amenity for the town. But the Powers-that-Be had other ideas. Bournemouth is nothing if not conservative. There had never been a zoo in the town, so they did not see why there should be one now. This is what is known by local councils as progress. Firstly, they said that the animals would be dangerous; then they said they would smell; and then, searching their minds wildly for ideas, they said they had not got any land anyway.

I began to get a trifle irritable. I am never at my best when dealing with the pompous illogicalities of the official mind. But I was beginning to grow worried in the face of such complete lack of co-operation. The animals were sitting in the back garden, eating their heads off and costing me a small fortune weekly in meat and fruit. The neighbours, now thoroughly indignant that we were not conforming to pattern, kept bombarding the local health authorities with complaints, so that on an average twice a week the poor inspector was forced to come up to the house, whether he wanted to or not. The fact that he could find absolutely nothing to substantiate the wild claims of the neighbours made no difference: if he received a complaint he had to come and investigate. We always gave the poor man a cup of tea, and he grew quite fond of some of the animals, even bringing his little daughter to see them. But I was chiefly worried by the fact that winter was nearly upon us, and the animals could not be expected to survive its rigors in an unheated marquee. Then Jacquie had a brilliant idea.

'Why not let's offer them to one of the big stores in town as a Christmas show?' she suggested.

So I rang every big store in town. All of them were charming but unhelpful; they simply had not the space for such a show, however desirable. Then I telephoned the last on my list, the huge emporium owned by J. J. Allen. They, to my delight, expressed great interest and asked me to go and discuss it with them. And 'Durrell's Menagerie' came into being.

A large section of one of their basements was set aside, roomy cages were built with tastefully painted murals on the walls depicting a riot of tropical foliage, and the animals were moved out of the cold and damp which had already started, into the luxury of brilliant electric light and a constant temperature. The charge for admission just covered the food bills, and so the animals were warm, comfortable and well fed without being a drain on my resources. With this worry off my mind I could turn my attention once more to the problem of getting my zoo.

It would be wearisome to go into all the details of frustration during this period, or to make a catalogue of the number of mayors, town councillors, parks superintendents and sanitary officers I met and argued with. Suffice it to say that I felt my brain creaking at times with the effort of trying to persuade supposedly intelligent people that a zoo in any town should be considered an attraction rather than anything else. To judge by the way they reacted one would have thought I wanted to set off an atomic bomb on one of the piers.

In the meantime the animals, unaware that their fate hung in the balance, did their best to make life exciting for us. There was, for example, the day that Georgina the baboon decided that she wanted to see a little more of Bournemouth than the inside of J. J. Allen's basement. Fortunately it was a Sunday morning, so there was no one in the store: otherwise I dread to think what would have happened.

I was sipping a cup of tea, just before going down to the store and cleaning and feeding the animals, when the telephone rang. Without a care in the world I answered it.

'Is that Mr Durrell,' inquired a deep, lugubrious voice.

'Yes, speaking.'

'This is the Police 'ere, sir. One of them monkeys of yours 'as got out, and I thought I'd better let you know.'

'Good God, which one is it?' I asked.

'I don't know, sir, really. It's a big brown one. Only it looks rather fierce, sir, so I thought I'd let you know.'

'Yes, thanks very much. Where is it?'

'Well, it's in one of the windows at the moment. But I don't see as 'ow it'll stay there very long. Is it liable to bite, sir?'

'Well, it may do. Don't go near it. I'll be right down,' I said, slamming down the receiver.

I grabbed a taxi and we roared down to the centre of the town, ignoring all speed limits. After all, I reflected, we were on police business of a sort. As I paid off the taxi the first thing that greeted my eyes was the chaos in one of the big display windows of Allen's. The window had been carefully set out to exhibit some articles of bedroom furniture. There was a large bed, made up, a tall bedside light and several eiderdowns tastefully spread over the floor. At least, that was how it had been when the window dresser had finished it. Now it looked as if a tornado had hit it. The light had been overturned and had burned a large hole in one of the eiderdowns; the bedclothes had been stripped off the bed and the pillow and sheets were covered with a tasteful pattern of paw marks. On the bed itself sat Georgina, bouncing up and down happily, and making ferocious faces at a crowd of scandalized church-goers who had gathered on the pavement outside the window. I went into the store and found two enormous constables lying in ambush behind a barricade of turkish towelling.

'Ah!' said one with relief, 'there you are, sir. We didn't like to try and catch it, see, because it didn't know us, and we thought it might make it worse, like.'

'I don't think anything could make that animal worse,' I said bitterly. 'Actually she's harmless, but she makes a hell of a row and looks fierce . . . it's all bluff, really.'

'Really?' said one of the constables, polite but unconvinced.

'I'll try and get her in the window there if I can, but if she breaks away I want you two to head her off. Don't, for the love of Allah, let her get into the china department.'

'She came through the china department already,' said one of the constables with gloomy satisfaction.

'Did she break anything?' I asked faintly.

'No, sir, luckily; she just galloped straight through. Me and Bill was chasing 'er, of course, so she didn't stop.'

'Well, don't let's let her get back in there. We may not be so lucky next time.'

By this time Jacquie and my sister Margo had arrived in another taxi, so our ranks had now swelled to five. We should, I thought, be able to cope with Georgina between us. I stationed the two constables, my sister and wife at suitable points guarding the entrance to the china department, and then went round and entered the window in which Georgina was still bouncing up and down on the ruined bed, making obscene faces at the crowd.

'Georgina,' I said in a quiet but soothing voice, 'come along then, come to Dad.'

Georgina glanced over her shoulder in surprise. She studied my face as I moved towards her, and decided that my expression belied my honeyed accents. She gathered herself and leapt through the air, over the still smouldering eiderdown, and grabbed at the top of the great rampart of turkish towelling that formed the background of the window display. This, not having been constructed to take the weight of a large baboon hurtling through the air, immediately collapsed, and Georgina fell to the ground under a cascade of many-hued towelling. She struggled madly to free herself, and just succeeded in doing so as I flung myself forward to catch her. She gave a hysterical squawk and fled out of the window into the interior of the shop. I unravelled myself from the towelling and followed her. A piercing shriek from my sister told me of Georgina's whereabouts; my sister always tends to go off like a locomotive in moments of crisis. Georgina had slipped past her and was now perched on a counter, surveying us with glittering eyes, thoroughly enjoying the game. We approached her in a grim-faced body. At the end of the counter, suspended from the ceiling, hung a Christmas decoration made out of holly, tinsel and cardboard stars. It was shaped somewhat like a chandelier, and looked, as far as Georgina was concerned, ideal for swinging. She poised herself on the end of the counter and as we ran forward she leaped up and grabbed at the decoration in a manner vaguely reminiscent of the elder Fairbanks. The decoration promptly gave way, and Georgina fell to the ground, leapt to her feet and galloped off wearing a piece of tinsel over one ear.

For the next half-hour we thundered to and fro through the deserted store, always with Georgina one jump ahead of us, as it were. She knocked down a huge pile of account books in the stationery department, paused to see if a pile of lace doilies was edible, and made a large and decorative puddle at the foot of the main staircase. Then, just as the constables were beginning to breathe rather stertorously and I was beginning to despair of ever catching the wretched animal, Georgina made a miscalculation. Loping easily ahead of us she came upon what looked like the perfect hiding-place constructed of rolls of linoleum arranged on end. She fled between the rolls and was lost, for the rolls had been arranged in the form of a hollow square, a three-sided trap from which there was no escape. Quickly we closed in and blocked the entrance to the linoleum trap. I advanced towards her, grim-faced, and she sat there and screamed wildly, begging for mercy. As I made a lunge to grab her she ducked under my hand, and as I swung round to prevent her escape I bumped into one of the massive rolls of linoleum. Before I could stop it this toppled forward like a gigantic trun-cheon and hit one of the constables accurately on the top of his helmet. As the poor man staggered backwards, Georgina took one look at my face and decided that she was in need of police protection. She rushed to the still swaying constable and wrapped her arms tightly round his legs, looking over her shoulder at me and screaming. I jumped forward and grabbed her by her hairy legs and the scruff of her neck, and dragged her away from the constable's legs.

'Cor!' said the constable, in a voice of deep emotion, 'I thought I'd 'ad me chips that time.'

'Oh, she wouldn't have bitten you,' I explained, raising my voice above Georgina's harsh screams. 'She wanted you to protect her from me.'

'Cor!' said the constable again. 'Well, I'm glad *that's* over.'

We put Georgina back in her cage, thanked the constables, cleared up the mess, cleaned and fed the animals and then went home to a well-earned rest. But for the rest of that day, every time the telephone rang I nearly jumped out of my skin.

Another animal that did his best to keep us on our toes was, of course, Cholmondely St John, the chimp. To begin with, after establishing himself in the house and getting my mother and sister well under control, he proceeded to catch a nasty chill that rapidly developed into bronchitis. Having recovered from this he was still very wheezy, and I therefore decreed that he should, for the first winter at any rate, wear clothes to keep him warm. As he lived in the house with us he already was wearing plastic pants and paper nappies, so he was used to the idea of clothes.

As soon as I had made this decision my mother, a delighted gleam in her eye, set to work, her knitting-needles clicking ferociously, and in record time had provided the ape with a variety of woolly pants and jerseys, in brilliant colours and the most complicated Fair-Isle patterns. So Cholmondely St John would loll on the window-sill of the drawing-room, nonchalantly eating an apple, clad in a different suit for each day of the week, completely ignoring the fascinated groups of local children that hung over our front gate and watched him absorbedly.

The attitude of people towards Cholmondely I found very interesting. Children, for example, did not expect him to be anything more than an animal with a curious resemblance to a human being, and with the ability to make them laugh. The adults who saw him, I'm afraid, were much less bright. On numerous occasions I was asked by apparently intelligent people whether he could talk. I always used to reply that chimps have, of course, a limited language of their own. But this is not what my questioners meant; they meant could he talk like a human being, could he discuss the political situation or the cold war, or some equally fascinating topic.

But the most extraordinary question I was ever asked about Cholmondely was asked by a middle-aged woman on the local golf-links. I used to take Cholmondely up there on fine days and let him scramble about in some pine trees, while I sat on the ground beneath, reading or writing. On this particular day Cholmondely had played for half an hour or so in the branches above me and then, growing bored, he had come down to sit on my lap and see if he could inveigle me into tickling him. Just at that moment this strange woman strode out of the gorse bushes and, on seeing Cholmondely and me, stopped short and looked at us. She displayed none of the surprise that most people evince at finding a chimpanzee in a Fair-Isle pullover occupying the golf-links. She came closer and watched Cholmondely closely as he sat on my lap. Then she turned to me and fixed me with a gimlet eye.

'Do they have souls?' she inquired.

'I don't know, madam,' I replied. 'I can't speak with any certainty for myself on that subject, so you can hardly expect me to vouch for a chimpanzee.'

'Um,' she said, and walked off. Cholmondely had that sort of effect on people.

Having Cholmondely living in the house with us was, of course, a fascinating experience. His personality and intelligence made him one of the most interesting animals I have ever kept. One of the things about him that impressed me most was his memory, which I considered quite phenomenal.

I possessed at that time a Lambretta and side-car, and I decided that, providing Cholmondely sat well in the side-car and didn't try to jump out, I would be able to take him for excursions into the countryside. The first time I introduced him to it, I took him for a round trip of the golf-links, just to see how he would behave. He sat there with the utmost decorum, watching the passing scenery with a regal air. Apart from a tendency to lean out of the side-car and try to grab any cyclist we overtook, his behaviour was exemplary. Then I drove the Lambretta down to the local garage to have her filled up with petrol. Cholmondely was as fascinated with the garage as the garage man was with Cholmondely. The ape leaned out of the side-car and carefully watched the unscrewing of the petrol tank; and the introduction of the hose and splash and gurgle of the petrol made him 'Ooo' softly to himself in astonishment.

A Lambretta can travel an incredible distance on a very small amount of petrol and, as I did not use it a great deal, about two weeks had passed before she needed filling up again. We had just come back from a local water-mill where we had been visiting Cholmondely's friend, the miller. This kind man, a great admirer of Cholmondely's, always had a brew of tea ready for us, and we would sit in a row above the weir, watching the moorhens paddling by, sipping our tea and meditating. On the way home from this tea party I noticed that the Lambretta was getting low on fuel, so we drove down to the garage.

As I was passing the time of day with the garage man, I noticed that he was gazing over my shoulder, a somewhat stupefied expression on his face. I turned round quickly to see what mischief the ape was up to. I found that Cholmondely had climbed out of the side-car on to the saddle, and was busy trying to unscrew the cap of the petrol tank. Now this was surely quite a feat of memory. Firstly, he had only seen the filling-up process once, and that had been two weeks previously. Secondly, he had remembered, out of all the various gadgets on the Lambretta, which was the correct one to open in these circumstances. I was almost as impressed as the garage man.

But the time Cholmondely impressed me most, not only with his memory but with his powers of observation, was on the occasions when I had to take him up to London, once to appear on TV and later for a lecture. My sister drove me up to London, while Cholmondely sat on my lap and watched the passing scenery with interest. About halfway to our destination I suggested that we stopped for a drink. You had to be rather careful about pubs when you had Cholmondely with you, for it was not every landlord that appreciated a chimpanzee in his private bar. Eventually we found a pub that had a homely look about it, and stopped there. To our relief, and Cholmondely's delight, we found that the woman who ran the pub was a great animal lover, and she and Cholmondely took an immediate fancy to each other. He was allowed to play catch-as-catch-can among the tables in the bar, he was stuffed with orange juice and potato crisps, he was even allowed to get up on the bar itself and do a war dance, thumping his feet and shouting 'Hoo ... Hoo ... Hoo.' In fact he and the landlady got on so well that he was very reluctant to leave the place at all. If he had been an RAC inspector he would have given that pub twelve stars.

Three months later I had to take Cholmondely up for the lecture; by that time I had forgotten all about the pub in which he had had such a good time, for we had, since then, been in many other licensed establishments which had given him a warm welcome. As we drove along Cholmondely, who was sitting on my lap as usual, started to bounce up and down excitedly. I thought at first he had seen a herd of cows or a horse, animals in which he had the deepest interest, but there was not a farm animal to be seen. Cholmondely went on bouncing, faster and faster, and presently started 'Oo ... ooing' to himself. I still could not see what was exciting him. Then his 'Ooing' rose to a screaming crescendo, and he leaped about on my lap in an ecstasy of excitement, and we rounded a corner and there, a hundred yards ahead, was his favourite pub. Now this meant that he had recognized the countryside we were passing through, and had connected it with his memory of the good time he had had in the pub, a mental process which I had not come across in any other animal. Both my sister and I were so shaken by this that we were very glad to stop for a drink, and let Cholmondely renew his acquaintance with his friend the landlady, who was delighted to see him again.

In the meantime I was still continuing my struggle to find my zoo, but my chance of success seemed to recede farther and farther each day. The collection had to be moved from J. J. Allen's, of course, but here Paignton Zoo came to my rescue. With extreme kindness they allowed me to board my collection with them, on deposit, until such time as I could find a place of my own. But this, as I say, began to seem more and more unlikely. It was the old story. In the initial stages of a project, when you need people's help most, it is never forthcoming. The only solution, if at all possible, is to go ahead and accomplish it by yourself. Then, when you have made a success of it, all the people who would not help you launch it gather round, slap you on the back and offer their assistance.

'There must be an intelligent local council *somewhere*,' said Jacquie one evening, as we pored over a map of the British Isles.

'I doubt it,' I said gloomily, 'and anyway I doubt whether I have the mental strength to cope with another round of mayors and town clerks. No, we'll just have to get a place and do it ourselves.'

'But you'll have to get their sanction,' Jacquie pointed out, 'and then there's Town and Country Planning and all that.'

I shuddered, 'What we should really do is to go to some remote island in the West Indies, or somewhere,' I said, 'where they're sensible enough not to clutter their lives with all this incredible red tape.'

Jacquie moved Cholmondely St John from the portion of the map on which he was squatting.

'What about the Channel Isles?' she asked suddenly.

'What about them?'

'Well, they're a very popular holiday resort, and they've got a wonderful climate.'

'Yes, it would be an excellent place, but we don't know anyone there,' I objected, 'and you need someone on the spot to give you advice in this sort of thing.'

'Yes,' said Jacquie, reluctantly, 'I suppose you're right.'

So, reluctantly (for the idea of starting my zoo on an island had a very strong appeal for me) we forgot about the Channel Islands. It was not until a few weeks later that I happened to be in London and was discussing my zoo project with Rupert Hart-Davis that a gleam of daylight started to appear. I confessed to Rupert that my chances of having my own zoo now seemed so slight that I was on the verge of giving up the idea altogether. I said that we had thought of the Channel Islands, but that we had no contact there to help us. Rupert sat up, and with an air of a conjurer performing a minor miracle, said he had a perfectly good contact in the Channel Islands (if only he was asked) and a man moreover who had spent his whole life in the islands and would be only too willing to help us in any way. His name was Major Fraser, and that evening I telephoned him. He did not seem to find it at all unusual that a complete stranger should ring him up and ask his advice about starting a zoo, which made me warm to him from the start. He suggested that Jacquie and I should fly across to Jersey and he would show us round the island, and give us any information he could. And this accordingly we arranged to do.

So we flew to Jersey. As the plane came in to land the island seemed like a toy continent, a patchwork of tiny fields, set in a vivid blue sea. A pleasantly carunculated rocky coastline was broken here and there with smooth stretches of beach, along which the sea creamed in ribbons. As we stepped out on to the tarmac the air seemed warmer, and the sun a little more brilliant. I felt my spirits rising.

In the car park Hugh Fraser awaited us. He was a tall, slim man, wearing a narrow-brimmed trilby tilted so far forward that the brim almost rested on his aquiline nose. His blue eyes twinkled humorously as he shepherded us into his car and drove us away from the airport. We drove through St Helier, the capital of the island, which reminded me of a sizeable English market town; it was something of a surprise to find, at a cross-roads, a policeman in a white coat and white helmet, directing the traffic. It suddenly gave the place a faintly tropical atmosphere. We drove through the town and then out along narrow roads with steep banks, where the trees leaned over and entwined branches, turning it into a green tunnel. The landscape, with its red earth and rich green grass, reminded me very much of Devon, but the landscape was a miniature one, with tiny fields, narrow valleys stuffed with trees, and small farmhouses built of the beautiful Jersey granite, which contains a million autumn tints in its surface where the sun touches it. Then we turned off the road, drove down a long drive and suddenly, before us, was Hugh's home, Les Augrès Manor.

The Manor was built like an E without the centre bar; the main building was in the upright of the E, while the two cross pieces were wings of the house, ending in two massive stone arches which allowed access to the courtyard. These beautiful arches were built in about 1660 and, like the rest of the building were of the lovely local granite. Hugh showed us round his home with obvious pride, the old granite cider-press and cow-sheds, the huge walled garden, the small lake with its tattered fringe of bulrushes, the sunken water-meadows with the tiny streams trickling through them. At last we walked slowly back under the beautiful archways and into the courtyard, flooded with sunshine.

'You know, Hugh, you've got a wonderful place here,' I said.

'Yes it is lovely . . . I think one of the loveliest Manors on the island,' said Hugh.

I turned to Jacquie. 'Wouldn't it make a wonderful place for our zoo?' I remarked.

'Yes it would,' agreed Jacquie.

Hugh eyed me for a moment. 'Are you serious?' he inquired.

'Well, I *was* joking, but it would make a wonderful site for a zoo. Why?' I asked.

'Well,' said Hugh, thoughtfully, 'I'm finding the upkeep too much for my resources, and I want to move to the mainland. Would you be interested in renting the place?'

'Would I?' I said. 'Just give me the chance.'

'Come inside, dear boy, and we'll discuss it,' said Hugh, leading the way across the courtyard.

So, after a frustrating year of struggling with councils and other local authorities, I had gone to Jersey, and within an hour of landing at the airport I had found my zoo.

FROM THE STATIONARY ARK:

Anyone who has had anything to do with zoos must admit, albeit reluctantly, that there is precious little art in zoo architecture. The average architect in a zoo behaves like a child with its first box of bricks and will, if left to himself, produce buildings that are about as much use as they would be if they had been designed by a mentally retarded infant of five.

The main problem with zoo architecture in the past, and to a large degree in the present, is that the cages and enclosures are designed by people for *people*. It may seem odd to stress it, but when designing anything in an animal collection, there are four things which should be considered, in this order of importance:

(a) The needs of the animal,
(b) the needs of the person looking after the animal,

(c) the public who wish to see the animal and,
(d) the aesthetic aims of the architect and of the gardener who has to tend it.

Looking around the average zoo, you will find, far too often, that this order of importance has been reversed. Thus you get an edifice which may be an architectural dream and wonderful from the public's point of view, but useless for both the animal and the staff. It is, if I may be permitted to coin a phrase, what I call 'anthropomorphic architecture' and the reason it comes into being is twofold.

Firstly, the architect *does* know what he and the public want, which is something that is large and pretty (a building that salves their conscience about the imagined rigours of captivity) but he does *not* know what the animal wants and as there seems to be, generally, a complete lack of liaison between the architect and the person responsible for the animal's welfare, these architectural monsters are born.

Now it would be as foolish to expect every zoo architect to have a zoological training, as it would be to expect honesty in every politician, but it does help if the architect knows the difference between a giraffe and a dormouse, in the same way as it helps if a politician knows right from wrong. In most cases it would appear (judging by the end product) that the architect is given a brief and then goes ahead and produces what he thinks is architecturally best, with little or no consideration for the animal or the staff. There are far too many modern zoo cages which are anything but ideal for the animals within them, yet, curiously enough, it is seldom these cages which are criticized by the public, as long as they are nice and clean. Because of this attitude, many zoos have been forced to build bigger and bigger cages for animals, which, in a great many cases, only use a fifth of the space provided and would probably feel much more secure in a smaller area.

I remember visiting a brand new elephant house with a very distinguished continental zoo director who believed that, when an architect was designing something in a zoo, the animal was the customer and its wishes and needs were of paramount importance. We stood for some considerable time in silence, gazing at this monstrous new edifice, and then my friend broke the silence, speaking in a hushed whisper.

'What is she for?' he inquired.

'Elephants,' I said succinctly.

'Elephants?' he said, his eyes widening in shocked amazement, 'elephants? But why is she shaped like this, why all these pointed bits on top, what they do?'

'The whole building, according to the architect, is supposed to represent a group of elephants at a water hole,' I said. My friend closed his eyes in anguish and muttered a particularly all-embracing curse on architects, in one of the lesser known Serbo-Croat dialects. The only word that emerged clearly was architect and this was expectorated with a venom that would have done credit to a Spitting cobra.

We went inside. It was rather like going into a deformed cathedral. My friend gazed at the comparatively small area left for the animals and at the enormously distorted maze which was allowed for the public, then he let his gaze wander up to where, high above, would have hung the bells, if this *had* been a cathedral. He shuddered and again called upon the assistance of some Serbo-Croat deity.

'What for the roof so high?' he asked me, an anyway tenuous grasp of the English tongue disintegrating under the shock of such architecture. 'What for the roof so high, uh? They think sometimes maybe the elephant is meaning to fly up at night and be roosting?'

Look around at the zoos of the world and you will find them filled with such architectural abortions. Unfortunately, they are still being ripped, untimely, from the architectural womb. The whole approach to the building of cages, enclosures and houses in zoos has been wrong for years and, to a large extent, still is. There are some zoos which have made major breakthroughs, but sadly, these cases are all too rare. In zoo design today, the first question that is asked is not what does the animal need, but what does the public want? In a well-run collection of animals, you should provide the following:

1. A cage which constitutes a territory seeming suitable to the animal and providing an area of security to which he can retreat when under stress.
2. A mate, or mates, considered suitable by the animal.
3. An adequate diet, which is considered interesting by the animal and nutritional by you.
4. As much freedom from boredom as possible, i.e. plenty of 'furniture' in the cages and, if possible, a neighbour or two to have exciting, acrimonious, but unsanguinary battles and disputes with.

But, because of the public's anthropomorphic attitude, we still get these terrible animal houses, the modern equivalent to the Hindu monkey temples, so beloved of the zoos in the nineteen hundreds and in which so many unfortunate and ungrateful Rhesus monkeys shivered their way to death.

The public's concern for captive animals is laudable, but, for the most part, misguided. They scarcely ever, in fact, complain about the things in zoos that they should complain about, but they get vociferously hysterical about the things that do not matter a damn to the animal.

People say that it is wrong to cage animals; it is wrong to imprison them; it is wrong to deprive them of their freedom. They seldom, if ever, criticize the cage; it is only the idea of the cage that they are against. The discovery that different animals have territories of different sorts and sizes, ranging from a few square feet to a few square miles, depending on the species, in the same way that human beings have back gardens, estates, counties and countries, is a comparatively new one, and we still have an enormous amount to learn about it. But it is this fact which must be borne in mind at all times when designing a cage or an enclosure for an animal. You are not necessarily depriving him of his liberty, for territory is a form of natural cage and the word 'liberty' does not have the same connotation for an animal as it does for a chest-beating liberal *Homo sapiens*, who can afford the luxury of abstract ideas. What you are, in fact, doing is much more important; you are taking away his *territory*, so you must take great care to provide him with an adequate substitute, or you will have a bored, sick or dead animal on your hands.

The thing that turns a cage into a territory may be something quite slight, but it need not be the size. It might be the shape of the cage, the number of branches or the lack of them, the absence or presence of a pond, a patch of sand, a chunk of log, which could make all the difference. Such a detail, trivial to the uninformed visitor, can help the animal consider this area his territory, rather than simply a place where he ekes out his existence. As I say, it is not necessarily size that is of prime importance. This is where the people who criticize zoos go wrong, for they generally have little idea of what circumscribed lives most animals lead. The monotony of the daily round of a great many wild animals would make the average Streatham bank clerk's everyday existence seem like the first five volumes of *The Hundred and One Nights*. The minuscule area in which some animals spend their entire lives is something that is not generally understood. In many cases, animals live, mate and die in an area that is relatively tiny, only moving outside it if some important ingredient is missing.

On the edge of a campsite I had in the West African rainforests there grew three trees, heavily covered with epiphytes and lianas. These trees, each about thirty feet high, standing cheek by jowl, represented the whole known world to a medium-sized pair of squirrels. In this tiny area they had everything they wanted. They had fruit and shoots and insects to eat, and they had water supplies in the shape of small pools of dew and rain, which collected where the branches joined the main trunks of the trees. Lastly, not to be overlooked, they had each other. I occupied that campsite for four months. The squirrels were very much in evidence, from first dawn till sunset, and at no time did I see them leave the three trees, except to chase off intruders of their own species.

The three essentials that these little rodents had were the same three as most probably govern the lives of all animals: the desire to reproduce their kind and the need for food and for water. Out of these things springs the claim to territory, and territory is a form of natural cage. I am not attempting to say that the critics of captive animals are wrong to criticize, I am merely saying that they are criticizing for the wrong reasons. It is the anthropomorphic approach that is so deadly.

Going on an animal-collecting expedition teaches you a lot about territory and also about the flight distance of animals. The flight distance is a term used to describe the distance that an animal allows between himself and an enemy before taking flight. Though it varies, all animals have this, even man. If you don't believe me, try going into a field with a bull and find out your flight distance for yourself. When you have got a newly caught wild animal, the most formidable task facing you is to persuade it to cut down its flight distance (you are the enemy, don't forget, and in constant close contact with it). You also have to provide it with a new territory.

Take, for example, a squirrel. Put a newly caught squirrel in a simple wooden box (which is what most travelling crates are) with a wire front and you will have an animal that leaps and scrabbles in terror every time you go near him. This will go on for months, perhaps for ever, for the simple reason that he is being deprived, at one stroke, of his flight distance and his territory. He cannot get away from your monstrous hand when it enters his Lilliputian world to clean and feed him.

Now, put the same squirrel in the same box, but provide a bedroom at one end, reached by a small hole just big enough to allow him to enter. Immediately the whole picture changes. He now has a secure area to which he can retreat when you invade his territory. From the calm of his bedroom, he can watch you clean out his cage and put in and take out his fruit and water pots, if not with equanimity then at least without too much alarm. It is important, of course, to leave the bedroom area as inviolate as possible to begin with, thus building up the animal's confidence. This is sometimes easier said than done, for some animals, like humans, are terrible hoarders and will carefully pile up in their bedroom that food which their stomachs cannot accommodate but which they feel sure will come in useful one day. When the scent of rotting leftovers becomes too all-pervading, you are forced to invade the bedroom area and clean it out, but the longer you can delay doing this, the better.

Once the animal is fully established, he will even come to look forward to your periodic invasion of his bedroom, for it means a fresh supply of banana leaves or grass, bringing with them tiny insects and seeds to be eaten, smells from the outside world to be snuffed and mused upon and then all the feverish excitement and activity that bedmaking involves.

I have found that this bedroom technique works excellently with most small mammals. I have had a wild squirrel settle down so well that after three days when I was forced to clean out his bedroom, he actually came into it and started to tear at the banana leaves and make his bed while I was still pushing them in. In the case of an extremely pugnacious and vociferous pygmy mongoose, he was convinced, within a couple of hours, not only that his bedroom should be inviolate but that his whole cage area should be as well. He accepted instantly that the cage was his territory and he defended it with the ferocity of a wounded tiger. It took endless and exhausting subterfuges to get him to one end of the cage so that I could put his food and water in at the other without risking a severed artery.

The size of the average travelling crate is governed by the fact that it is safer to transport animals in small, rather than large, cages, for, should the cages be moved by unskilled labour (which, unfortunately, they frequently are) and carelessly handled or dropped in consequence, the animal stands much less chance of being injured in a small crate. You will generally find that an animal, having occupied a cage for some months, gains so strong a feeling of security from it, despite its small dimensions, that, in many cases, on arrival at the zoo it refuses to leave the travelling crate for more spacious quarters. The travelling box has successfully become its territory and the boundaries it knows and feels safe in, where it is assured of food and water.

The new cage, be it fifty times as big, does not, at first glance, offer these things. It merely holds out the promise of that thing about which human beings get so excited, greater freedom. But this is the last thing that the animal wants; he wants security and this he has already in his small travelling crate. In many cases, the crate has to be left inside the more spacious zoo cage for several days, sometimes for weeks, until the conservative and cautious creature decides to include the large cage in his territory. Even when he has accepted the larger cage, should he feel frightened, he will make a beeline for the smaller one, for it is there that he feels at home.

When collecting in West Africa once, we were brought some Demidoff's bushbabies. They were brought in by a hunter, at the very last moment, as we were moving down country to catch our ship and, although I purchased them, I had nothing to keep them in except a rather ancient native wickerwork fish trap, measuring some two feet long by six inches in diameter. Fortunately, the Demidoff's bushbaby is the smallest of the bushbabies (being about the size of a golden hamster that has been on a strict diet), and so these three specimens fitted very well into the fish trap, which I had filled with dried banana leaves. The Demidoffs are one of the loveliest of the bushbabies – enchanting little creatures with huge dark eyes, delicate ears, soft greeny-grey fur and the swift, dainty movements of thistledown blown by the wind.

When we reached the coast (only three days later), I built a proper cage for my Demidoffs and transferred them to it. Mercifully, I had not thrown away the fish trap, for as soon as they were in their new cage the bushbabies went into a decline. They refused all food and huddled miserably in their bedroom, staring at me with great soulful eyes, like a trio of banished fairies. In desperation I returned them to the fish trap, whereupon they revived instantly and started to feed and behave normally. On the voyage to England, the fish trap (not having been designed for this sort of thing) started to disintegrate and had to be patched up with bits of string to prevent it from falling apart. On arrival, the Demidoffs were united in their disapproval of the zoo cage, which was approximately fifty times bigger than the fish trap, and resisted being evicted from their wicker home with great stubbornness.

The fish trap had to be hung on the wall of the new cage, and the Demidoffs lived in it for a year before venturing out into the more spacious cage. Even then, they still spent most of their time in the remains of the fish trap and resisted all attempts to wean them on to a better built, more spacious and hygienic basket. Eventually, after two years, the fish trap, which the Demidoffs had taken only three days to decide was home, finally fell to pieces, but by this time the enchantingly stubborn little creatures had become used to their new quarters.

FROM MENAGERIE MANOR:

I know that it is a confession of acute and depraved eccentricity, but nevertheless I must admit that I am fond of reptiles. They are not, I grant you, over-burdened with intelligence. You do not get the same reaction from them that you would from a mammal, or even a bird, but still I like them. They are bizarre, colourful, and in many cases graceful, so what more could you want?

Now, the majority of people will confess to you (as though it were something quite unique) that they have an 'instinctive' loathing for snakes, and with much eye-rolling and grimacing they will give you many reasons for their fear, ranging from the sublime ('It's instinctive') to the ridiculous ('They're all sort of slimy' etc). I have been, at one time or another, bored by so many snake-complex admissions that as soon as the subject of reptiles crops up in conversation with anyone I want to run away and hide. Ask the average person his views on snakes and he will, within the space of ten minutes, talk more nonsense than a brace of politicians.

To begin with, it is not 'natural' for human beings to fear snakes. You might just as well say that they are naturally afraid of being run over by a bus. Most people, however, are convinced they are born with a built-in anti-snake feeling. This can be quite simply disproved by handing a harmless snake to a child who is too young to have had its head filled with a lot of nonsense about these creatures; the child will hold the reptile and play with it quite happily and without a trace of fear. I remember once putting this point to a woman who had been gurgling on about her snake phobia for what seemed like years. She was most indignant. 'I've never been taught to fear snakes, I've always been like that,' she said haughtily, and then added in triumph, 'and my mother was like that, too.' Faced with such logic, what could one reply?

People's fears of snakes seem to be based on a series of misconceptions. The most common one is the conviction that all these creatures are poisonous. In actual fact, the non-poisonous ones outnumber the poisonous ones by about ten to one. Another popular idea is that these reptiles are slimy to touch, whereas snakes are dry and cold, and feel no different from a pair of snake-skin shoes or a crocodile-skin handbag. Yet people will insist that they cannot touch a snake because of its sliminess, and think nothing of handling a wet cake of soap.

Our reptile house is fairly small, but we have a pretty good cross-section of reptiles and amphibia on show. I derive a lot of innocent amusement out of going in there when it is crowded and listening to the general public airing its ignorance with an assurance that is breathtaking. For instance, the snake's tongue: this is purely a scent organ with which the creature smells, hence the way it is flicked rapidly in and out of the mouth; it is also used as a feeler, in the same way that a cat uses its whiskers. The snake experts, however, who visit the reptile house know better. 'Cor, Em,' someone will shout excitedly, 'come and look at this snake's sting . . . Coo, wouldn't like to be stung by *that*!' And Em will hurry over and peer horrified at the innocent grass snake, and then give a delicious shudder. All reptiles can, of course, spend long periods completely immobile, when even their breathing is difficult to detect, unless you look closely. The classic remark was delivered by a man who, having peered into several cages in which the reptiles lay unmoving, turned to his wife with an air of one who has been swindled, and hissed, 'They're *stuffed*, Milly.'

A snake moving along the ground or through the branches of a tree is one of the most graceful sights in the world, and when you consider that the creature is walking with its ribs the whole thing becomes even more remarkable. If you watch a moving snake carefully, you can sometimes see the ribs moving beneath the skin as the snake draws itself along. The creature's unblinking stare (another thing to which people object) is due not to the fact that the snake is trying to hypnotize you, but simply to its having no eyelids. The eye is covered with a fine, transparent scale, like a watch-glass. This is very clearly noticed when a snake sheds its skin, which they all do periodically. The skin comes loose around the lips, and then, by rubbing itself against rocks or branches, the snake gradually peels it off.

If you examine this shed skin, you can see that the eye scales have been shed as well.

All snakes are adapted for feeding in the same way, but their methods of obtaining their food vary. The non-poisonous ones and the constrictors (such as the pythons) grab their prey with their mouths, and then try to throw two or three coils of their body round the victim as rapidly as possible, thus holding and crushing at the same time. The poisonous ones, on the other hand, bite and then wait for the poison to take effect, which is generally very soon. Once the prey has undergone its last convulsions, it can be eaten. The poison fangs, of course, are in the upper jaw, and usually near the front of the mouth. When not in use, they fold back against the gum, like the blade of a penknife; as the snake opens its mouth to strike, they drop down into position. The fangs are hollow, like a hypodermic needle, or else they have a deep groove running down the back. The poison sac, to which they are connected, lies above the gum. As the snake bites, the poison is forced out and trickles down the groove or hollow in the fang and so into the wound. However, whatever the method of attack, once the prey is dead, the swallowing process is the same in all snakes. The lower jaw is jointed to the upper one in such a way that it can be dislocated at will, and, of course, the skin of the mouth, throat, and body is extremely elastic, so the snake can swallow a creature considerably larger than its own head. Once the food is in the stomach, the slow process of digestion starts. Any portions of the animal that are impossible to assimilate, such as hair, are regurgitated in the form of pellets at a later date. On one occasion a large python was killed, and in its stomach were found four round balls of hair, the size of tennis balls and very hard. On being cut open, each one was found to contain the hoof of a wild pig. These sharp hooves could have damaged the lining of the python's stomach, and so each one had been carefully covered with a thick, smooth layer of hair.

In the majority of zoos nowadays dead creatures are fed to the snakes. This is not because it is better for the snakes, or that they prefer it, but simply because of misplaced kindness on the part of the general public, who imagine that a white rat or a rabbit suffers terribly when put into a cage with a snake. That this is nonsense I have proved to my complete satisfaction, for I have seen, in a Continental zoo, a rabbit perched on the back of a python (obviously not hungry), cleaning its whiskers with tremendous sangfroid. The director of the zoo told me that when white rats were given to the snakes, it was imperative that they should be removed if they were not eaten straight away; otherwise they proceeded to gnaw holes in the snake's body.

Gerry continued his expeditions around the world, now with several purposes. While collecting animals for his own zoo, he had to gather material for his books, his main source of income, in order to repay the loan he had cajoled from his publisher for setting up the zoo, which at that time was hardly making ends meet and for which Gerry was also dipping into his pocket. He began filming in earnest, not only intending to sell the footage to replenish his coffers, but also to bring to a wider audience the wonders of wildlife and wild places.

His sense of the tragedy of extinction is expressed in the account, not of animals, but of people – the vanished tribes of Patagonia. His belief in the potential of captive breeding as a powerful tool to thwart animal extinctions is revealed in the story of a big flightless rail from New Zealand and the struggles to help it survive. But for all the serious pressures of this period, Gerry's descriptions of animals, from cats to platypuses, lost none of their appeal.

FROM THE WHISPERING LAND:

By the following day the news had spread through the village that there had arrived a mad *gringo* who was willing to pay good money for live animals, and the first trickle of specimens started. The first arrival was an Indian carrying, on the end of a length of string, a coral snake striped in yellow, black and scarlet, like a particularly revolting Old School tie. Unfortunately, in his enthusiasm, the Indian had tied the string too tightly about the reptile's neck, and so it was very dead.

I had better luck with the next offering. An Indian arrived clasping a large straw hat tenderly to his bosom. After a polite exchange of greetings I asked to see what he had so carefully secured in his hat. He held it out, beaming hopefully at me, and then looking into the depths of the hat I saw reclining at the bottom, with a dewy-eyed expression on its face, the most delightful kitten. It was a baby Geoffroy's cat, a small species of wild cat which is getting increasingly rare in South America. Its basic colouring was a pale fawny yellow, and it was dappled all over with neat, dark brown spots. It regarded me with large bluey-green eyes from the interior of the hat, as if pleading to be picked up. I should have known better. In my experience it is always the most innocent-looking creatures that can cause you the worst damage. However, misled by its seraphic expression, I reached out my hand and tried to grasp it by the scruff of the neck. The next moment I had a bad bite through the ball of my thumb and twelve deep red grooves across the back of my hand. As I withdrew my hand, cursing, the kitten resumed its innocent pose, apparently waiting to see what other little game I had in store for it. While I sucked my hand like a half-starved vampire, I bargained with the Indian and eventually purchased my antagonist. Then I tipped it, hissing and snarling like a miniature jaguar, out of the hat and into a box full of straw. There I left it for an hour or so to settle down. I felt that its capture and subsequent transportation in a straw hat might be mainly responsible for its fear and consequent bad temper, for the creature was only about two weeks old, as far as I could judge.

When I thought it had settled down and would be willing to accept my overtures of friendship, I removed the lid of the box and peered in hopefully. I missed losing my left eye by approximately three millimetres. I wiped the blood from my cheek thoughtfully; obviously my latest specimen was not going to be easy. Wrapping my hand in a piece of sacking I placed a saucer of raw egg and minced meat in one corner of the box, and a bowl of milk in the other, and then left the kitten to its own devices. The next morning neither of the two offerings of food had been touched. With a premonition that this was going to hurt me more than the kitten, I filled one of my feeding-bottles with warm milk, wrapped my hand in sacking and approached the box.

Now I have had, at one time and another, a fair amount of experience in trying to get frightened, irritated or just plain stupid animals to feed from a bottle, and I thought that I knew most of the tricks. The Geoffroy's kitten proceeded to show me that, as far as it was concerned, I was a mere tyro at the game. It was so lithe, quick and strong for its size that after half an hour of struggling I felt as though I had been trying to pick up a drop of quicksilver with a couple of crowbars. I was covered in milk and blood and thoroughly exhausted, whereas the kitten regarded me with blazing eyes and seemed quite ready to continue the fight for the next three days if necessary. The thing that really irritated me was that the kitten had – as

I knew to my cost – very well-developed teeth, and there seemed no reason why it should not eat and drink of its own accord, but, in this stubborn mood, I knew that it was capable of quite literally starving itself to death. A bottle seemed the only way of getting any nourishment down it. I put it back in its box, washed my wounds, and was just applying plaster to the deeper of them when Luna arrived, singing cheerfully.

'Good morning, Gerry,' he said, and then stopped short and examined my bloodstained condition. His eyes widened, for I was still bleeding profusely from a number of minor scratches.

'What's this?' he asked.

'A cat . . . *gato*,' I said irritably.

'Puma . . . jaguar?' he asked hopefully.

'No,' I said reluctantly, '*chico gato montes*.'

'*Chico gato montes*,' he repeated incredulously, 'do this?'

'Yes. The bloody little fool won't eat. I tried it on the bottle, but it's just like a damned tiger. What it really needs is an example . . .' my voice died away as an idea struck me. 'Come on, Luna, we'll go and see Edna.'

'Why Edna?' inquired Luna breathlessly as he followed me down the road to Helmuth's flat.

'She can help,' I said.

'But, Gerry, Helmuth won't like it if Edna is bitten by a *gato montes*,' Luna pointed out in Spanish.

'She won't get bitten,' I explained. 'I just want her to give me a kitten.'

Luna gazed at me with dark, puzzled eyes, but the conundrum was too much for him, and so he merely shrugged and followed me round to Helmuth's front door. I clapped my hands and went into Helmuth's and Edna's comfortable sitting-room, where Edna was ensconced over a huge pile of socks, darning placidly and listening to the gramophone.

'Hullo,' she said, giving us her wide, attractive smile, 'the gin is over there, help yourself.'

Edna had a beautiful and placid nature: nothing seemed to worry her unduly. I am sure that if you walked into her sitting-room with fourteen Martians in tow she would merely smile and point out the location of the gin.

'Thank you, dear,' I said, 'but I didn't come for gin, strange though it may sound.'

'It does sound strange,' agreed Edna, grinning at me mischievously. 'Well, if you don't want gin, what do you want?'

'A kitten.'

'A kitten?'

'Yes . . . you know, a small cat.'

'Today Gerry is *loco*,' said Luna with conviction, pouring out two liberal measures of gin and handing one to me.

'I have just bought a baby *gato montes*,' I explained to Edna. 'It's extremely wild. It won't eat by itself, and this is what it did to me when I tried to feed it on the bottle.' I displayed my wounds. Edna's eyes widened.

'But how big is this animal?' she asked.

'About the size of a two-week-old domestic cat.'

Edna looked stern. She folded up the sock she was darning.

'Have you put disinfectant on those cuts?' she inquired, obviously preparing herself for a medical orgy.

'Never mind the cuts . . . I washed them . . . But what I want from you is a kitten, an ordinary kitten. Didn't you say the other day that you were infested with kittens over here?'

'Yes,' said Edna, 'we have plenty of kittens.'

'Good. Well, can I have one?'

Edna considered

'If I give you a kitten will you let me disinfect your cuts?' she asked cunningly. I sighed.

'All right, blackmailer,' I said.

So Edna disappeared into the kitchen quarters, from whence came a lot of shrill exclamations and much giggling. Then Edna returned with a bowl of hot water and proceeded to minister unto my cuts and bites, while a procession of semi-hysterical Indian maids filed into the room, carrying in their arms groups of kittens of all shapes and colours, from ones still blind to ones that were half grown and looked almost as wild as my Geoffroy's cat. Eventually I chose a fat, placid female tabby which was approximately the same size and age as my wild cat, and carried it back in triumph to the garage. Here I spent an hour constructing a rough cage, while the tabby kitten purred vigorously and rubbed itself round my legs, occasionally tripping me up. When the cage was ready I put the tabby kitten in first, and left it for an hour or so to settle down.

Most wild animals have a very strong sense of territory. In the wild state, they have their own particular bit of forest or grassland which they consider their own preserve, and will defend it against any other member of their own species (or other animals sometimes) that tries to enter it. When you put wild animals into cages the cages become, as far as they are concerned, their territory. So, if you introduce another animal into the same cage, the first inmate will in all probability defend it vigorously, and you may easily have a fight to the death on your hands. So you generally have to employ low cunning. Suppose, for example, you have a large vigorous creature who is obviously quite capable of looking after itself, and it has been in a cage for a period of a few weeks. Then you get a second animal of the same species, and you want to confine them together, for the sake of convenience. Introduce the new specimen into the old one's cage, and the old one may well kill it. So the best thing to do is to build an entirely new cage, and into this you introduce the weaker of the two animals. When it has settled down, you then put the stronger one in with it. The stronger one will, of course, still remain the dominant animal, and may even bully the weaker one, but as far as he is concerned he had been introduced into someone else's territory, and this takes the edge off his potential viciousness. It's a sort of Lifemanship that any collector has to practise at one time or another.

In this case I was sure that the baby Geoffroy's was quite capable of killing the domestic kitten, if I introduced the kitten to *it*, instead of the other way round. So, once the tabby had settled down, I seized the Geoffroy's and pushed it, snarling and raving, into the cage, and stood back to see what would happen. The tabby was delighted. It came forward to the angry Geoffroy's and started to rub itself against its neck, purring loudly. The Geoffroy's, taken aback by its greeting as I had hoped, merely spat rather rudely, and retreated into a corner. The tabby, having made the first overtures of friendship, sat down, purring loudly, and proceeded to wash itself with a self-satisfied air. I covered the front of the cage with a piece of sacking and left them to settle down, for I was sure now that the Geoffroy's would do the tabby no real harm.

That evening, when I lifted the sacking, I found them lying side by side, and the Geoffroy's, instead of spitting at me as it had done up until now, contented itself with merely lifting its lip in a warning manner. I carefully inserted a large bowl of milk into the cage, and a plate containing the finely-chopped meat and raw egg, which I wanted the Geoffroy's to eat. This was the crucial test, for I was hoping that the tabby would fall upon this delicious fare and, by example, encourage the Geoffroy's to eat. Sure enough, the tabby, purring like an ancient outboard engine, flung itself at the bowl of milk, took a long drink and then settled down to the meat and egg. I had retreated to a place where I could see without being seen, and I watched the Geoffroy's carefully. To begin with it took no interest at all, lying there with half-closed eyes. But eventually the noise the tabby was making over the egg and meat – it was a rather messy feeder – attracted its attention. It rose cautiously and approached the plate, while I held my breath. Delicately it sniffed round the edge of the plate, while the tabby lifted a face that was dripping with raw egg and gave a mew of encouragement, slightly muffled by the portion of meat it had in its mouth. The Geoffroy's stood pondering for a moment, and then, to my delight, sank down by the plate and started to eat. In spite of the fact that it must have been extremely hungry it ate daintily, lapping a little raw egg, and then picking up a morsel of meat which it chewed thoroughly before swallowing. I watched them until, between them, they had cleaned both plates, then I replenished them with more milk, egg and meat, and went to bed well satisfied. The next morning both plates were spotless, and the Geoffroy's and the tabby were locked in each other's arms, fast asleep, their stomachs bulging like two little hairy balloons. They did not wake up until midday, and then they both looked distinctly debauched. But when they saw me approaching with the plates of food they both displayed considerable interest, and I knew that my battle with the Geoffroy's was won.

*　　*　　*

Early the next morning, while it was still dark, I was awoken by Huichi [owner of a ranch in Patagonia] moving around the kitchen, whistling softly to himself, clattering the coffee-pot and cups, trying to break in on our slumbers gently. My immediate reaction was to snuggle down deeper under the pile of soft, warm, biscuit-coloured guanaco skins that covered the enormous double-bed in which Jacquie and I were ensconced. Then, after a moment's meditation, I decided that if Huichi was up I ought to be up as well; in any case, I knew I should have to get up in order to rout the others out. So, taking a deep breath, I threw back the bed-clothes and leapt nimbly out of bed. I have rarely regretted an action more: it was rather like coming freshly from a boiler-room and plunging into a mountain stream.

With chattering teeth I put on all the clothes I could find, and hobbled out into the kitchen. Huichi smiled and nodded at me, and then, in the most understanding manner, poured two fingers of brandy into a large cup, filled it up with steaming coffee and handed it to me. Presently, glowing with heat, I took off one of my three pullovers, and took a malicious delight in making the rest of the party get out of bed.

We set off eventually, full of brandy and coffee, in the pale daffodil-yellow dawn light and headed towards the place where the penguins were to be found. Knots of blank-faced sheep scuttled across the nose of the Land-Rover as we drove along, their fleeces wobbling as they ran, and at one point we passed a long, shallow dew-pond, caught in a cleft between the gentle undulation of hills, and six flamingos were feeding at its edge, pink as cyclamen buds. We drove a quarter of an hour or so, and then Huichi swung the Land-Rover off the main track and headed across country, up a gentle slope of land. As we came to the top of the rise, he turned and grinned at me.

'Ahora,' he said, 'ahora los pinguinos.'

Then we reached the top of the slope and there was the penguin colony.

Ahead of us the low, brown scrub petered out, and in its place was a great desert of sun-cracked sand. This was separated from the sea beyond by a crescent-shaped ridge of white sand-dunes, very steep and some two hundred feet high. It was in this desert area, protected from the sea wind by the encircling arms of the dunes, that the penguins had created their city. As far as the eye could see on every side the ground was pock-marked with nesting burrows, some a mere half-hearted scrape in the sand, some several feet deep. These craters made the place look like a small section of the moon's surface seen through a powerful telescope. In among these craters waddled the biggest collection of penguins I had ever seen, like a sea of pygmy headwaiters, solemnly shuffling to and fro as if suffering from fallen arches due to a lifetime of carrying overloaded trays. Their numbers were prodigious, stretching to the furthermost horizon where they twinkled black and white in the heat haze. It was a breath-taking sight. Slowly we drove through the scrub until we reached the edge of this gigantic honey-comb of nest burrows and then we stopped and got out of the Land-Rover.

We stood and watched the penguins, and they stood and watched us with immense respect and interest. As long as we stayed near the vehicle they showed no fear. The greater proportion of birds were, of course, adult;

but each nesting burrow contained one or two youngsters, still wearing their baby coats of down, who regarded us with big, melting dark eyes, looking rather like plump and shy debutantes clad in outsize silver-fox furs. The adults, sleek and neat in their black and white suits, had red wattles round the base of their beaks, and bright, predatory, street-pedlar eyes. As you approached them they would back towards their burrows, twisting their heads from side to side in a warning display, until sometimes they would be looking at you completely upside down. If you approached too close they would walk backwards into their burrows and gradually disappear, still twisting their heads vigorously. The babies, on the other hand, would let you get within about four feet of them, and then their nerve would break and they would turn and dive into the burrow, so that their great fluffy behinds and frantically flapping feet was all that could be seen of them.

At first the noise and movement of the vast colony was confusing. As a background to the continuous whispering of the wind was the constant peeting of the youngsters, and the loud prolonged, donkey-like bray of the adults, standing up stiff and straight, flippers spread wide, beaks pointing at the blue sky as they brayed joyfully and exultingly. To begin with you did not know where to look first, and the constant movement of the adults and young seemed to be desultory and without purpose. Then after a few hours of getting used to being amongst such a huge assemblage of birds, a certain pattern seemed to emerge. The first thing that became obvious was that most of the movement in the colony was due to adult birds. A great number stood by the nest burrows, obviously doing sentry duty with the young, while among them vast numbers of other birds passed to and fro, some making their way towards the sea, others coming from it. The distant sand-dunes were freckled with the tiny plodding figures of penguins, either climbing the steep slopes or sliding down them. This constant trek to and fro to the sea occupied a large portion of the penguins' day, and it was such a tremendous feat that it deserves to be described in detail. By carefully watching the colony, day by day, during the three weeks we lived among it, we discovered that this is what happened:

Early in the morning one of the parent birds (either male or female) would set out towards the sea, leaving its mate in charge of the nestlings. In order to get to the sea the bird had to cover about a mile and a half of the most gruelling and difficult terrain imaginable. First they had to pick their way through the vast patchwork of nesting burrows that made up the colony, and when they reached the edge of this – the suburbs, as it were – they were faced by the desert area, where the sand was caked and split by the sun into something resembling a gigantic jig-saw puzzle. The sand in this area would, quite early in the day, get so hot that it was painful to touch, and yet the penguins would plod dutifully across it, pausing frequently for a rest, as though in a trance. This used to take them about half an hour. But, when they reached the other side of the desert they were faced with another obstacle, the sand-dunes. These towered over the diminutive figures of the birds like a snow-white chain of Himalayan mountains, two hundred feet high, their steep sides composed of fine, loose shifting sand. We found it difficult enough to negotiate these dunes, so it must have been far worse for such an ill-equipped bird as a penguin.

When they reached the base of the dunes they generally paused for about ten minutes to have a rest. Some just sat there, brooding, while others fell forwards on to their tummies and lay there panting. Then, when they had rested, they would climb sturdily to their feet and start the ascent. Gathering themselves, they would rush at the slope, obviously hoping to get the worst of the climb over as quickly as possible. But this rapid climb would peter out about a quarter of the way up; their progress would slow down, and they would pause to rest more often. As the gradient grew steeper and steeper they would eventually be forced to flop down on their bellies, and tackle the slope that way, using their flippers to assist them in the climb. Then, with one final, furious burst of speed, they would triumphantly reach the top, where they would stand up straight, flap their flippers in delight, and then flop down on to their tummies for a ten-minute rest. They had reached the halfway mark and, lying there on the knife-edge top of the dune, they would see the sea, half a mile away, gleaming coolly and enticingly. But they had still to descend the other side of the dune, cross a quarter of a mile of scrub-land and then several hundred yards of shingle beach before they reached the sea.

Going down the dune, of course, presented no problem to them, and they accomplished this in two ways, both equally amusing to watch. Either they would walk down, starting very sedately and getting quicker and quicker the steeper the slope became, until they were galloping along in the most undignified way, or else they would slide down on their tummies, using their wings and feet to propel their bodies over the surface of the sand exactly as if they were swimming. With either method they reached the bottom of the dune in a small avalanche of fine sand, and they would get to their feet, shake themselves, and set off grimly through the scrub towards the beach. But it was the last few hundred yards of beach that seemed to make them suffer most. There was the sea, blue, glittering, lisping seductively on the shore, and to get to it they had to drag their tired bodies over the stony beach, where the pebbles scrunched and wobbled under their feet, throwing them off balance. But at last it was over, and they ran the last few feet to the edge of the waves in a curious crouching position, then suddenly straightened up and plunged into the cool water. For ten minutes or so they twirled and ducked in a shimmer of sun ripples, washing the dust and sand from their heads and wings, fluttering their hot, sore feet in the water in ecstasy, whirling and bobbing, disappearing beneath the water, and popping up again like corks. Then, thoroughly refreshed, they would set about the stern task of fishing, undaunted by the fact that they would have to face that difficult journey once again before the food they caught could be delivered to their hungry young.

Once they had plodded their way – full of fish – back over the hot terrain to the colony, they would have to start on the hectic job of feeding their ravenous young. This feat resembled a cross between a boxing- and an all-in wrestling-match, and was fascinating and amusing to watch. There was one family that lived in a burrow close to the spot where we parked the Land-Rover each day, and both the parent birds and their young got so used to our presence that they allowed us to sit and film them at a distance of about twenty feet, so we could see every detail of the feeding process very clearly. Once the parent bird reached the edge of the colony it had to run the gauntlet of several thousand youngsters before it reached its own nest-burrow and babies. All these youngsters were convinced that, by launching themselves at the adult bird in a sort of tackle, they could get it to regurgitate the food it was carrying. So the adult had to avoid the attacks of these fat, furry youngsters by dodging to and fro like a skilful centre-forward on a football field. Generally the parent would end up at its nest-burrow, still hotly pursued by two or three strange chicks, who were grimly determined to make it produce food. When it reached home the adult would suddenly lose patience with its pursuers, and, rounding on them, would proceed to beat them up in no uncertain fashion, pecking at them so viciously that large quantities of the babies' fluff would be pecked away, and float like thistledown across the colony.

Having routed the strange babies, it would then turn its attention to its own chicks, who were by now attacking it in the same way as the others had done, uttering shrill wheezing cries of hunger and impatience. It would squat down at the entrance to the burrow and stare at its feet pensively, making motions like someone trying to stifle an acute attack of hiccups. On seeing this the youngsters would work themselves into a frenzy of delighted anticipation, uttering their wild, wheezing cries, flapping their wings frantically, pressing themselves close to the parent bird's body, and stretching up their beaks and clattering them against the adult's. This would go on for perhaps thirty seconds, when the parent would suddenly – with an expression of relief – regurgitate vigorously, plunging its beak so deeply into the gaping mouths of the youngsters that you felt sure it would never be able to pull its head out again. The babies, satisfied and apparently not stabbed from stem to stern by the delivery of the first course, would squat down on their plump behinds and meditate for a while, and their parent would seize the opportunity to have a quick wash and brush up, carefully preening its breast-feathers, picking minute pieces of dirt off its feet, and running its beak along its wings with a clipper-like motion. Then it would yawn, bending forward like someone attempting to touch his toes, wings stretched out straight behind, beak gaping wide. Then it would sink into the trance-like state that its babies had attained some minutes earlier. All would be quiet for five minutes or so, and then suddenly the parent would start its strange hiccupping motions again, and pandemonium would break out immediately. The babies would rouse themselves from their digestive reverie and hurl themselves at the adult, each trying its best to get its beak into position first. Once more each of them in turn would be apparently stabbed to the heart by the parent's beak, and then once more they would sink back into somnolence.

The parents and young who occupied this nest-burrow where we filmed the feeding process were known, for convenient reference, as the Joneses. Quite close to the Joneses' establishment was another burrow that contained a single, small and very undernourished-looking chick whom we called Henrietta Vacanttum. Henrietta was the product of an unhappy home-life. Her parents were, I suspected, either dimwitted or just plain idle, for they took twice as long as any other penguins to produce food for Henrietta, and then only in such minute quantities that she was always hungry. An indication of her parents' habits was the slovenly nest-burrow, a mere half-hearted scrape, scarcely deep enough to protect Henrietta from any inclement weather, totally unlike the deep, carefully dug villa-residence of the Jones family. So it was not surprising that Henrietta had a big-eyed, half-starved, ill-cared-for look about her that made us feel very sorry for her. She was always on the look-out for food, and as the Jones parents had to pass her front door on their way to their own neat burrow, she always made valiant attempts to get them to regurgitate before they reached home.

These efforts were generally in vain, and all Henrietta got for her pains was a severe pecking that made her fluff come out in great clouds. She would retreat, disgruntled, and with anguished eye watch the two disgustingly fat Jones babies wolfing down their food. But one day, by accident, Henrietta discovered a way to pinch the Jones family's food without any unpleasant repercussions. She would wait until the parent Jones had started the hic-cupping movements as a preliminary to regurgitation, and the baby Joneses were frantically gyrating round, flapping their wings and wheezing, and then, at the crucial moment, she would join the group, carefully approaching the parent bird from behind. Then, wheezing loudly, and opening her beak wide, she would thrust her head either over the adult's shoulder, as it were, or under its wing, but still carefully maintaining her position behind the parent so that she should not be recognized. The parent Jones, being harried by its gaping-mouthed brood, its mind fully occupied with the task of regurgitating a pint of shrimps, did not seem to notice the introduction of a third head into the general mêlée that was going on around it. And when the final moment came it would plunge its head into the first gaping beak that was presented, with the slightly desperate air of an aeroplane passenger seizing his little brown paper bag at the onset of the fiftieth air-pocket. Only when the last spasm had died away, and the parent Jones could concentrate on external matters, would it realize that it had been feeding a strange offspring, and then Henrietta had to be pretty nifty on her great, flat feet to escape the wrath. But even if she did not move quickly enough, and received a beating up for her iniquity, the smug look on her face seemed to argue that it was worth it.

In the days when Darwin had visited this area there had still been the remnants of the Patagonian Indian tribes left, fighting a losing battle against extermination by the settlers and soldiers. These Indians were described as being uncouth and uncivilized and generally lacking in any quality that would qualify them for a little Christian charity. So they vanished, like so many animal species when they come into contact with the beneficial influences of civilization, and no one, apparently, mourned their going. In various museums up and down Argentina you can see a few remains of their crafts (spears, arrows, and so on) and inevitably a large and rather gloomy picture purporting to depict the more unpleasant side of the Indians' character, their lechery. In every one of these pictures there was shown a group of long-haired, wild-looking Indians on prancing wild steeds, and the leader of the troupe inevitably had clasped across his saddle a white woman in a diaphanous garment, whose mammary development would give any modern film star pause for thought. In every museum the picture was almost the same, varying only in the number of Indians shown, and the chest expansion of their victim. Fascinating though these pictures were, the thing that puzzled me was that there was never a companion piece to show a group of civilized white men galloping off with a voluptuous Indian girl, and yet this had happened as frequently (if not more frequently) than the rape of white women. It was a curious and interesting sidelight on history. But nevertheless these spirited but badly-painted portraits of abduction had one interesting feature. They were obviously out to give the worst possible impression of the Indians, and yet all they succeeded in doing was in impressing you with a wild and rather beautiful people, and filling you with a pang of sorrow that they were no longer in existence. So, when we got down into Patagonia I searched eagerly for relics of these Indians, and questioned everyone for stories about them. The stories, unfortunately, were much of a muchness and told me little, but when it came to relics, it turned out, I could not have gone to a better place than the penguin metropolis.

One evening, when we had returned to the *estancia* after a hard day's filming and were drinking *maté* round the fire, I asked Señor Huichi – *via* Marie – if there had been many Indian tribes living in those parts. I phrased my questions delicately, for I had been told that Huichi had Indian blood in him, and I was not sure whether this was a thing he was proud of or not. He smiled his slow and gentle smile, and said that on and around his *estancias* had been one of the largest concentrations of Indians in Patagonia, in fact, he went on, the place where the penguins lived still yielded evidence of their existence. What sort of evidence, I asked eagerly. Huichi smiled again, and, getting to his feet he disappeared into his darkened bedroom. I heard him pull a box out from under his bed, and he returned carrying it in his hands and placed it on the table. He removed the lid and tipped the contents out on to the white tablecloth, and I gasped.

I had seen, as I say, various relics in the museums, but nothing to compare with this; for Huichi tumbled out on to the table a rainbow-coloured heap of stone objects that were breathtaking in their colouring and beauty. There were arrowheads ranging from delicate, fragile-looking ones the size of your little fingernail, to ones the size of an egg. There were spoons made by slicing in half and carefully filing down big sea-shells; there were long, curved stone scoops for removing the edible molluscs from their shells; there were spearheads with razor-sharp edges; there were the balls for the *boleadoras*, round as billiard-balls, with a shallow trough running round their equators, as it were, which took the thong from which they hung; these were so incredibly perfect that one could hardly believe that such precision could be achieved without a machine. Then there were the purely decorative articles: the shells neatly pierced for ear-rings, the necklace made of beautifully matched green, milky stone rather like jade, the seal-bone that had been chipped and carved into a knife that was obviously more ornamental than useful. The pattern on it was simple arrangements of lines, but carved with great precision.

I sat poring over these objects delightedly. Some of the arrowheads were so small it seemed impossible that anyone could create them by crude chipping, but hold them up to the light and you could see where the delicate wafers of stone had been chipped away. What was more incredible still was that each of these arrowheads, however small, had a minutely serrated edge to give it a bite and sharpness. As I was examining the articles I was suddenly struck by their colouring. On the beaches near the penguins almost all the stones were brown or black; to find attractively coloured ones you had to search. And yet every arrowhead, however small, every spearhead, in fact every piece of stone that had been used had obviously been picked for its beauty. I arranged all the spear- and arrowheads in rows on the tablecloth, and they lay there gleaming like the delicate leaves from some fabulous tree. There were red ones with a darker vein of red, like dried blood; there were green ones covered with a fine tracery of white; there were blue-white ones, like mother-of-pearl; and yellow and white ones covered with a freckling of blurred patterns in blue or black where the earth's juices had stained the stone. Each piece was a work of art, beautifully shaped, carefully and minutely chipped, edged and polished, constructed out of the most beautiful piece of stone the maker could find. You could see they had been made with love. And these, I reminded myself, were made by the barbarous, uncouth, savage and utterly uncivilized Indians for whose passing no one appeared to be sorry.

Huichi seemed delighted that I should display such obvious interest and admiration for his relics, and he went back into the bedroom and unearthed another box. This one contained an extraordinary weapon carved from stone: it was like a small dumb-bell. The central shaft which connected the two great, misshapen balls of stone fitted easily into the palm of your hand, so that then you had a great ball of stone above and below your fist. As the whole thing weighed about three pounds it was a fearsome weapon, capable of splitting a man's skull like a puffball. The next item in the box – which Huichi reverently unwrapped from a sheet of tissue paper – looked as though, in fact, it had been treated with this stone club. It was an Indian skull, white as ivory, with a great splinter-edged gaping hole across the top of the cranium.

Huichi explained that over the years, whenever his work had taken him to the corner of the *estancia* where the penguins lived, he had searched for Indian relics. He said that the Indians had apparently used that area very extensively, for what particular purpose no one was quite sure. His theory was that they had used the great flat area where the penguins now nested as a sort of arena, where the young men of the tribe practised shooting with bow and arrow, spear-throwing, and the art of entangling their quarry's legs with the *boleadoras*. On the other side of the great sand-dunes, he said, were to be found huge piles of empty sea-shells. I had noticed these great, white heaps of shells, some covering an area of a quarter of an acre and about three feet thick, but I had been so engrossed in my filming of the penguins that I had only given them a passing thought. Huichi's theory was that this had been a sort of holiday resort, as it were, the Margate of the Indians. They had come down there to feed on the succulent and plentiful shellfish, to find stones on the shingle beach from which to make their weapons, and a nice flat area on which to practise with these weapons. What other reason would there be for finding these great piles of empty shells, and, scattered over the sand-dune and shingle patches, such a host of arrow- and spearheads, broken necklaces, and the occasional crushed skull? I must say Huichi's idea seemed to me to be a sensible one, though I suppose a professional archaeologist would have found some method of disproving it. I was horrified at the thought of the number of delicate and lovely arrowheads that must have been splintered and crushed beneath the Land-Rover wheels as we had gaily driven to and fro over the penguin town. I resolved that the next day, when we had finished filming, we would search for arrowheads.

As it happened, the next day we had only about two hours' decent sunshine suitable for filming, and so the rest of the time we spent crawling over the sand-dunes in curious prenatal postures, searching for arrowheads and other Indian left-overs. I very soon discovered that it was not nearly as easy as it seemed. Huichi, after years of practice, could spot things with uncanny accuracy from a great distance.

'*Esto, una,*' he would say, smiling, pointing with the toe of his shoe at a huge pile of shingle. I would glare at the area indicated, but could see nothing but unworked bits of rock.

'*Esto,*' he would say again, and bending down pick up a beautiful leaf-shaped arrowhead that had been within five inches of my hand. Once it had been pointed out, of course, it became so obvious that you wondered how you had missed it. Gradually, during the course of the day, we improved, and our pile of finds started mounting, but Huichi still took a mischievous delight in wandering erect behind me as I crawled laboriously across the dunes, and, as soon as I thought I had sifted an area thoroughly, he would stoop down and find three arrowheads which I had somehow missed. This happened with such monotonous regularity that I began to wonder, under the influence of an aching back and eyes full of sand, whether he was not palming the arrowheads, like a conjuror, and pretending to find them just to pull my leg. But then my unkind doubts were dispelled, for he suddenly leant forward and pointed at an area of shingle I was working over.

'*Esto,*' he said, and, leaning down, pointed out to me a minute area of yellow stone protruding from under a pile of shingle. I gazed at it unbelievingly. Then I took it gently between my fingers and eased from under the shingle a superb yellow arrowhead with a meticulously serrated edge. There had been approximately a quarter of an inch of the side of the arrowhead showing, and yet Huichi had spotted it.

However, it was not long before I got my own back on him. I was making my way over a sand-dune towards the next patch of shingle, when my toe scuffed up something that gleamed white. I bent down and picked it up, and to my astonishment found I was holding a beautiful harpoon-head about six inches long, magnificently carved out of fur seal bone. I called to Huichi, and when he saw what I had found his eyes widened. He took it from me gently and wiped the sand off it, and then turned it over and over in his hands, smiling with delight. He explained that a harpoon-head like this was one of the rarest things you could find. He had only ever found one, and that had been so crushed that it had not been worth saving. Ever since he had been looking, without success, for a perfect one to add to his collection.

Presently it was getting towards evening, and we were all scattered about the sand-dunes hunched and absorbed in our task. I rounded a spur of sand and found myself in a tiny valley between the high dunes, a valley decorated with two or three widened and carunculated trees. I paused to light a cigarette and ease my aching back. The sky was turning pink and green as it got towards sunset time, and apart from the faint whisper of the sea and the wind it was silent and peaceful. I walked slowly up the little valley, and suddenly I noticed a slight movement ahead of me. A small, very hairy armadillo was scuttling along the top of the dunes like a clockwork toy, intent on his evening search for food. I watched him until he disappeared over the dunes and then walked on. Under one of the bushes I was surprised to see a pair of penguins, for they did not usually choose this fine sand to dig their nest burrows in. But this pair had chosen this valley for some reason of their own, and had scraped and scrabbled a rough hole in which squatted a single fur-coated chick. The parents castanetted their beaks at me and twisted their heads upside down, very indignant that I should disturb their solitude. I watched them for a moment, and then I noticed something half hidden in the pile of sand which they had dug out to form their nest. It was something smooth and white. I went forward and, despite the near hysterics of the penguins, I scraped away the sand. There lying in front of me was a perfect Indian skull, which the birds must have unearthed.

I sat down with the skull on my knee and smoked another cigarette while I contemplated it. I wondered what sort of a man this vanished Indian had been. I could imagine him, squatting on the shore, carefully and cleverly chipping minute flakes off a piece of stone to make one of the lovely arrowheads that now squeaked and chuckled in my pocket. I could imagine him, with his fine brown face and dark eyes, his hair hanging to his shoulders, his rich brown guanaco skin cloak pulled tight about him as he sat very straight on a wild, unshod horse. I gazed into the empty eye-sockets of the skull and wished fervently that I could have met the man who had produced anything as beautiful as those arrowheads. I wondered if I ought to take the skull back to England with me and give it a place of honour in my study, surrounded by his artistic products. But then I looked around, and decided against it. The sky was now a vivid dying blue, with pink and green thumb-smudges of cloud. The wind made the sand trickle down in tiny rivulets that hissed gently. The strange, witch-like bushes creaked pleasantly and musically. I felt that the Indian would not mind sharing his last resting place with the creatures of what had once been his country, the penguins and the armadillos. So I dug a hole in the sand and placing the skull in it I gently covered it over. When I stood up in the rapidly gathering gloom the whole area seemed steeped in sadness, and the presence of the vanished Indians seemed very close. I could almost believe that, if I looked over my shoulder quickly, I would see one on horseback, silhouetted against the coloured sky. I shrugged this feeling off as fanciful, and walked back towards the Land-Rover.

As we rattled and bumped our way back in the dusk towards the *estancia*, Huichi, talking to Marie, said very quietly:

'You know, *señorita*, that place always seems to be sad. I feel the Indians there very much. They are all around you, their ghosts, and one feels sorry for them because they do not seem to be happy ghosts.'

This had been my feeling exactly.

Before we left the next day I gave Huichi the harpoon-head I had found. It broke my heart to part with it, but he had done so much for us that it seemed very small return for his kindness. He was delighted, and I know that it is now reverently wrapped in tissue-paper in the box beneath his bed, not too far from where it ought to be, buried on the great shining dunes, feeling only the shifting sand as the penguins thump solidly overhead.

FROM TWO IN THE BUSH:

In 1948 a discovery was made in New Zealand that shook the ornithological world out of its usual comatose condition in an incredible manner – no less than the discovery (or re-discovery) of a bird that had vanished, a bird that had, for the last fifty years, been believed to be extinct. It was, to give it its full title, the Notornis or Takahe (*Notornis mantelli*), and the whole history of this bird is one of the most fascinating in the annals of ornithology.

The first Takahe was discovered in 1850, and excited even the staid naturalists of those days. The bird had been known to the Maoris from both North and South Islands, but in North Island it was only known from fossil remains. In South Island, the Maoris said, the Takahe had been common, particularly around the shore of Te Anau and Manapouri, two large glacial lakes. It was so common, in fact, that the Maoris used to organize annual hunts during the winter, when the snows up in the mountains drove the birds down to lower levels in search of food, but by the time the Europeans came to the area, only fossil remains could be found. Then, in 1849, the first live one was caught on Resolution Island in Dusky Sound by a party of sealers, who did what human beings usually do in these circumstances: they ate it. Two years later another Takahe was discovered and presumably suffered the same fate, but fortunately the skins of both these birds were obtained by a gentleman called Mantell, who sent them to the Natural History Museum in London. For twenty-eight years after this the Takahe vanished again, as mysteriously as it had reappeared, then, in 1879, another specimen was caught near Lake Te Anau, and in 1898 yet another was caught by a dog in the same vicinity. Now it seemed as though the Takahe was really extinct, that it had followed in the footsteps of that other famous flightless bird, the Dodo, for fifty years passed and there was no sign of it at all.

But there was a Dr G. B. Orbell who did not believe that the Takahe had suffered the fate of the Dodo, and in 1948 he set out on an expedition to see if he could find it. The place he chose was an old glacial valley which lay high up in the mountains on the western shores of Lake Te Anau. His expedition was not a success for, apart from seeing some ill-defined footprints and hearing some unusual bird calls, he found no proof that the Takahe was still in existence. Nothing daunted, he went back to the valley seven months later, and there he found a small breeding colony of the elusive bird. This is the sort of discovery that every naturalist dreams of making, but only one in a million achieves, and so I can understand and envy the delight which Dr Orbell must have felt when he caught his first glimpse of a real, live Takahe. The day after his discovery, of course, the reappearance of the Takahe was headline news all over the world, and the

New Zealand Government, fearing a sudden influx of sightseers, ornithologists and other fellow travellers into this tiny valley thus – disturbing the colony – stepped in with commendable promptitude and immediately declared the whole area a vast sanctuary, making it out of bounds to anyone who was not an accredited scientist or naturalist, and even their visits were under Government and Wildlife Department supervision. So the Takahe (numbering, as far as could be judged, between thirty and fifty birds) was secure in its own sanctuary at last, a sanctuary measuring some seven hundred square miles.

Shortly after we had arrived in Wellington I had met Gordon Williams, who, at the time the Takahe was rediscovered, was a biologist attached to the New Zealand Wildlife Service. He told me about the second part of the Takahe story, which was, if anything, even more remarkable than the first.

The birds in their remote valley were certainly anything but safe, in spite of the fact that the whole area had been designated a sanctuary and no unauthorized person was let in. To begin with, their numbers were minute and it was quite possible for a sudden influx of the introduced stoat and weasel to wipe them out, or for a similar influx of introduced deer or opossums to do much the same thing by their damage to the trees, thus altering the whole habitat of the bird. So, once again, one of New Zealand's native birds was being threatened by introduced animals. It was obviously impossible to patrol the valley to make sure that predators, deer and opossums did not get into it, so there was only one thing to do to ensure the safety of the Takahe, and that was to try to establish a breeding colony of them in captivity; but this was not quite so easy as it appeared on the surface. First, a site for the experiment had to be chosen which closely resembled the Takahe Valley; then public opinion had to be weaned on to the side of the experimenters, for a lot of well-meaning people – not fully understanding the ramifications of the problems and the dangers that faced the newly rediscovered birds – were against 'putting them in cages'. The first problem was solved by finding a very suitable area up at Mount Bruce, some eighty miles from Wellington, and public opinion was at last persuaded that the whole scheme was for the good of the birds. So Operation Takahe came into being.

Now, as Gordon Williams explained, came the hardest part of all. In those days the only way to get into and out of the valley was to climb from the shores of Lake Te Anau up the steep, thickly forested slopes over extremely difficult terrain until you reached the narrow gorge entering the valley, two thousand five hundred feet above. This was difficult enough (as previous expeditions had found out) even if you were just going up there to film or collect scientific data; but to climb up there, collect live Takahe and bring them down again, was a feat that would make even the most hardened animal collector blanch. It was obvious that these difficulties ruled out the capture and transportation of fully adult birds, for everything taken up into or brought down out of the valley had to be transported by pack, and it was felt that the adult birds would not survive the journey; therefore, the only thing to do was to get chicks. Now this decision in itself brought up a whole host of new problems; firstly the chicks would have to have a foster-mother and it seemed that bantams, the time-honoured domestic breed of fowl for this job, were the ideal choice. But even the most phlegmatic of bantams was not going to take kindly to suddenly having a lot of Takahe chicks shoved under her, and being told to keep them warm. So the answer was to get Takahe eggs and put them under bantams, but then, as somebody pointed out, even the most well-behaved bantam, brimming over with mother love, could hardly be expected to sit tight on the eggs while being bumped and jolted all the way up to and down from Takahe Valley. Gloom and despair settled over the instigators of Operation Takahe and it seemed as if it really was going to be impossible to get any of the birds out of the valley to safety. Then somebody (I suspect Williams himself, for he was so desperately keen on the project) suggested that the bantams be 'brain-washed' – that is to say, that a series of bantams be taught to sit tight on a nest of eggs no matter *what* the circumstances were. It was a long shot but well worth trying, and now began a careful selection of bantams. Out of a hundred or so, a handful were chosen either for their dim-wittedness or their basically phlegmatic characters, and these birds had to undergo what was, to all intents and purposes, a sort of avian assault course. They each had a clutch of chicken eggs to sit on in a cardboard box, and once they were sitting firmly they were then subjected to every form of shock that they might have to cope with on their trip to and from the valley. The boxes were jolted about, they were dropped, they were driven in cars over bumpy roads, taken in trains, speedboats and aeroplanes. Gradually the bantams of weaker moral fibre started to crack, and desert their eggs, so that at the end of the experiment only three were left. Of these, one was chosen for the simple reason that, sitting on her eggs in a cardboard box, she had been placed on top of a car and a low branch had swept box, bantam and eggs straight off the roof – a piece of basic training that had not been included in the curriculum. The box, after rolling over and over for several yards, came to a halt the wrong way up, but when it was opened they found the bantam still sitting on her eggs with grim determination – and not one of the eggs was broken, for presumably they had been cushioned against the shock by her body. So this dutiful bantam was chosen for the task of being the most important member of the Operation Takahe expedition.

It must have been a nerve-racking trip for the members of the team. Firstly, they had no means of knowing that a bantam who had behaved so beautifully down below was going to behave in the same way up in the valley, and they all knew that if they failed in their mission there would be such a sentimental public outcry that their chances of having a second attempt would be nil. To their infinite relief and credit, however, the whole thing went off without a hitch. The Takahe eggs were obtained, the bantam sat like a rock, and after giving a day or so to make sure, they started down the hazardous, slippery mountainside towards Lake Te Anau. Once they reached the shores of the lake there was a speedboat waiting to rush their precious cargo to the nearest road; here the bantam and eggs were put in a car and dashed down to Picton, there to be loaded on to a plane that flew them to Wellington; then another car ride, and at last the faithful bantam and her eggs were safely installed in the sanctuary at Mount Bruce. After this epic and nerve-racking trip, all the team could do was sit back and wait for the eggs to hatch, while offering up prayers that they would be fertile. In due course, however, two chicks hatched, and the team and the bantam began to look rather smug about the whole business. At last, they felt, they had achieved success. But now a new obstacle reared its ugly head. The bantam foster-mother, of course, treated the Takahe chicks exactly as if they were her own. She led them about, scratching up the leafmould vigorously and pecking at whatever tit-bits appeared, fondly imagining that the baby Takahes – like bantam chicks – would learn by her example, but the Takahes were *not* bantam chicks and followed their foster-mother about in a bewildered fashion, piping for food but unable to learn the bantam method of feeding. It was obvious that the female Takahe *feeds* her babies, and does not show them *how* to feed for themselves as the chicken does. Now the problem of feeding them was in itself a task, for it was found that baby Takahes do not gape at the mother as normal birds would do; the food is offered in the mother's beak and the babies take it from there in a sideways manner. At length a satisfactory method was worked out: the Takahe chicks were fed on blow flies and similar delicacies impaled on the end of a pencil. With this method of food intake and with the bantam to supply them with mother love and warmth at night, they grew and throve.

*　　　*　　　*

After tea, David [Fleay, an Australian naturalist, at his animal sanctuary in Queensland] took us to see the animal for which he is most famous; the unbelievable Duck-Billed Platypus. Although the Platypus has been written up *ad nauseam*, it *is* such an incredible creature that it's worth running over its more startling features once again. The rubbery beak and the webbed feet are like a duck's; the body is covered with a short and exceedingly soft fur like that of a mole; the short, somewhat paddle-shaped tail resembles that of a beaver; on the hind legs the male is armed with spurs that contain a poison almost as virulent as that of a snake; finally, as if all that was not enough, it is a mammal (which means that it is warm-blooded and suckles its young on milk) but the young are hatched out of eggs. The Platypus, incidentally, has no teats like a normal mammal, but merely an area of spongy skin through which it exudes the milk which the young ones then lap up. It is a strictly insectivorous creature, feeding on fresh-water crayfish, worms and grubs, and consuming its own weight in these delicacies each night. It is this prodigious appetite that is one of the many reasons that Platypus are so difficult to keep in captivity.

David's pair were housed in his specially designed Platypusary. This was a large, shallow pond, at one end of which were the wooden sleeping quarters – shallow boxes filled with hay connected to the pond by long wooden tunnels lined with Sorbo rubber. The reason for this is that in the wild state the Platypus burrows are narrow, and when the animal wends its way up the burrow to its bedroom the surplus moisture in its fur is squeezed out by contact with the walls of the burrow: in captivity, David has found that it is best to line the tunnels with hay or Sorbo rubber, which will perform the same function, for should a Platypus reach his bedroom with his fur still damp he will almost inevitably catch a chill and die. The Platypuses were not in their pond when we arrived at the Platypusary, so

David obligingly opened up a bedroom, plunged his hand into the crisp hay bed, and pulled one out for our inspection.

Now, although I had never seen a live Platypus, I had, over the years, seen films and photographs of them; I knew about their curious anatomy, how many eggs they lay, what they feed on, and so on. In fact I felt I knew the Platypus fairly well, but as I gazed at the creature wriggling in David's hands I suddenly realized that all my study of the Platypus over the years had left me completely unprepared for one thing: the personality of the beast. The curve of the beak gave it a benign and perpetual smile, and its round, brown, boot-button eyes gleamed with personality. It looked, quite frankly, like one of Donald Duck's nicer relatives clad in a fur coat some three sizes too large for it. You almost expected it to quack and in fact the noise it did make resembled the disgruntled growl of an indignant broody hen. David placed the Platypus on the ground and it waddled about eagerly, with movements reminiscent of a baby otter, snuffling interestedly at every object it came across.

David has not only kept and bred the Platypus in captivity (the first man to do so) but he has twice undertaken the hazardous task of accompanying Platypus to the New York Zoological Society. When you consider the organization involved in such a venture, the mind boggles: the thousands of worms, crayfish and frogs to be obtained for the journey; the special Platypusary that has to be built; the slow and careful conditioning of the animals to prepare them for the trip, for Platypuses are immensely highly strung and any upset can make them go off their food and die. It says much for David's abilities and patience that on both occasions he landed his charges alive and well, and they lived successfully for a number of years in the United States.

'You know, there was a very odd rumour circulating in England during the war,' I said to David. 'It was about 1942, if I remember right. Someone told me that a Platypus was being sent to the London Zoo, but I heard no more about it, so I suppose it was only a rumour. Do you know anything about it?'

'That wasn't a rumour,' said David grinning, 'that was a fact.'

'What,' I asked in astonishment, 'ferrying Platypus about in the middle of a world war?'

'Yes,' said David, 'sounds a bit mad, doesn't it? Suddenly, in the middle of the war, Winston Churchill decided that he wanted a Platypus. Whether he thought it would be good for morale, or a good propaganda story, or whether he just wanted a Platypus, I don't know; anyway, I was approached by Menzies and given the job of catching the animal, getting it used to captivity and preparing it for the voyage. Well, I got a nice young male and after keeping him for six months I thought he was about ready for the voyage. I'd briefed an apprentice on the ship about keeping the animal, and given him masses of written instructions as well. The whole ship was intensely interested in the scheme and I got wonderful co-operation, so eventually the Platypus sailed on the *Port Phillip*.'

David paused and gazed thoughtfully down at the Platypus, which was endeavouring to eat his shoe; then he bent and picked it up carefully by its tail and slid it into its bedroom.

'Do you know,' he continued, 'they got that Platypus right across the Pacific, through the Panama Canal, across the Atlantic and then – two days out from Liverpool – there was a submarine alert. Well, they had to drop depth charges, of course. As I told you, a Platypus is highly temperamental and very susceptible to noise; the depth charges exploding were the last straw as far as the animal was concerned, and it just died. Two days out from Liverpool!'

To me the whole story was one of the most gloriously Quixotic things I had ever heard. Humanity being torn asunder by the most terrible war in history, and in the middle of it Churchill, with his cigar, trenchantly demanding a Platypus (of all things), and on the other side of the world David carefully and patiently training a young Platypus and preparing it for the long voyage through submarine-infested waters. What a pity the story did not have a happy ending. But, even so, what a magnificently idiotic thing to do at that time. I doubt whether Hitler, even in his saner moments, would have ever had the delightful eccentricity of mind to ask for a Duck-Billed Platypus in the middle of the war.

PART THREE

1965–1985

Silverback!

A silverback is a male gorilla in his prime, on whose great, broad, silvery back rests all the responsibilities of leading his band, providing direction and comfort, protecting it and enlarging it. Gerry's flowing mane of blond hair turned to silver during this period and his greying beard completed the image of a silverback. His burdens were enormous – writing and filming to keep the zoo and himself afloat and then to promote and expand the conservation work, guiding the young Wildlife Preservation Trusts, the charitable organizations born out of Jersey Zoo, through the early days of skinny budgets and sceptics and the later days of starting conservation projects in the animals' countries of origin.

Gerry met these responsibilities in a number of ways. His writings during this period were at their most diverse, including pre-1945 experiences, as well as current travels to a multiplicity of destinations – trips for animal-collecting, conservation planning, natural history filming and fund-raising. He tried his hand at faction and fiction in short stories and novels, with charming results, and he wrote an overview of his conservation work.

The selections here are intended to reflect the variety and energy infusing Gerry's life during these heady and hectic two decades. His books are fewer than in the previous period, for he was dealing with so much more than his writing, but the selections record the highlights: the start of the breeding group of Jersey Zoo's gorillas, eventually made famous by the heroics of its own silverback, Jambo; the acquisition of the best and brightest patron any organization could have, the Princess Royal; the bursting on the scene of one of the funniest 'factional' characters, Ursula; the fascination with the most magical, yet seriously threatened ecosystems of the world – coral reefs and tropical rainforests, the former first encountered in Mauritius during the trip that gave rise to the Trusts' overseas conservation work; and our amazing visit to the then USSR in pre-Gorbachev days and the frustrations of tracking down a hibernating bear.

FROM THE STATIONARY ARK:

The complexities of successful marriage among animals is shown by the difficulties we had with our gorilla group, for in trying to establish these creatures we ran the gamut of practically everything that could happen . . . we acquired the female N'Pongo when she was an estimated two and a half years old. We then obtained Nandi, another female, slightly younger. N'Pongo, from the first, was a charming extrovert with great gaiety of disposition and firm ideas about her own importance. Though she liked Nandi from the moment of introduction, N'Pongo made it quite clear that it was *her* zoo that they were living in, the staff were *her* friends and Nandi would do well to remember it. She was too charming and good-natured an ape to develop into a sadistic bully, as many animals would have done in the circumstances, and she treated Nandi with great affection but considerable firmness. Thus, for five years the relationship was one of mutual affection and regard, with N'Pongo in many ways taking the place of the male. The relationship, in fact, was one which, in a girls' school, might have been described as unhealthy.

It was at this point that we were having so much trouble getting a male. It began to look as though N'Pongo and Nandi would have to end their days as virgin spinsters, a thought that was naturally abhorrent to us. It was then that Ernst Lang offered us Jambo. This was an enormous piece of luck from many points of view. Lang had been the first person in Europe to breed and successfully rear a gorilla, the famous Goma, and since that remarkable breakthrough (for gorillas were one of those difficult beasts that it was said could not be bred in captivity), his gorilla family had gone from strength to strength. Jambo was one of the males born into the family. Not only was he zoo-bred, but he himself was the father of a young male, the mother of which was his sister. This meant that Jambo was no callow teenager whose knowledge of sex was confined to perverted peeps at the health and strength magazines; he was a fertile male who knew how to mate.

This is very important, for there are many things in the apes' world that are learned by example, and successful copulation seems to be one of them. An ape reared without contact with a herd seems to be singularly inept and, in some cases, a totally unsuccessful lover, simply because he was never shown. Jambo had not only been shown by his enormous father, Achilla, but had proved that he had paid proper attention to the demonstration. His final qualification was that he was just the right age to become N'Pongo's and Nandi's husband. Lang had extolled his virtues in letters and, rather in the manner of the early royal marriages, photographs had been exchanged. We were told that Jambo was exceptionally powerful and exceedingly handsome, black but comely and with a rather humorous expression. We all thought he was perfect. Now we had to wait to see if the two females agreed.

Introducing animals is a heart-stopping business. Will they attack each other and, if so, will the hose pipes, the buckets of water, the pitchforks, be of the least avail? If not, will they simply ignore each other, or will they ignore each other to begin with and then attack each other later, when one has been lulled into a sense of false security? If they do ignore each other, does this mean that they might grow to like each other later on, or were all one's trouble and expense in vain? Anybody who cherishes the idea that all individuals of the species are bound to be alike in given circumstances, should have been there to watch the introduction of Jambo to N'Pongo and Nandi. It was a classic in every sense of the word.

We had confined the females in one of the three sections of the bedroom so that, through the barred divisions, they could look into the third bedroom into which we were going to release Jambo. Between the male and the females would lie a section of the bedrooms and two sets of bars. This would, we felt, act as a buffer state until we got some idea of all three participants' reactions to the whole idea. N'Pongo and Nandi could tell something curious was going on by all the untoward activity, but they had no idea what, since Jambo was still invisible in his travelling crate.

The moment arrived, the slide on Jambo's crate was lifted, the door to the bedroom slid open and Jambo, massive and black as coal, reeking with the garlic-smell of gorilla sweat, swaggered, hunching his shoulders like a professional heavyweight, into the cage. He gave one swift, all-embracing glance around him, saw the females, but made no sign. He squatted for a moment to gaze around him in a lordly fashion before starting a slow perambulation around the bedroom, examining every nook and cranny with interest but still totally ignoring the two females. The effect of all this on the females was fascinating. Both of them, when they heard the slide, had come forward and peered, but when Jambo sauntered, dark and handsome, into their line of vision, the reaction of each one was totally unexpected by us.

We had thought that, if either of them displayed immediate interest, it would be the basically friendly extrovert N'Pongo. Nandi always tended to be suspicious and kept herself to herself. But the moment Jambo strolled into view, N'Pongo took one good look at him and then turned and walked off, showing by the set of her broad back a measureless disdain. She expressed quite firmly a total lack of interest in the opposite sex and Jambo in particular. The effect on the antisocial Nandi was quite different and charmingly comic. She was a little way away from the bars, squatting on her haunches, when Jambo came into view. She took one look at the massive shape and reacted in much the same way as a teenage girl might if her favourite pop star suddenly walked into her bedroom, clad in nothing but a guitar. The expression on her face was one of incredulity and wonder; nothing in her previous life had prepared her for this miracle. No one had told her that such a thing as a handsome male gorilla existed. She took one look at Jambo and fell instantly and irrevocably in love.

I am sorry if this sounds unscientific and anthropomorphic, but in the dry and pedantic jargon of the biologist there is no way to describe it. She shuffled her way to the bars, never taking her eyes off this wonderful apparition, and clung on to them in a rather desperate sort of way, gazing wide-eyed and immobile at the apparently disinterested Jambo. She sat in a trance, drinking in his every movement. Once, during the course of investigations, he disappeared behind the wall for a few moments. Her distress was immediate; she ran to and fro, trying to see where he had gone. Eventually, when he did not reappear, she came to the conclusion that he had gone out through the slide into the outdoor area. Instantly she ran to her own slide, bent down and tried to peer under it. Fortunately for her peace of mind, Jambo reappeared, nonchalantly sucking a piece of orange and ignoring Nandi's display of uncontrolled passion. Relieved to see him again, she once more took up her station at the bars and gazed at him reverently and adoringly. N'Pongo, meanwhile, had eaten a few nuts, peered out of the window at us and finally lain down on her shelf, utterly ignoring the presence of a male in their midst.

When they were finally allowed in with each other, both females carried on in much the same way. It was obvious that N'Pongo, for so many years the queen of all she surveyed, viewed the newcomer with suspicion and jealousy but with a certain caution too. She decided to continue her policy of pretending that the eighteen-stone Jambo did not exist. Nandi, on the other hand, behaved, if possible, in an even more inane manner now that she could get close to the object of her passion. She would squat within a foot or so of him, gazing at him raptly, her eyes shining with affection. After a time, when Jambo lay in the sun and allowed her to groom him, her joy knew no bounds and she would lean up against his massive body, with a look of besotted pride on her face that was so human it was laughable. N'Pongo was somewhat distressed by this liaison, but she still maintained her domination over Nandi. However, there now developed an unfortunate association between N'Pongo and Jambo.

Jambo, for all his experience, was still very young and full of what can only be described as youthful high spirits and crude humour. He knew N'Pongo disliked him, and this aroused in him a sort of devilment. He would practise all sorts of schoolboy pranks, which, as we know, can become very wearing to the nerves. He would jump out on her suddenly when she least expected it, or, sauntering past, would suddenly rush at her and pull her hair. Immediately N'Pongo would attack him and he would run off. This teasing would go on until N'Pongo was in a towering rage and would pursue him, screaming abuse, accompanied by Nandi who, rather half-heartedly, took her part. But it was obvious that Nandi would consider such attentions from Jambo as a pleasure and privilege and was somewhat puzzled by N'Pongo's reaction.

Jambo, of course, like all practical jokers, did not know when to stop. He never actually hurt N'Pongo, except for a few minor bites and scratches (nothing by gorilla play standards), but as soon as he found that he could make her lose her temper, he teased her unmercifully. N'Pongo began to have the hangdog air of the wife of a professional humorist and, what was worse, she started to lose condition. Reluctantly we had to separate her from Jambo, allowing them into the outer areas separately and dividing Nandi's time between the two so that Jambo would not get bored and N'Pongo not become too jealous.

Then N'Pongo came into season and suddenly it was vouchsafed to her what a male gorilla, even an irritating practical joker male gorilla, was for. With complete shamelessness she would solicit him through the bedroom bars and, when they were allowed in with each other, copulation took place almost at once. During the whole time she was in season, N'Pongo tolerated

Jambo. Although she did not display quite the hero worship of Nandi, she nevertheless abandoned herself to the carnal delights in the most whole-hearted fashion. Then, the moment she was out of season, she resumed her former relationship with Jambo. Once again they had to be separated. Though she became more tolerant of Jambo as the months passed, she still only really had time for him when she was in season. It would have made things much easier for us if she had lived in harmony with him, but we had to be thankful for small mercies. At least she had mated with him and that was the main thing. Nandi, too, had received his attention when in season, and so now all we could do was wait and hope that both females would be fertile, give birth successfully and, most important, prove to be good mothers.

At long last, from the latest batch of urine samples that had been sent off to the laboratories, came back the exciting news that both females were pregnant. The first one to give birth was Nandi. This, our first gorilla birth, was a never-to-be-forgotten occasion. Apart from the importance of the birth itself, gorillas have only been bred since the 1960s and only forty-seven of them have been reared successfully. We hoped that there were going to be no complications because it was Nandi's first baby. With the aid of a closed-circuit television we had installed in the den, a twenty-four-hour watch was possible and thanks to this we noticed that Nandi was starting her labour at eight o'clock one night. Operation Gorilla came into force at once.

Over the months, as Nandi and N'Pongo had grown more and more rotund, we had been making our preparations to try to cover all eventualities. We could not assume that both gorillas were going to be good mothers, nor could we assume that the births were going to be easy and normal; so everything, from the possibility of having to do a caesarean section to taking the babies away and hand-rearing them, had to be taken into consideration and planned for.

The most likely event was that we would have to remove Nandi's infant and hand-rear it. This being so, a room in the manor was prepared as a nursery. It had a built-in airing cupboard, washbasin and cupboard space, and in this room were installed our two Oxygenair baby incubators and, for use when the babies grew older, large wickerwork clothesbaskets to act as sleeping quarters and a playpen. The nursery was heated by a thermo-statically controlled radiator and kept at between 70° and 75°F. In addition, we installed a washing machine for nappies and a tumbler clothes dryer. Of course, we had to lay in a stock of oddments ranging from baby oil, baby lotion and nappies, to feeding bottles, thermometers and plastic pants. In spite of the fact that the outlay had been considerable, we hoped we would not have to use any of it.

By the time Nandi started to strain at eight o'clock that fateful night, we felt we had taken every precaution that was humanly possible. Now it was up to Nandi and we could only watch and be ready to help, should it be necessary.

It was a nerve-racking time. The interval from the moment we noticed the first straining until the moment Nandi had the baby in her arms lasted nine hours and twenty-four minutes – an unprecedented length of time according to the observations we had of gorilla births in other zoo collections. The baby was what is known as a ventex presentation – that is to say, it was born face downward instead of face upward – and, as such, it inevitably produced an unnaturally prolonged labour. There was one point (when Nandi had already beaten the record for the longest labour so far observed) when we seriously and reluctantly started thinking in terms of a caesarean section, but we eventually decided against it, as Nandi, although in pain and restive, was in good physical condition. We decided to wait, for a caesarean section is not an operation you undertake unless you have to. Luckily, Nandi gave birth before reaching the time limit we had set.

From the commencement of labour until the moment of birth, every move that Nandi made was recorded; a total of 260 observations, which make up one of the most comprehensive scientific coverages of a gorilla birth ever made. Nandi cleaned up the baby very well and then ate the placenta and membranes. She held the infant close to her body and with great tenderness, so we had high hopes that all was going to be well. But then we came up against the usual stumbling block. Nandi had no idea that the baby should feed. Four hours after birth, the baby, a male, tried to suckle but was pulled off the nipple by Nandi.

The maximum recorded time that a baby gorilla had been left with its mother before being removed for hand-rearing was thirty-two hours, but our baby was so strong and so eager to feed that we left him with Nandi for forty hours. Still she would not let the infant suckle. Reluctantly we loaded the capture-dart gun, tranquillized Nandi and removed the baby. He was taken up to the nursery (beautifully decorated with cut-out pictures of Walt Disney characters on the walls and ceiling, so that the babies' eyes would have something to focus on) and installed in the incubator. The baby's first few feeds, which he took greedily, consisted of glucose and water; after that he was started on SMA, a dried milk used for human babies, and rapidly gained weight. We christened him Assumbo after an area in the Cameroons, which is the most westerly part of Africa in which lowland gorillas are found. He proved to be an exceptionally good baby.

Three months later, it was N'Pongo's turn. Unfortunately, she gave no preliminary signs that she was going to commence labour and, as we had had several dates recorded as possible birth dates, we were taken by surprise. The first we knew of it was at eight o'clock in the morning, when our curator of mammals, Quentin Bloxam, came on duty and found N'Pongo sitting on her shelf, totally ignoring her baby, which was lying on the floor, waving its arms about and whimpering. N'Pongo had eaten the placenta, cleaned up the baby and then, feeling that that was the extent of her obligations to the future of the gorilla race, had placed it on the floor and left it to its own devices. Quentin opened the slide leading into the outside area, and N'Pongo walked past the squealing infant without even a glance and went outside. It was obvious that, as far as she was concerned, it was now up to us. Quentin rescued the yelling baby, and it joined Assumbo in the next-door incubator. It proved to be a male as well, so we christened it Mamfe, again after a place in the Cameroons that I had used as a base camp on my collecting trips in West Africa.

The two boys grew apace and eventually graduated from incubator to basket and playpen and (when they got too boisterous) to a cage in the Mammal House. Here, with access to sunshine and fresh air, they grew even more quickly, beating up their toys and thumping their chests like adult gorillas in an effort to prove to us how powerful and savage they were, a boast belied by their enchanting woolly looks and the humorous glint in their eyes.

They had hardly settled down in their new quarters when the nursery was filled again, for, once more, Nandi and N'Pongo, within a few weeks of each other, had their second infants. Once more, we had, unfortunately, to take them away. Nandi's second baby was a female, called Zaire, and was the cause of much rejoicing, for in gorilla births in captivity there has been, up to now, a preponderance of males. N'Pongo's second offspring was a male, Tatu, probably the handsomest baby we have yet had and the image of his father. As I write this, Nandi is pregnant for the third time and I have no doubt that N'Pongo will follow suit. If these two births are successful, it will mean that we will have had six gorillas in three years, which cannot be considered bad going by any standards, when you remember that the first gorilla birth was recorded in 1956, just about twenty-one years ago and that there have only been seventy-four successful births to date. It is to be hoped that we can keep at least a trio of these or subsequent youngsters to form a potential breeding group for the future, when Jambo and N'Pongo and Nandi are past breeding age. The object of the exercise is to have our breeding groups self-sustaining, so that not only will it be unnecessary to catch gorillas in the wild again, but, from our breeding pool, we will be able to supply other zoos.

FROM THE ARK'S ANNIVERSARY:

By now, the early seventies, our breeding successes with rare animals were excellent, and the list of species in our care had grown considerably. This was mostly the result of my own collecting expeditions, but also of purchasing animals from other zoos or even dealers. At that time the commercial trade in rare animals was not illegal, as it is today, and purchase was often the only way to obtain specimens to set up a breeding group. I felt that a good home at the Jersey Zoo, where the animals would prosper and reproduce, was infinitely preferable to their languishing in dealers' shops or potty little menageries. (Today, of course, we and most other reputable zoos exchange or lend rare animals, with no money changing hands.) We still suffered from that chronic disease, lack of funds, but we were moving forward and our reputation was gradually increasing so that people outside the zoo world were beginning to understand what our motives were and not only to applaud our successes but to be generous in their contributions to our work.

It was at this time, just as I was taking off for my little house in the south of France to earn my living by writing a book, that I learnt that the island was going to be honoured by a visit from Princess Anne. At everyone's insistence, I phoned up the powers-that-be who organize such events and asked innocently if they intended bringing the princess to the manor house to meet the animals. I was only inquiring, I said, because I had intended to take off for France but would, of course, delay my departure if Her Royal Highness intended to grace us with her presence. The powers were shocked. Show the princess the zoo? Never! Her schedule was far too tight. Besides, they had other much more stimulating treats for her to enjoy, like the new sewage works (I think it was) for example. Slightly miffed that we were considered of secondary interest to a sewage works, I reported back and our Council said that this was ridiculous. I must phone up again. So I did and said I hoped they were quite sure, as I was going to France and there I intended to remain until I had finished my book. No, came the reply. The princess's interests lay in sewage rather than the salvation of obscure forms of animal life. So I went to France.

I was just getting into my stride in Chapter Two when I got a frantic phone call from Jersey. The princess had asked to see the zoo. Would I please be present? No, I said, I would not. I had been told she would not visit the zoo. I had come to France and there I intended to remain, writing for my bread and butter. I had, of course, every intention of returning, but I felt piqued at their inefficiency and intended to let them stew in their own juice for a bit. There were more phone calls. Bribery, blackmail, flattery and cajolery had no effect. Finally, when it seemed that everyone was going to commit suicide en masse, I said I would condescend to return. Down in the south of France, I could hear the sigh of relief emanating from Jersey.

I had never been involved in such a visit before. My only contact with royalty had been peripheral, waving a small paper Union Jack on the outskirts of a crowd of some hundred thousand on an occasion in London in my youth. I had no idea of the complexity of it, the intensive searches by detectives of every nook and cranny (I asked if they wanted to search the gorillas, but they refused), everyone with stopwatches timing each step of the way. They had allotted twenty-five minutes for me to show the princess 700 animals spread out over twenty-odd acres and explain the functions of the Trust. I felt it would not do my peace of mind any good to inquire how much time they had allotted to the new sewage works.

It was obvious that the visit would have to be taken at a canter rather than a slow, civilized trot, and so it was essential to try to choose the animals in which the princess would be most interested and, moreover, to have them bunched together. The imminent approach of royalty has an odd effect on one, I discovered. What was I going to say to her? All of a sudden our achievements and our aspirations seemed as interesting as a vicar's sermon. The whole thing seemed a great mistake. I wished I was back in France, but I was stuck with it. Waiting for the car to arrive, I felt like someone going on stage for the first time, hands like windmill sails, feet like Thames barges filled with glue, and a vacancy of mind achieved only by having a thorough lobotomy. The moment she left the car and I bowed over her hand, all my whimsies were washed away. I was taking around a beautiful, elegant, highly intelligent woman who asked unexpected questions, who was interested. I wished the retinue of powers-that-be would go away as they shuffled and twittered nervously behind us and, more fervently, I wished the press would go away as they crouched, clicking like a field of mentally defective crickets in front of us. I think this was the combination that was my undoing, that made me commit the gaffe of all gaffes.

We were approaching a line of cages and in one of them, at that time, we had a magnificent male mandrill, whose name was Frisky. He was – and it is a term you can use only for a mandrill – in full bloom. The bridge of his nose, the nose itself and the lips were scarlet as any anointment by lipstick. On either side of his nose were bright, cornflower blue welts. His face, with these decorations, framed in gingery-green fur and a white beard, looked like some fierce *juju* mask from an ancient tribe, whose culinary activities included gently turning their neighbours into pot roasts. However, if Frisky's front end was impressive, as he grunted and showed his teeth at you, when he swung round he displayed a posterior which almost defied description. Thinly haired in greenish and white hair, he looked as though he had sat down on a newly painted and violently patriotic lavatory seat. The outer rim of his posterior was cornflower blue (as were his genitals) and the inner rim was a virulent sunset scarlet. I had noticed that the women I had taken around before had been more impressed by Frisky's rear elevation than the front and I had worked out a silly routine which I now – idiotically – employed. As we approached the cage, Frisky grunted and then swung around to display his sunset rear.

'Wonderful animal, ma'am,' I said to the princess. 'Wouldn't you like to have a behind like that?'

Behind me, I could hear an insuck of breath and a few despairing squeals, as from dying fieldmice, which emanated from the entourage. I realized, with deep gloom, that I had said the wrong thing. The princess examined Frisky's anatomy closely.

'No,' she said, decisively, 'I don't think I would.'

We walked on.

After she had left, I had several large drinks to steady myself and then faced up to the fact that I had – still sticking to the animal motif – made a sow's ear out of a silk purse. I had intended to ask the princess if she would become our patron, but what chance now? What princess in her right mind would consider this when the leading figure in the organization had asked her if she would not consider exchanging her own adequate anatomy for that of a mandrill? One could not apologize, the deed was done.

Some weeks later, prodded by everybody, I wrote and asked the princess if she would become our patron. To my incredulity and delight she replied that she would. I am not sure how much he had to do with it, but I took Frisky a packet of Smarties – whose virulent colours so closely resembled his own – as a thank-you gift.

FROM FILLETS OF PLAICE:

In my early twenties quite a number of personable young ladies drifted in and out of my life and none of them made a very deep impression upon me with the exception of Ursula Pendragon White. She popped in and out of my life for a number of years with monotonous regularity, like a cuckoo out of a clock, and of all the girl friends I had, I found that she was the only one who could arouse feeling in me that ranged from alarm and despondency to breathless admiration and sheer horror.

Ursula first came to my attention on the top of a Number 27 bus that was progressing in a stately fashion through the streets of Bournemouth, that most salubrious of seaside resorts, where I then lived. I occupied the back seat of the bus while Ursula and her escort occupied the front seat. It is possible that my attention would not have been attracted to her if it hadn't been for her voice which was melodious and as penetrating and all-pervading as the song of a roller canary. Looking around to find the source of these dulcet Roedean accents I caught sight of Ursula's profile and was immediately riveted. She had dark, naturally curly hair, which she wore short in a sort of dusky halo round her head, and it framed a face that was both beautiful and remarkable. Her eyes were enormous and of that very deep blue, almost violet colour, that forget-me-nots go in the sun, fringed with very dark, very long lashes, and set under very dark, permanently raised eyebrows. Her mouth was of the texture and quality that should never, under any circumstances, be used for eating kippers or frogs' legs or black pudding, and her teeth were very white and even. But it was her nose that was breath-taking; I had never seen a nose like it. It was long, but not too long, and combined three separate styles. It started off by being Grecian in the strict classical sense, but at the end the most extraordinary things happened to it. It suddenly tip-tilted like the nose of a very elegant Pekingese, and then it was as though somebody had delicately sliced off the tip of the tilt to make it flat. Written down baldly like this it sounds most unattractive, but I can assure you the effect was enchanting. Young men took one look at Ursula's nose and fell deeply and blindly in love with it. It was a nose so charming and so unique that you could not wait to get on more intimate terms with it. So entranced was I by her nose that it was some moments before I came to and started eavesdropping on her conversation. It was then that I discovered another of Ursula's charms, and that was her grim, determined, unremitting battle with the English language. Where other people meekly speak their mother tongue in the way that it is taught to them, Ursula adopted a more militant and Boadicea-like approach. She seized the English language by the scruff of the neck, as it were, and shook it thoroughly, turned it inside out, and forced words and phrases to do her bidding, forced them to express things they were never meant to express.

Now she leant forward to her companion and said, apropos of something they had been discussing when I had got on the bus, 'And Daddy says it's a half a dozen of one and a dozen of the other, but I don't think so. There's fire without smoke and *I* think somebody ought to tell her. Don't you?'

The young man, who looked like a dyspeptic bloodhound, seemed as confused at this statement as I was.

'Dunno,' he said. 'Ticklish situation, eh?'

'There's nothing funny about it, darling. It's serious.'

'Some people,' said the young man with the air of a Greek philosopher vouchsafing a pearl of wisdom, 'some people never let their right hand know what their left hand is doing.'

'My dear!' said Ursula, shocked, 'I never let either of my hands know what I'm doing, but that's not the point. What I say is ... Oocoo! This is where we get off. Darling, hurry up.'

I watched her as they threaded their way down the bus. She was tall, carelessly but elegantly dressed, with one of those willowy, coltish figures that turn young men's thoughts to lechery, and she had long and beautifully shaped legs. I watched her get down on to the pavement and then, still talking animatedly to her companion, disappear among the crowds of shoppers and holiday-makers.

I sighed. She was such a lovely girl that it seemed cruel of fate to have given me a tantalizing glimpse of her and then to whisk her out of my life. But I was wrong, for within three days Ursula had been whisked back into my life, where she remained, intermittently, for the next five years.

I had been invited to a friend's house to celebrate his birthday, and as I entered the drawing-room I heard the clear, flute-like voice of the girl on the bus.

'I'm just a natural voyeur,' she was saying earnestly to a tall young man. 'Travel is in my blood. Daddy says I'm the original rolling moss.'

'Happy birthday,' I said to my host. 'And in return for this extremely expensive present I want you to introduce me to the girl with the extraordinary nose.'

'What, Ursula?' he asked in surprise. 'You don't want to meet *her*, do you?'

'It's my greatest ambition in life,' I assured him.

'Well, on your own head be it,' he said. 'If she takes you up she'll drive you mad. The local asylum is already bursting with her various boy friends.'

We moved across the room to the girl with the ravishing nose.

'Ursula,' said my friend, trying to keep the surprise out of his voice, 'here's somebody who wants to meet you. Gerry Durrell . . . Ursula Pendragon White.'

Ursula turned and enveloped me in a blue stare of prickling intensity, and gave me a ravishing smile. Her nose, seen full-face, was even more enchanting than seen profile. I gazed at her and was lost.

'Hullo,' she said. 'You're the bug boy, aren't you?'

'I would prefer to be known as the elegant, handsome, witty, devil-may-care man-about-town,' I said regretfully. 'But if it is your wish that I be the bug boy, then the bug boy I shall be.'

She gave a laugh that sounded like sleigh-bells.

'I'm sorry,' she said. 'That was rude of me. But you are the person who likes animals, aren't you?'

'Yes,' I admitted.

'Then you're just the person I want to talk to. I've been arguing with Cedric for days about it. He's terribly stubborn, but I know I'm right. Dogs *can* have inhibitions, can't they?'

'Well . . .' I said judiciously, 'if you beat them seven days a week . . .'

'No, no, *no!*' said Ursula impatiently, as to a dim-witted child, '*inhibitions.* You know, they can see ghosts and tell when you're going to die, and all that sort of thing.'

'Don't you mean premonitions?' I suggested tentatively.

'No, I don't,' said Ursula sharply. 'I mean what I say.'

After we had discussed the noble qualities of dogs and their soothsaying prowess for some time, I cunningly steered the conversation on to music. There was a concert on at the Pavilion for which I had managed to acquire seats, and I thought that this would be a very dignified and cultural way of beginning my friendship with Ursula. Did she, I asked, like music?

'I simply *adore* it,' she said, closing her eyes blissfully. 'If music be the bowl of love, play on.'

She opened her eyes and beamed at me.

'Don't you mean . . .' I began unguardedly.

From being warm and blurred as love-in-the-mist, Ursula's eyes suddenly became as sharp and angry as periwinkles under ice.

'Now don't *you* start telling me what I mean,' she said mutinously. 'All my boy friends do it and it makes me *wild*. They go on correcting and correcting me as though I was an . . . an exam paper or something.'

'You didn't let me finish,' I said blandly. 'I was about to say, "Don't you mean that your love of music is so great that you would accept with delight an invitation to a concert at the Pavilion tomorrow afternoon?"'

'Ooooo!' she exclaimed, her eyes glowing. 'You haven't got tickets, have you?'

'It's the accepted way of getting into a concert,' I pointed out.

'You are *clever*. I tried to get some last week and they were sold out. I'd *love* to come!'

As I left, feeling very pleased with myself, my host asked me how I had got on with Ursula.

'Wonderfully,' I said, elated with my success. 'I'm taking her out to lunch tomorrow and then to a concert.'

'What?' exclaimed my host in horror.

'Jealousy will get you nowhere,' I said. 'You're a nice enough chap in your humble, uncouth way, but when it comes to attractive girls like Ursula you need a bit of charm, a bit of the old bubbling wit, a touch of the *je ne sais quoi*.'

'I cannot do it,' said my host. 'In spite of your appalling arrogance. I cannot let *you*, a friend of mine, rush headlong into one of the blackest pits of hell without stretching out a hand to help save you.'

'What are you talking about?' I asked, genuinely interested, for he seemed serious.

'Listen,' he said earnestly, 'be warned. The best thing would be for you to phone her up this evening and tell her you've got flu or rabies or something, but I know you won't do that. You're besotted. But for heaven's sake, take my advice. If you take her out to lunch, keep her away from the menu, unless somebody's just died and left you a couple of hundred pounds. She has an appetite like a particularly rapacious python, and no sense of money. As to the concert ... well, don't you realize, my dear fellow, that the Pavilion authorities go pale and tremble at the mere mention of her name? That they have been trying for years to think of a legal way of banning her from attending concerts?'

'But she said she was very fond of music,' I said uneasily.

'So she is, and it has a horrifying effect upon her. But not nearly as horrifying an effect as she has on music. I've seen the leader of the orchestra in tears, gulping sal volatile like a baby sucking its bottle, after a performance of *The Magic Flute*. And it's rumoured, I think quite rightly, that the conductor's hair went white overnight after she'd attended a performance of Stravinsky's *Rite of Spring*. Don't you realize that when Eileen Joyce gave a recital here and Ursula attended she had such a detrimental effect upon that unfortunate pianist that she *forgot to change her dress* between pieces?'

'It ... it could have been an oversight,' I said.

'An oversight! An oversight? Tell me, have you ever known Eileen Joyce to run out of *dresses*?'

I must confess he had me there.

He propelled me with the gentleness of a kindly hangman to the front door.

'Don't forget,' he said in a low voice, squeezing my arm with sympathy, 'I'm your friend. If you need me, phone me. Any hour of the day or night. I'll be here.'

A friendly gesture from a red ruffed lemur, a primate unique to Madagascar,
and one of the many species on the decline in that country due to loss of habitat.
(© *Robert Rattner*)

With me in the Rockies, on location for filming *The Amateur Naturalist* in 1983. Gerry loved riding, and as a teenager taught American GIs in Britain in the early 1940s.

At a sanctuary near Hwange National Park, Zimbabwe, for young black rhinos orphaned by poachers. We were on a lecture tour in Zimbabwe in 1987, when there were just under 4,000 black rhinos left in the world. Today there are less than 2,600.

With the film team, taking a coconut break, en route to our aye-aye hunting grounds in the northeast of Madagascar in 1990. *R to l:* Mickey Tostevin (sound man), 'Cap'n' Bob Evans (producer), John Hartley and Tiana (driver). (© *Lee Durrell*)

LEFT: The aye-aye, a most extraordinary lemur and target of Gerry's 1990 collecting and filming expedition to Madagascar, which was his last. The breeding group in Jersey is thriving, but the outlook for this animal in Madagascar is bleak. (© *James Morgan*)

ABOVE: Gerry championed all animals – not just big, beautiful ones but also the small, obscure and less than appealing ones, like this Mallorcan midwife toad. Thought to be extinct, but rediscovered in minuscule numbers in 1980, a recovery programme in collaboration with the Spanish government has ensured its survival. (© *Quentin Bloxam*)

FAR LEFT: The golden lion tamarin of Brazil, a species surely saved by the concerted effort of zoo-based conservationists, combining breeding programmes with field research and community action. Tamarins from Jersey Zoo were the first captive-bred pair of liberated animals to produce young in the wild. (© *Mark Pidgeon*)

LEFT: The 'golden' fruit bat from Rodrigues, a tiny island in the Indian Ocean. There were about 120 of these left when Gerry learned of their plight in the mid-1970s. Now there are more than 1,500 wild bats, thanks to reforestation and education programmes. (© *John Hartley*)

ABOVE: Gerry with John Hartley, who came to Jersey Zoo aged seventeen in 1961. John started working with reptiles, but became Trust Secretary in 1968, and Gerry's personal assistant in 1976. This is the entrance to a rainforest reserve in Madagascar, one of the locations for a television series made in Madagascar and Mauritius in 1981. (© *Lee Durrell*)

Checking a trap for the giant jumping rat, one of the most appealing but little-known creatures of Madagascar, in the Kirindy Forest in the west. (© *Lee Durrell*)

A recently freed Mauritius kestrel taking food from the hand in 1990. Only four birds were known to exist in 1976, but today there are 350 flying free in Mauritius, thanks to the breeding and release programme.

BELOW: With infant cotton-top tamarins, one of the many species of South American monkey whose wild numbers dropped dramatically because of the trade for pets and medical research subjects. They are still on the decline due to loss of habitat. (© *Phillip Coffey*)

RIGHT: With a Russian desman, an aquatic insectivore, captured during the flooding of the Oka River in Russia. The desman is endangered because its soft, silky fur is much prized and its marshy habitat is being destroyed. (© *John Hartley*)

One of the gentle lemurs we collected from Lac Alaotra, Madagascar's most important rice-producing region, was a tiny baby which had to be dropper-fed until Gerry persuaded an old female gentle lemur to look after it. The exponential growth of rice fields at the expense of this lemur's marsh habitat spells doom for it and many other marsh-land species unique to the region. (© *Lee Durrell*)

BELOW: With a young skua on Unst in the Shetland Islands during filming for *The Amateur Naturalist*. (© *Lee Durrell*)

Les Augrès Manor, a typical Jersey manor house, viewed through the wrought-iron 'dodo' gate into the forecourt. Les Augrès is the nerve centre of the Jersey Zoo and headquarters of the Jersey Wildlife Preservation Trust, and the dodo is our symbol. (© *Phillip Coffey*)

With the reconstructed skeleton of a common dodo, *Raphus cucullatus*, a species exterminated within a hundred years of its discovery by the ignorant and greedy hand of our own species. The dodo was a powerful symbol to Gerry, representing the kind of travesty his work was designed to prevent. (© *Phillip Coffey*)

And he shut the front door firmly in my face and left me to walk home, curiously disquieted.

But the following morning my spirits had revived. After all, I thought, Ursula was an exceptionally lovely girl and I was quite sure that anyone as attractive as that could not behave in the boorish manner that my friend had described. Probably he had tried to date her and she, being wise as well as beautiful, had given him the brush-off. Comforting myself with this thought, I dressed with unusual care and went down to the railway station to meet her. She had explained that, living out in Lyndhurst in the New Forest, she had to come into Bournemouth by train because 'Daddy always uses the Rolls when I want it.' On the platform I awaited the arrival of the train anxiously. Whilst I was rearranging my tie for the twentieth time I was accosted by an elderly lady, a pillar of the local church, who was, unaccountably, a friend of my mother's. I stood, shifting nervously from one foot to the other, wishing the old harridan would go away, for when meeting a new girl friend for the first time, the last thing one wants is a sanctimonious and critical audience. But she clung like a leech and was still telling me about her latest jumble sale when the train dragged itself, chugging and grimy, into the station. I was giving scant attention to her story of what the vicar said. I was too busy looking at the opening carriage doors and trying to spot Ursula.

'And the vicar said, "I, myself, Mrs Darlinghurst, will tell the bishop about your selfless dedication to the organ fund." He has no need to say it, of course, but I thought it was most Christian of him, don't you?'

'Oh, yes . . . yes . . . Most, er, perceptive of him.'

'That's what I thought. So I said to him, "Vicar," I said, "I'm only a humble widow . . ."'

What other secrets of her private life she had vouchsafed to the vicar I was never to learn, because from behind me came an earsplitting scream of recognition.

'Darling! *Darling*, I'm here,' came Ursula's voice.

I turned round, and only just in time, for Ursula flung herself into my arms and fastened her mouth on mine with the avidity of a starving bumble-bee sighting the first clover flower of the season. When I finally managed to extricate myself from Ursula's octopus-like embrace I looked round for Mrs Darlinghurst, only to find her retreating along the platform, backwards, with a look on her face of one who, having led a sheltered life, suddenly finds himself confronted with the more unsavoury aspects of a Roman orgy. I smiled feebly at her, waved goodbye, and then, taking Ursula firmly by the arm, steered her out of the station while endeavouring to remove what felt like several pounds of lipstick from my mouth.

Ursula was dressed in a very smart blue outfit that highlighted her unfairly enormous eyes, and she wore elegant white lace gloves. Over her arm she carried a curious basket like a miniature hamper with a large handle, which presumably contained sufficient cosmetics to withstand a siege of several years.

'Darling,' she said, peering raptly into my face, 'I *am* going to enjoy this. Such a lovely day! Lunch alone with you, and then the concert ... Uhhmmm! *Paradise!*'

A number of men in the ticket hall, on hearing her invest the word 'paradise' with a sort of moaning lechery that had to be heard to be believed, looked at me enviously, and I began to feel better.

'I've booked a table . . .' I began.

'Darling,' interrupted Ursula, 'I simply *must* go to the loo. There wasn't one on the train. Buy me a newspaper so I can go.'

Several people stopped and stared.

'Hush!' I said hurriedly. 'Not so loud. What do you want a newspaper for? They have paper in the loos.'

'Yes, but it's so *thin*, darling. I like a nice thick layer on the seat,' she explained, in a clear voice that carried like a chime of bells on a frosty night.

'On the seat?' I asked.

'Yes. I *never* sit on the seat,' she said. 'Because I knew a girl once who sat on a loo seat and got acme.'

'Don't you mean acne?' I asked, confused.

'No, *no!*' she said impatiently. 'Acme. You come out all over in the most hideous red spots. Do hurry and buy me a newspaper, darling. I'm simply *dying.*'

So I bought her a paper and watched her disappear into the ladies, flourishing it as a deterrent to germs, and I wondered if any one of her numerous boy friends had ever described her as the acme of perfection.

She emerged, several minutes later, smiling and apparently germ-free, and I bundled her into a taxi and drove her to the restaurant. When we got there and had established ourselves the waiter unfurled two enormous

menus in front of us. Remembering my friend's advice I removed the menu
deftly from Ursula's hands.

'I'll choose for you,' I said. 'I'm a gourmet.'

'Are you really?' said Ursula. 'But you're not Indian, are you?'

'What has that got to do with it?' I inquired.

'Well, I thought they came from India,' she said.

'What? Gourmets?' I asked, puzzled.

'Yes,' she said. 'Aren't they those people that spend all their time looking
at their tummy?'

'No, no. You're thinking of something quite different,' I said. 'Anyway,
be quiet and let me order.'

I ordered a modest but substantial lunch and a bottle of wine to go with
it. Ursula chattered on endlessly. She had an enormous variety of friends,
all of whom she expected you to know, and whose every concern was of
interest to her. From the stories that she told, it was obvious that she spent
the greater part of her life trying to reorganize the lives of her friends,
whether they wanted her to or not. She babbled on like a brook and I
listened entranced.

'I'm very worried about Toby,' she confided to me over the prawn cocktail. 'I'm very worried about him indeed. I think he's got a secret passion
for someone and it's just eating him away. But Daddy doesn't agree with
me. Daddy says he's well on the way to being an incoherent.'

'An incoherent?'

'Yes. You know, he drinks too much.'

So rich is the English language, I reflected, that this word could, in fact,
with all fairness, be used to describe a drunk.

'He ought to join Incoherents Anonymous,' I said without thinking.

'What are they?' asked Ursula, wide-eyed.

'Well, they're a sort of secret society of ... of ... um ... incoherents,
who try and help each other to ... well, to give it up and become ... um
... become ...'

'Become coherents!' said Ursula with a squeak of delight.

I must confess this end result had escaped me.

Later on, over her filet mignon, she leant forward and fixed me with her
blue, intense stare.

'Do you know about Susan?' she whispered. Her whisper was more clearly
audible than her normal voice.

'Er . . . no,' I confessed.

'Well, she became pregnant. She was going to have an *illiterate baby*.'

I pondered this news.

'With modern methods of education . . .' I began.

'Don't be silly! She didn't use *anything*,' whispered Ursula. 'That's what's so *stupid*. And her father, naturally, said he wasn't going to have a lot of illiterates darkening *his* hearth.'

'Naturally,' I said. 'It would turn it into a sort of Do-the-girls Hall.'

'Exactly!' she said. 'So her father said she must have an ablution.'

'To wash away sin?' I inquired.

'No, silly! To get rid of the baby.'

'And did she have it?' I asked.

'Yes. He sent her up to London. It cost an awful lot of money and the poor dear came back looking terrible. I do think her father was unfair.'

By this time most of the other tables in the restaurant were listening to our conversation with bated breath.

Over coffee Ursula was telling me a long and very involved story about some friend of hers who was in dire distress, whom she had wanted to help. I hadn't listened with any great attention until she suddenly said, 'Well, I couldn't do anything about it *then*, because Mummy was in bed with a cold and Daddy wanted me to cook him an early lunch because he was taking the bull to the vet to have him castigated. And so . . .'

'Your father was doing *what*?' I asked.

'Taking the bull to the vet to have him castigated. He was getting terribly fierce and dangerous.'

How, I wondered, enraptured by the thought, did one castigate a fierce and dangerous bull? But I was too wise to ask Ursula.

'Look, hurry up and finish your coffee,' I said. 'Otherwise we'll be late for the concert.'

'Ooo, yes,' she said. 'We mustn't be late.'

She gulped down her coffee and I paid the bill and ushered her out of the restaurant. We walked through what are laughingly called the Pleasure Gardens of Bournemouth among the faded rhododendrons and the paddling pool, and came eventually to the Pavilion.

As we made our way to our seats, Ursula insisted on taking her miniature hamper with her.

'Why don't you leave it in the cloakroom?' I asked, for it was a fairly bulky object.

'I don't trust cloakrooms,' said Ursula darkly. 'They do strange things in cloakrooms.'

In order to save embarrassment I didn't inquire what strange things they did in cloakrooms, and we got into our seats and wedged the hamper between our legs.

Gradually the Pavilion filled with the normal crowd of earnest music lovers. And when the leader of the orchestra appeared, Ursula joined in the clapping with great vigour and then she leaned across to me and said, 'I think he's such a handsome conductor, don't you?'

I didn't feel that at that moment I should correct her. Presently the conductor came on and again Ursula threw herself into the applause with great enthusiasm and settled back with a deep sigh. She glanced at me and gave me a ravishing smile.

'I *am* going to enjoy this, darling,' she said.

The concert was a hotchpotch of Mozart, a composer I am very fond of. I soon discovered what my friends had meant about Ursula's distressing effect upon music. Should there be the slightest pause for one brief second in the music, Ursula's hands were up and clapping. Soon, after people had been hissing and shushing us, I became quite adroit at catching her hands as they came up to clap in the middle of a piece. Each time she would turn anguished eyes on me and say, 'Darling, I'm *sorry*. I thought he'd finished.'

It was, I think, after the fourth piece that I felt the basket move. At first I thought I was mistaken but I pressed my leg against it and, sure enough, it was vibrating. I looked at Ursula, who had her eyes closed and was waving her forefinger in the air in time to the music.

'Ursula!' I whispered.

'Yes, darling,' she said, without opening her eyes.

'What have you got in your basket?' I asked.

She opened her eyes, startled, and looked at me.

'What do you mean?' she said defensively.

'There is something moving in your basket,' I said.

'Hush!' came a chorus of angry voices around us.

'But it can't be,' she said, 'unless the pill's worn off.'

'*What* have you got in your basket?' I asked.

'Oh, it's nothing. It's just a present for somebody,' she said.

She leant down and fumbled at the lid, raised it, and then lifted out of it a minute, snow-white Pekingese with enormous black eyes.

To say I was shocked would be putting it mildly. After all, the concert-goers in Bournemouth took their music very seriously, and the last thing that they wanted or, indeed, would have allowed, was a dog in the sacred precincts of the Pavilion.

'Oh, damn!' said Ursula, looking at the Pekingese's rather charming little snub nose. 'The pill's worn off.'

'Look, put him back in the basket!' I hissed.

'Hush!' said everybody around us.

Ursula bent down to put the puppy back into the basket and he yawned voluptuously into her face and then gave a sudden and unexpected wiggle. She dropped him.

'Oooo!' she squeaked. 'I dropped him! I dropped him!'

'Shut up!' I said.

'Hush!' said everyone around us.

I reached down to try and find the puppy, but, obviously exhilarated by the fact that he had been released from his prison, he had trotted down the row through the forest of legs.

'What are we going to *do*?' said Ursula.

'Look, just shut up! Shut up and leave it to me,' I said.

'Hush!' said everybody around us.

We hushed for a minute while I thought frantically. How could I possibly find a Pekingese puppy amongst all those seats and legs without disrupting the entire concert?

'We'll have to leave it,' I said. 'I'll look for him after everybody's gone, after the concert.'

'You can't!' said Ursula. 'You simply can't leave him, poor little thing. He might get trodden on and hurt.'

'Well, how do you expect me to find him?' I asked.

'Hush!' said everybody around us.

'He's got all tangled up in the seats and the legs and things,' I said.

'But darling, you *must* find him. He'll get terribly, terribly lonely,' she said.

There must have been all of seven hundred people in the hall.

'All right,' I said. 'I'll pretend I'm going to the loo.'

'What a good idea,' said Ursula, beaming. 'I think he went down that way.'

I got to my feet and ran the gauntlet of outraged faces and mumbled profanity as I worked my way down the row and out into the aisle. There, I saw just ahead of me the Pekingese puppy, squatting down as boy puppies do before they've learnt to cock their leg, decorating the red carpet with a little sign of his own. I went forward cautiously and grabbed at him. I caught him, but as I lifted him up he uttered a loud and piercing scream that was clearly audible even above the rather exuberant piece of music that the orchestra was playing. There was a great rustle as people turned round indignantly to look in my direction. The puppy continued his screams. I stuffed him unceremoniously under my coat, and, almost at a run, I left the concert hall.

I went to the cloakroom, where, fortunately, I knew the girl in charge.

'Hullo,' she said. 'You leaving already? Don't you like the concert?'

'No ... it's ... it's a question of force of circumstances,' I said. I pulled the puppy out from my jacket and held it up in front of her.

'Would you look after this for me?' I asked.

'Oh, isn't he sweet!' she said. 'But you didn't have him in there, did you? Dogs are not allowed you know.'

'Yes, I know,' I said. 'He just got in by mistake. He belongs to a friend of mine. Would you look after him till after the concert?'

'Of course I will,' she said. 'Isn't he sweet?'

'He's not terribly sweet when he's in a concert hall,' I said.

I handed the puppy over to her tender care and went back and stood quietly in the shadows until the orchestra had finished the piece that they were playing. Then I made my way back to Ursula.

'Have you got him, darling?' she asked.

'No, I haven't,' I said. 'I put him in charge of the cloakroom attendant. She's a friend of mine.'

'Are you sure he'll be all right?' she asked, obviously with dark thoughts about what they did in cloakrooms to Pekingese puppies.

'He'll be perfectly all right,' I said. 'He'll be loved and cherished until after the concert. I can't think what induced you to bring a dog to a concert.'

'But, darling,' she said, 'I meant him as a present for a friend of mine. I ... I meant to tell you only you talked so much that I couldn't get a word in edgeways. I want to take him after the concert.'

'Well, don't, for heaven's sake, do it again,' I said. 'The Pavilion is not a place for dogs. Now let's relax and try and enjoy the rest of the concert, shall we?'

'Of course, darling,' she said.

When the concert was over and Ursula had, as she put it, clapped herself hoarse, we extricated the puppy from the cloakroom and put it back in its basket and made our way out through the throngs of music lovers avidly discussing the prowess of the Bournemouth Symphony Orchestra.

'Darling, I *did* enjoy that,' said Ursula. 'It's all those archipelagos. They go running up my spine. There's nothing like Beethoven, is there?' she asked loudly and clearly, hanging on my arm like a fragile maiden aunt, gazing earnestly into my eyes, and clasping in one hand the programme, which had embossed in large letters on the front, 'A Concert of Mozart'.

'Absolutely nothing,' I agreed. 'Now, what about this puppy?'

'Well,' she said, 'I want to take him to a friend of mine who lives on the outskirts of Poole. Her name is Mrs Golightly.'

'I'm not at all surprised,' I said. 'But why do you want to take the puppy to Mrs Golightly?'

'She needs it,' said Ursula. 'She needs it desperately. You see, she's just lost her own Bow-wow.'

'She's lost her what?' I asked.

'Her Bow-wow,' said Ursula.

'You mean her dog?' I asked.

'Yes,' said Ursula. 'That's what he was called – Bow-wow.'

'And so she needs another one?' I said.

'Of course,' said Ursula. 'She doesn't *want* one, but she needs one.'

'Are you, um, giving her this puppy because you think she needs one?' I inquired.

'But of course! Anyone with half an eye could see she needs one,' said Ursula.

'It strikes me,' I said, 'that you spend most of your time interfering in your friends' affairs when they don't really want it.'

'Of course they want it,' said Ursula earnestly. 'They want it but they don't *realize* that they want it.'

I gave up.

'All right,' I said. 'Let's go to Poole.'

So we went. When we got to Poole, Ursula dived immediately into the back streets and eventually ended up at one of those tiny little houses, two up and two down, that stare frostily at each other across streets. This one had a highly polished brass door-knob and I noticed that the step was a beautiful white as evidence of hard scrubbing on someone's part. Ursula banged vigorously with the knocker and presently the door was opened by a tiny, grey, frail old lady.

'Why, Ursula!' she said. 'Miss Ursula, it's you!'

'Emma, darling!' said Ursula and enveloped this fragile wisp of a person in a vast embrace.

'We've come to visit you,' she said, unnecessarily. 'This is Gerry.'

'Oh, do . . . do come in,' said the little old lady, 'but I do wish you'd let me know. I'm all untidy and the house is in such a mess.'

She ushered us into a living-room full of the most ugly furniture I have ever seen in my life, that glowed with love and polish. It spoke of the most impeccable bad taste. It was a room which had been cherished as things are cherished in a museum. Nothing was out of place; everything glittered and gleamed and the air smelt faintly of furniture polish and antiseptic. Carefully arranged on the upright piano, which didn't look as though it had ever been used, were a series of photographs; two of them were portraits of a heavily moustached gentleman standing rather rigidly, and the rest were of a rather fluffy mongrel in various attitudes. Most of them were blurred and out of focus, but it was quite obvious that the moustached gentleman took second place to the dog. This, I suspected, must have been Bow-wow.

'Do sit down. Do sit down,' said the little old lady. 'I must make you a cup of tea. I've got some cake. What a merciful thing, I made a cake only the other day. You will have a slice of cake and a cup of tea?'

My one desire at the precise moment was for several very large pints of beer, but I said that I would be delighted with tea.

Over tea and a slice of sponge cake that was as light and frothy as a pound of lead, Ursula chattered on. It was obvious that Emma Golightly had, at some time, been somebody in her father's household for whom she quite obviously had a great affection. It was extraordinary to watch the effect of Ursula's exuberance on Emma. When she opened the door to us, her face had been grey and gaunt and now it was flushed and smiling and she was obviously injected with some of Ursula's enthusiasm.

'Yes, yes!' she kept saying, 'and do you remember the time . . .'

'But of course!' Ursula said.

'And then do you remember that other time when . . .' And so it went on interminably.

But it was as though this rather fragile little old lady had been given a transfusion. I almost expected to look at Ursula and find her drained completely of blood.

Eventually, with masterly adroitness, Ursula steered the subject on to Bow-wow.

'Er, Gerry doesn't know about Bow-wow,' she said, looking at Emma commiseratingly. 'You tell him.'

Emma's eyes filled with tears.

'He was a wonderful dog,' she said. 'A wonderful dog. Really, you know, he could almost speak . . . almost speak, he really could. And then, one day, I let him out and some bloke in a car came down here and knocked him over. Didn't even stop . . . he didn't even stop. I took him to the vet . . . he was all covered with blood. I took him to the vet and I said . . . I'll pay anything, anything to keep him alive. 'Cos, you see, after my husband died, he was all I had. And he was a lovely dog, he really was. You would have loved him if you'd known him. And he was all covered with blood and he didn't seem to be suffering much, but they said there was nothing they could do. They said the kindest thing would be to put him out of his misery. Well, now, he'd been my companion ever since my husband died. For . . . for years I'd . . . I'd had him . . . For nearly twelve years. And so you can imagine it was a bit of a shock to me. So as they said it was the only thing to do, I said, "Well, all right, well – go ahead and do it." And so they . . . they put him down.'

She paused for a moment and blew her nose vigorously.

'It must have been a great shock to you,' I said.

'Oh, it was. It was a tremendous shock. It was like taking away part of my life, because, as I said to you, ever since my husband died he'd really been my only companion.'

I wasn't quite sure how to continue this conversation, because it was quite obvious that if Emma went on talking about Bow-wow she would break down and I didn't know how we could cope with that situation. But at that moment Ursula unveiled her guns.

'*Darling* Emma,' she said, 'it's *because* of the way you treated Bow-wow . . . the way that you looked after him and gave him such a happy life . . . it's for that reason that I want to . . . I want to ask you a *very great favour*. Now please say no, but I do wish that you'd consider it.'

'A favour, Miss Ursula?' said Emma. 'Of course I'll do you a favour. What do you want?'

'Well,' said Ursula, prevaricating like mad, 'this friend of mine has got this puppy and unfortunately, owing to illness in the family – his wife is desperately, *desperately* ill – he can't give it the attention that it really deserves, and so – just for a week or so – he wants somebody to look after it. Somebody who'll love it and give it the affection it needs. And immediately I thought of you.'

'Oh,' said Emma, 'a puppy? Well, I . . . I don't know. I mean, after Bow-wow . . . you know, you don't seem to want another dog, somehow.'

'But this is only a *puppy*,' said Ursula, her eyes brimming. 'Only a tiny, *tiny* little puppy. And it's only for a week or so. And I'm sure that you could look after it so *marvellously*.'

'Well, I don't know, Miss Ursula,' said Emma. 'I . . . I wouldn't like to have another dog.'

'But I'm not asking you to *have* it,' said Ursula. 'I'm just asking you to look after it for this poor man whose wife is terribly, *terribly* ill. He's torn between his wife and his dog.'

'Ah,' said Emma. 'Just as I was when Bill was ill. I remember it now. I sometimes didn't know whether to take Bow-wow out for a walk or stay with Bill, he was that sick. Well, what sort of a dog is it, Miss Ursula?'

'I'll show you,' said Ursula. She bent down and opened the basket. The Pekingese was lying curled up, exhausted by his cultural afternoon at the Pavilion, sound asleep. She picked him up unceremoniously by the scruff of his neck and held him up before Emma's startled eyes.

'Look at him,' said Ursula. '*Poor little thing.*'

'Oh,' said Emma. 'Oh, poor little thing.' She echoed Ursula unconsciously.

Ursula attempted to cradle the puppy in her arms and he gave her, to my satisfaction, a very sharp bite on the forefinger.

'*Look* at him,' she said, her voice quivering, as he struggled in her arms. 'A poor little dumb animal that doesn't really know whether he's coming or going. He's been wrenched away from the family life that he is used to. Surely you will take pity on him, Emma?'

I began to feel that the whole scene was beginning to take on the aspect of something out of *Jane Eyre*, but I was so fascinated by Ursula's technique that I let her go on.

'This tiny waif,' she said, extricating her finger with difficulty from his champing jaws, 'this tiny waif wants only a little bit of companionship, a little bit of help in his moment of strife . . . As, indeed, does my friend.'

'Well, I'll give you the fact that he's very, very nice,' said Emma, obviously moved.

'Oh, he is,' said Ursula, clamping her hand firmly over his mouth so that he couldn't bite her again. 'He's absolutely charming, and I believe – I'm not sure, but I believe – he's house-trained . . . Just for a week, dear Emma. Can't you possibly see your way to . . . to . . . to putting him up, as it were, as though he was a paying guest or something like that?'

'Well, I wouldn't do it for everybody,' said Emma, her eyes fastened, mesmerized, on the wriggling fat-tummied, pink-tummied puppy with his great load of white fur and his great bulbous black eyes. 'But seeing as he seems a nice little dog, and as it's you that's asking . . . I'm . . . I'm . . . willing to have him for a week.'

'Darling,' said Ursula. 'Bless you.'

She whipped the puppy hastily back into his hamper because he was getting out of control. Then she rushed across and threw her arms round Emma and kissed her on both cheeks.

'I always knew,' she said, peering into Emma's face with her brilliant blue searchlight gaze that I knew could have such devastating effect, 'I knew that you, of *all* people, would not turn away from a tiny little puppy like this in his hour of need.'

The curious thing was that she said it with such conviction that I almost got out my handkerchief and sobbed.

So eventually, refusing the offer of another cup of tea and another slice of indigestible cake, we left. As we walked down the road towards the station Ursula wrapped her arm round me and clutched me tight.

'Thank you *so* much, darling,' she said. 'You were a great help.'

'What do you mean, a great help?' I said. 'I didn't do anything.'

'No, but you were there. Sort of . . . a sort of a force, a presence, you know?'

'Tell me,' I said, interested, 'why you want to inflict this poor woman with that vindictive little puppy when she obviously doesn't require one?'

'Oh, but you don't know about Emma,' said Ursula. Which was quite true because I didn't.

'Tell me,' I said.

'Well,' she began. 'First of all, her husband got ill and then they got Bow-wow and then her attention was divided between the husband and Bow-wow, and then the husband died and she channelled all her recuperance, or whatever you call it, into Bow-wow. And then Bow-wow got knocked down and since then she's been going steadily downhill. My dear, you could *see* it. Every time I came to visit her I could see that she was getting more and more sort of, well . . . you know, old and haggish.'

'And how do you think the puppy is going to help her?' I inquired.

'Of course it's going to help her. It's the most savage puppy of the litter. It's bound to bite the postman or the greengrocer or somebody who delivers something, and it's got very long hair for a Peke and it's going to shed that all over the place, and it's not house-trained so it's going to pee and poo all over the place, dear.'

'Just a minute,' I said, interrupting, 'do you think this is a very wise gift to give a fragile old lady who's just lost her favourite Bow-wow?'

'But my dear, it's the *only* gift,' said Ursula. She stopped, conveniently under a street lamp, and her eyes gazed up at me.

'Bow-wow used to be exactly the same. He left hair all over the place, and if she didn't let him out he'd pee in the hall, and she'd complain for days . . . Gives her something to do. Well, since her husband died and Bow-wow died she's got nothing to do at all and she was just going into a sort of . . . a sort of grey *decline*. Now, with this new puppy, he'll bite her and he'll bite everyone else. They'll probably have court cases and he'll put his hair all over the place and he'll pee on the carpet and she'll be as delighted as anything.'

I gazed at Ursula and for the first time I saw her for what she was.

'Do you know,' I said, putting my arms round her and kissing her, 'I think you're rather nice.'

'It's not a question of niceness,' said Ursula, disrobing herself on me, as it were. 'It's not a question of niceness. She's just a pleasant old lady and I want her to have fun while she's still alive. That puppy will give her tremendous fun.'

'But you know, I would never have thought of that,' I said.

'Of *course* you would, darling,' she said, giving me a brilliant smile. 'You're so clever.'

'Sometimes,' I said as I took her arm and walked her down the street, 'sometimes I begin to wonder whether I am.'

The next few months had many halcyon days for me. Ursula possessed a sort of ignorant purity that commanded respect. I very soon found that in order to avoid embarrassment it was better to take her out into the countryside rather than confine her to a restaurant or theatre. At least in the countryside the cuckoos and larks and hedgehogs accepted her for what she was, a very natural and nice person. Take her into the confines of Bournemouth society and she dropped bricks at the rate of an unskilled navvy helping on a working site.

However, even introducing Ursula to the wilds was not without its hazards. I showed her a tiny strip of woodland that I'd discovered which had, at that time, more birds' nests per square inch than any other place I knew. Ursula got wildly excited and peered into nests brim-full of fat, open-mouthed baby birds or clutches of blue and brown eggs, and ooo'd over them delightedly. Nothing would content her but that I had to visit the place every day and phone her a long report on the progress of the various nests. A few weeks later I took her down to the place again and we discovered, to our horror, that it had been found, presumably by a group of schoolboys, and they had gone systematically through the whole of the woodland and destroyed every nest. The baby birds were lying dead on the ground and the eggs had all been taken. Ursula's anguish was intense. She sobbed uncontrollably with a mixture of rage and grief and it was a long time before I could comfort her.

She was still racked with occasional shuddering sobs when I ushered her into the spit and sawdust Bar of the Square and Compass, one of my favourite pubs in that region. Here, in this tiny bar, all the old men of the district would gather every evening, great brown lumbering shire horses of men, their faces as wrinkled as walnuts, their drooping moustaches as crisp and white as summer grass with frost on it. They were wonderful old men and I thought to meet them would take Ursula's mind off the ravaged nests. I was also interested to see what sort of reaction her presence would create.

To begin with, they sat stiff, silent, and suspicious, their hands carefully guarding their tankards, staring at us without expression. They knew me but now I had introduced an alien body into their tiny, smoke-blurred bar and, moreover, a very attractive and feminine body. This was heresy. The unwritten law was that no woman entered that bar. But Ursula was completely unaware of this or, if not unaware, undaunted by it. She powdered her nose, gulped down a very large gin in record time, and turned her brilliant melting blue eyes on the old men. Within a few minutes she had them relaxed and occasionally, half guiltily, chuckling with her. Then she spied the black board in the corner.

'Oooh!' she squeaked delightedly, 'tiddleywinks!'

The old men exchanged looks of horror. Then they all looked at the oldest member of the group, an eighty-four-year-old patriarch who was, I knew, the local champion of this much beloved game.

'No, Miss,' he said firmly, 'that's shove ha'penny.'

'Do teach me to play it,' said Ursula, gazing at him so adoringly that his brown face went the colour of an overripe tomato.

'Yes, go on, George, teach the Miss,' the other old men chorused, delighted that George was colouring and shuffling like a schoolboy.

Reluctantly, he lumbered to his feet and he and Ursula moved over to the table where the shove ha'penny board lay in state.

As I watched him teaching her I realized, not for the first time, the deviousness of women in general and of Ursula in particular. It was perfectly obvious that she not only knew how to play shove ha'penny but probably could have beaten George at it. But her fumbling attempts to learn from him and the sight of him patting her shoulder with his enormous carunculated hand as gently as though he were patting a puppy were a delight to watch. Ursula lost gracefully to him and then insisted on buying drinks all round – for which I had to pay since she had no money.

By now, the old men, flushed and enthusiastic, were practically coming to blows over who should play her next. Ursula, armed with her indispensable evening newspaper, disappeared briefly into the ladies before coming back to challenge all comers.

George, wiping the froth off his magnificent moustache, lowered himself on to the oak trestle beside me and accepted a cigarette.

'A fine young woman, sir,' he said, 'a very fine young woman, even though she's a foreigner.'

The curious thing is that he did not use the term foreigner in the way that most villagers in England would use it to describe somebody who had not actually been born in the village. He was firmly convinced by Ursula's particular brand of English that she must indeed come from the Continent or some savage place like that. I did not disillusion him.

I had known Ursula for about a year when one day she phoned me and dropped a bombshell.

'Gerry!' The voice was so penetrating that I had to hold the receiver away from my ear. It could only be Ursula.

'Yes,' I said resignedly.

'Darling, it's *me*, Ursula.'

'I never would have guessed it,' I said. 'You're so much quieter, so much more dulcet. That soft voice, like the cooing of a sucking dove . . .'

'Don't be *silly*, darling. I phoned you up because I've got the most *wonderful* news and I wanted *you* to be the first to know,' she said breathlessly.

What now, I wondered? Which one of her numerous friends had achieved some awful success due to her Machiavellian plottings?

'Tell me all,' I said, resigning myself to at least half an hour of telephone conversation.

'Darling, I'm *engaged*,' said Ursula.

I confess that my heart felt a sudden pang and a loneliness spread over me. It was not that I was in love with Ursula; it was not that I wanted to marry her – God forbid! – but suddenly I realized that I was being deprived of a charming companion. I was being deprived of somebody who could always lighten my gloom, and somebody who had given me so many hours of pleasure. And now she was engaged, doubtless to some hulking idiot, and all this, our lovely friendship, would change.

'Darling?' said Ursula. 'Darling? Are you still there?'

'Yes,' I said. 'I'm still here.'

'But, darling, you sound so glum. Is anything the matter? I thought you'd be *pleased*!' Her voice sounded plaintive, uncertain.

'I am pleased,' I said, trying to cast away selfishness, trying to cast away the remembrance of Ursula telling me of a friend who'd gone to Venice and who'd had a gondolier every night. 'Really, my love, I'm as pleased as punch. Who is the unlucky man?'

'It's Toby,' she said. 'You know Toby.'

'But I thought he was an incoherent?' I said.

'No, no, silly. Not that Toby, a completely *different* one.'

'I'm glad of that. I thought that if he was an incoherent he would have had difficulty in proposing.'

'Darling, you don't sound a bit like *you*,' she said, her voice worried and subdued. 'Are you angry with me for getting engaged?'

'Not at all,' I said acidly. 'I'm delighted to know that you've found somebody who can stop you talking long enough to propose. *I* never could.'

'Ooooo!' said Ursula. 'You're jealous! Darling, how wonderful! I never knew you wanted to propose to me. When was it?'

'Frequently,' I said, tersely, 'but fortunately I managed to stamp the desire underfoot.'

'Oh, darling, I *am* sorry. Are you going to go all silent and withdrawn and morass?'

'I've not the slightest intention of turning myself into a bog for your benefit,' I said with some asperity.

'Oh, darling, don't be so *silly*. I thought you'd be *pleased*. As a matter of fact I was hoping we could meet . . .' Her voice trailed away.

What a cad I was being, I reflected. What a monstrous, inhuman cad. Here was the girl virtually asking me to set the seal on her nuptials and here was I behaving like a fifteen-year-old. I was contrite.

'Of course we can meet, my sweet,' I said. 'I'm sorry I was rude. It's just that I can't get used to the idea of you being engaged. Where do you want to meet?'

'Oh, darling, *that's* better. Why don't we dance away the evening? Let's go to the Tropicana . . . *Do* let's, darling!'

Dance away the evening until ten o'clock, I thought to myself. The Tropicana was a particularly revolting nightclub of the sort that blossom suddenly like puffballs and have their brief moment of contributing to human misery and then mercifully disappear into obscurity. Of all the places she could have suggested Ursula could not have picked one that I disliked more.

'Right,' I said with enthusiasm, 'but can we have dinner first?'

'Oh darling, *yes*. Where?'

'How about the Grill room? I'll book a table.'

'*Daarling!*' breathed Ursula. 'The *first* place we had lunch together. Darling, you *are* romantic.'

'Not particularly. It's just the only place that serves good food,' I said austerely.

'Darling, I *love* you . . . even if you *are* oppressive. Lovely food, and then dancing. Oh, I'll meet you at the Grill at eight, darling, I can't *tell* you how pleased I am that you're pleased. I *love* you and *love* you for ever.'

I put the phone back and realized what I'd lost.

I realized what I'd lost even more when I met her, for she brought her fiancé with her. He was a handsome young man, quite obviously besotted by Ursula, with a very limited vocabulary. But he seemed nice enough. The Grill room, as I had rather suspected, was packed and so the three of us had to sit uncomfortably at a table designed for two. Toby didn't have very much to say for himself but that scarcely mattered as Ursula talked quite enough for two of them. When we'd finished dinner we went on to the Tropicana where the band was blaring. Here, Toby and I solemnly took it in turns to propel Ursula, chattering madly, round and round the floor. It was a thoroughly miserable evening, from my point of view. After that, I didn't see Ursula for a long time. I heard that she'd eventually got married and that she'd had a baby. I felt that, now she was safely ensconced on her wedding bed, she would drift out of my life altogether. But again I was wrong. One day the phone rang, and it was Ursula.

'Darling! It's *me*, Ursula!' she said.

'Good heavens!' I said, surprised. 'Where have you been all these years?'

'Darling, I got *married*,' she said. 'I've had a baby.'

'So I heard,' I said. 'Congratulations.'

'Darling, I've been stuck down in the country for so long. I've got to come into Bournemouth today to do some shopping. I wondered whether we could meet?'

'Are you bringing your husband with you?' I asked cautiously.

'No, darling, I'm just coming on my own,' she said.

'Well, in that case, by all means let us meet. I will buy you lunch. But first I'll meet you in the Cadena for coffee.'

'Marvellous, darling. I'll be there at eleven o'clock,' she said.

At eleven o'clock promptly she appeared through the doors of the Cadena café and I could see instantly that she was well on the way to expecting her second child. Apart from the protuberance of her stomach she had a glowing air about her, like rose petals in sunshine.

'Darling!' she screamed. 'Darling! *Darling!*'

She flung her arms round me and gave me a prolonged kiss of the variety that is generally cut out of French films by the English censor. She made humming noises as she kissed, like a hive of sex-mad bees. She thrust her body against mine to extract the full flavour of the embrace and to show me that she really cared, really and truly. Several elderly ladies and what appeared to be a brigadier who had been preserved (like a plum in port) stared at us with fascinated repulsion. You could tell from their expressions that they expected me to rip her clothes off her and rape her there, on the sacred floor of the Cadena. I tore myself loose from her with an effort.

'I thought you were married,' I said.

'I *am*, darling,' she said. 'Don't you think my kissing's improved?'

'Yes,' I said. 'Sit down and have some coffee.'

'Can I have an ice cream?' she asked.

'All right,' I said.

I ordered a coffee and an ice cream.

'Well, I must say, you're looking blooming,' I said.

'Do you think so?'

'I think you're looking wonderful. I see you're going to have another one.'

She took a large mouthful of ice cream and spoke through it rather indistinctly.

'Children are absholutely marvelloush.'

'So I believe,' I said.

She swallowed her mouthful of ice cream and leant forward and tapped my wrist with her moist spoon to gain my full attention.

'Do you know what they say?' she inquired in her penetrating voice.

Every table in the restaurant suspended operations and waited expectantly. I felt I might as well be hung for a sheep as for a lamb.

'No,' I said. 'What do they say?'

'Why,' she said, waving her spoon happily, 'contraception is a woman's work.'

We had coffee and then I took Ursula shopping, and later we went to lunch.

'Do you miss me, darling?' she inquired as she sipped at her wine.

'Of course I miss you,' I said. 'You were always one of my favourite girl friends.'

'Isn't it a pity that one can't have boy friends *and* be married?' she said.

'Well, you can always try,' I suggested.

'Oh, no, I couldn't do that,' she said. 'But you *are* sweet.'

'Think nothing of it,' I said.

'Anyway, I don't suppose you'd like me now,' she said, wistfully. 'I've reformed. I've become very dull.'

'Do you think so?' I asked, thinking how vital and sweet she was still.

'Oh, yes,' she said, looking at me solemnly with her great blue eyes. 'I'm afraid I'm now what they call one of the petty beaujolais.'

'Yes, but a vintage year,' I said, raising my glass.

FROM GOLDEN BATS AND PINK PIGEONS:

Outside the french windows that led from the sitting-room of the hotel suite lay a spacious and cool veranda. Step off this, and one walked twenty yards or so across coarse grass planted with tall casuarina trees that sighed like lovers in the wind, until one came to the wide, frost-white beach with its broken necklace of corals and coloured shells, lying wavering across the shoreline. In the distance lay the reef, white and thunderous with surf, and beyond it the royal blue of the Indian Ocean. Between the white beach, decorated with its biscuit-brittle graveyard of coral fragments, and the wide reef with its ever-changing flower bed of foam, lay the lagoon. Half a mile of butterfly-blue water, smooth as a saucer of milk, clear as a diamond, which hid an enchanted world like none other on earth.

Any naturalist who is lucky enough to travel, at certain moments has experienced a feeling of overwhelming exultation at the beauty and complexity of life, and a feeling of depression that there is so much to see, to observe, to learn, that one lifetime is an unfairly short span to be allotted for such a paradise of enigmas as the world is. You get it when, for the first time, you see the beauty, variety and exuberance of a tropical rainforest, with its cathedral maze of a thousand different trees, each bedecked with gardens of orchids, epiphytes, enmeshed in a web of creepers; an interlocking of so many species that you cannot believe that number of different forms have evolved. You get it when you see for the first time a great concourse of mammals living together, or a vast, restless conglomeration of birds. You get it when you see a butterfly emerge from a chrysalis; a dragonfly from its pupa; when you observe the delicate, multifarious courtship displays, the rituals and taboos, that go into making up the continuation of a species. You get it when you first see a stick or a leaf turn into an insect, or a piece of dappled shade into a herd of zebras. You get it when you see a gigantic school of dolphins stretching as far as the eye can see, rocking and leaping exuberantly through their blue world; or a microscopic spider manufacturing from its frail body a transparent, apparently never-ending line that will act as a transport as it sets out on its aerial exploration of the vast world that surrounds it.

But there is one experience, perhaps above all others, that a naturalist should try to have before he dies, and that is the astonishing and humbling experience of exploring a tropical reef. It seems that in this one action you use nearly every one of your senses, and one feels that one could uncover hidden senses as well. You become a fish, hear, and see and feel as much like one as a human being can; yet at the same time you are like a bird, hovering, swooping and gliding across the marine pastures and forests.

I had obtained my first taste of this fabulous experience when I was on the Great Barrier Reef in Australia but there, unfortunately, we had only masks and no snorkels, and my mask let in water. To say that it was frustrating, was putting it mildly, for there below me was this fascinating, multi-coloured world and I could only obtain glimpses of it, the duration of which was dependent upon how long I could hold my breath and how long it took my mask to fill and drown me. The tantalizing glimpses I *did* get of this underwater world were unforgettable and I determined to do it properly at the first available opportunity. This came in Mauritius, for there at the Le Morne Brabant Hotel, the lagoon and its attendant reef were literally on my doorstep. I could not have been closer without moving my bed into it.

The first morning, I made myself a pot of tea and carried it out on to the veranda, together with one of the small, sweet Mauritian pineapples. I sat eating and watching the boats arrive further down the beach, each piloted by handsome, bright-eyed, long-haired fishermen ranging from copper-bronze to soot-black in colour, wearing a variety of clothing in eye-catching colours that shamed the hibiscus and bougainvillaea flowers that flamed in the gardens. Each boat was loaded down with a cargo of snow-white pieces of coral and multi-coloured, pard-spotted cowries and cone shells. From sticks stuck in the gunwales hung necklaces of tiny shells like glittering rainbows. The sun had just emerged from the mountains behind the hotel. It turned the sky and the horizon powder-blue, gilded a few fat, white clouds that sailed in a slow flotilla across the sky, gave a crisp, white sparkle to the foam on the reef and turned the flat, still lagoon transparent sapphire.

Almost as soon as I had seated myself on the veranda, the table at which I sat had become covered with birds, anxious to share with me whatever breakfast I had. There were mynahs with neat, black and chocolate plumage and banana yellow beaks and eyes; Singing finches, the females a delicate leaf-green and pale, butter-yellow, and the males, by contrast, strident sulphur-yellow and black; and the Whiskered bulbuls, black and white, with handsome scarlet whiskers and tail flash. They all had a drink out of the milk jug, decided the tea was too hot and then sat, looking longingly at my fruit. I extracted the last of the juicy core from the glypterdont skin of the pineapple and then placed the debris on the table where it immediately became invisible under a fluttering, bickering mass of birds.

I finished my tea and then, taking my mask and snorkel, made my way slowly down to the shore. I reached the sand and the ghost crabs (so transparent that when they stopped moving and froze, they disappeared) skittered across the tide ripples and dived for safety into their holes. At the rim of the lagoon, the sea lapped very gently at the white sand, like a kitten delicately lapping at a saucer of milk. I walked into the water up to my ankles and it was as warm as a tepid bath.

All round my feet on the surface of the sand were strange decorations that looked as though someone had walked through the shallow water and traced on the sandy bottom the blurred outlines of a hundred starfish. They lay arm to arm, as it were, like some strange, sandy constellation. The biggest measured a foot from arm tip to arm tip, and the smallest was about the size of a saucer.

Curious about these ghostly sand starfish, I dug an experimental toe under one and hooked upwards. It came out from under its covering and floated briefly upwards, shedding the film of sand that had been lightly covering it and revealing itself to be a fine, robust starfish of a pale, brick-pink, heavily marked with a dull, white and red speckling. Though they looked attractively soft and velvety – like a star you put on top of a Christmas tree – they were, in fact, hard and sandpaperish to the touch. The one I had so rudely jerked out of its sandy bed with my toe performed a languid cartwheel in the clear water and drifted down on to the bottom, landing on its back. Its underside was a pale, yellowish ivory, with a deep groove down each arm that looked like an open zip-fastener. Within this groove, lay its myriad feet – tiny tentacles some four millimetres long, ending in a plate-shaped sucker. Each foot could be used independently so that there was a constant movement in the grooves and the tentacles contracted and expanded, searching for some surface on which the suckers could fasten.

Discovering none, and presumably concluding that it was upside down, the starfish curled the extreme tip of one arm under itself. Finding a foothold, it then curled its arm further in an effortless, boneless sort of way. At the same time, it curled under the two arms on either side of the first one, and slowly and gently, the animal started to lift itself with this triangle of arms. The arms on the opposite side of its body curled and spread upwards like the fingers of a hand to support it, and soon the body was vertical like a wheel, supported by the ever stiffening arms. The arms on the furthest side now spread wide and the body sank towards them slowly and gracefully like a yogi completing a complicated and beautiful asana. The body was now turned upright; it remained only for the starfish to pull out its remaining arms from underneath it and the animal was the right side up. The whole action had been performed with a slow-motion delicacy of movement that would have brought tears to the eyes of any ballet dancer.

Now, however, the starfish did something that no ballerina, be she ever so talented, could have emulated. It lay on the sand and simply disappeared. Before my eyes, it vanished and left behind it, like the Cheshire cat left its smile, merely a vague outline, the suggestion of a starfish, as it were, embossed upon the sand. What had happened, of course, was that while the starfish remained apparently unmoving, its hundreds of little feet, out of sight beneath it, were burrowing into the sand, so the animal simply sank from view and the white grains drifted to cover it. The whole thing, from the moment I had unearthed the creature until it disappeared, had taken no longer than two minutes.

I had approached the lagoon with every intention of plunging in and swimming out to deep water, but I had already spent five minutes watching the ghost crabs, five minutes admiring the necklace of flotsam washed up by the tide, and another two minutes standing ankle-deep in the water watching what was obviously a guru starfish attaining a sort of sandy nirvana. During this time, the fishermen, perched like some gay parrots in their boats, had been regarding me with the same avid interest as I had bestowed upon the natural history of the shoreline. Their curiosity had been well concealed, however, and there had been no attempt to solicit my custom for their wares in the tiresome way that is indulged in by pedlars in other countries. Mauritians were too polite for that. I waved at them and they all waved back, grinning broadly.

Determined not to be sidetracked again, I waded out waist-deep into the water, put on my mask and plunged my head under the water to get my head and back wet and protect it a little from the sun, which was hot even at that early hour. As my mask dipped below the surface, the sea seemed to disappear and I was gazing down at my feet in the submarine territory that immediately surrounded them.

Instantly I forgot my firm resolve to swim out into deeper water, for I was surrounded by a world as bizarre as any science fiction writer had thought up for a Martian biology. Around my feet, a trifle close for comfort, lay six or seven large, flattish sea urchins, like a litter of hibernating hedge-hogs with bits of seaweed and coral fragments enmeshed in their spines so that, until one looked closely, they appeared to be weed-covered lumps of dark lava. Entwined between them were several curious structures, lying on the sand in a languid manner, like sunbathing snakes. They were tubes some four feet long and about four inches in circumference. They looked like the submarine parts of a strange vacuum cleaner, apparently jointed every three inches and manufactured out of semi-opaque, damp brown paper that had started to grow a sort of furry fungus at intervals along its length.

At first, I could not believe that these weird objects were alive. I thought they must be strange, dead strands of some deep-sea seaweed now washed into the shallows by the tide, to roll and undulate helplessly on the sand to the small movements of the sea. Closer inspection showed me that they were indeed alive, unlikely though it seemed. *Sinucta muculata*, as this strange creature is called, is really a sort of elongated tube, which sucks in water at one end and with it microscopic organisms, and expels the water at the other.

As well as Sinucta, I saw some old friends lying about, placid on the sea bed – the sea slug that I had known from my childhood in Greece, thick, fat, warty creatures, a foot long, looking like a particularly revolting form of liver sausage. I picked one up; it was faintly slimy, but firm to the touch, like decaying leather. I lifted it out of the water and it behaved exactly as its Mediterranean cousins did. It ejected a stream of water with considerable force, at the same time becoming limp and flaccid in my hand. Then, having exhausted this form of defence, it tried another one. It suddenly voided a stream of a white substance that looked like liquid latex and was sticky beyond belief, the slightest portion adhering to your skin more tenaciously than Sellotape.

I could not help feeling that this was a rather futile form of defence for should an enemy be attacking, this curtain of adhesive, rubber-like solution would only serve to bind it more closely to the sea slug. However, it seemed unlikely that any weapon as complex as this would have been evolved in a creature so primitive unless it had fulfilled a necessary purpose. I released the slug and he floated to the bottom, to roll gently on to the sand, fulfilling the gay, vibrant, experience-full life that sea slugs lead, which consists of sucking the water in at one end of their being and expelling it at the other, while being rolled endlessly by the tide.

Reluctantly, I dragged my attention away from the creatures that lived in the immediate vicinity of my feet, and launched myself on my voyage of exploration. That first moment, when you relax and float face downwards, and, under the glass of your mask, the water seems to disappear, is always startling and uncanny. You suddenly become a hawk, floating and soaring over the forests, mountains and sandy deserts of this marine universe. You feel like Icarus, as the sun warms your back, and below you, the multi-coloured world unfolds like a map. Though you may float only a few feet above the tapestry, the sounds come up to you muted as if floating up from a thousand feet in still air, as you might be suspended and hear sounds of life in the toy farms and villages below a mountain. The scrunch of the gaudy parrot fish, rasping at the coral with its beak; the grunt or squeak or creakings of any one of a hundred fish, indignantly defending their territory against invaders; the gentle rustle of the sand moved by tides or currents; a whisper like the feminine rustle of a thousand crinolines. These and many more noises drift up to you from the sea bed.

At first, the sandy bottom was flat, littered with the debris of past storms and hurricanes; lumps of coral now covered with weed, and the abode of a million creatures; pieces of pumice stone. On the sand, lay battalions of huge, black sea urchins, with long, slender spines that move constantly like compass needles. Touch one of them, and the spines moving gently to and fro suddenly become violently agitated, waving about with ever-increasing speed like mad knitting needles. They were very fragile as well as being sharp, so that if they penetrated your skin, they broke off. They also stained the immediate area of the puncture, as though you had been given a minute injection of Indian ink. Although they looked black, when the sunlight caught them, you found that they were a most beautiful royal blue with a green base to each spine. This species was fortunately flamboyant enough to be very obvious and, although some lay in crevices and under coral ledges, the majority lay on the sand, singly or in prickly groups, and were very apparent.

Interspersed with these were more of the elongated hosepipes and a further scattering of sea slugs. These, however, appeared to be of a different species. They were very large, some of them eighteen inches long and a mottled, yellowish-green. They also seemed much smoother and fatter than their black cousins, most of them being some four or five inches in diameter. I dived down to pick up one of these dim and unattractive creatures. As I was swimming to the surface with him, he first of all squirted water in the usual way and then, finding this did not make me relinquish my grip on his fat body, exuded his sticky rubber.

I was astonished at the attractive effect it had under water. When the sea slug used this, his ultimate deterrent, in the air, it came out simply as a sort of squishy, white, sticky stream, but viewed under water, the same phenomenon was different and beautiful. The substance was revealed as being composed of fifty or more separate strands, each the thickness of fine spaghetti and about eight inches long. One end remained attached to the beast while the filaments at the other end curved out and floated in the water like a delicate white fountain. Whether these strands had the power to sting and perhaps paralyse small fish, I don't know. One could touch them without feeling anything or getting any irritation, but certainly, spread out in a graceful spray, the tentacles presented much more of an adhesive hazard to an enemy than I had thought.

I swam on and, quite suddenly, like a conjuring trick, I found I was swimming through and over a large school of extraordinary-looking fish. There were about fifty of them; each measured some three to four feet long and was coloured a neutrally-transparent grey, so that it was almost invisible. Their mouths protruded almost into an elongated spike, as did their tails, so that it was difficult to tell at first glance which way they were pointing until you saw their round, rather oafish eyes staring at you with caution. They had obviously been doing something very strenuous and were now exhausted. They hung, immobile in the water, facing the current, meditating. They were most orderly for they hung in the water in ranks, like well-drilled, if somewhat emaciated soldiers. It was interesting to note that they hung in exactly the right juxtaposition to each other, like troops on parade, so many feet between the fish in front and behind, and the same distance between the one above and the one below and the ones on each side. My sudden presence caused a certain amount of panic in their ranks, like someone marching out of step on an Armistice Day parade, and they swam off in confusion. As soon as they put enough distance between themselves and me, they re-formed ranks, turned to face the tide, and went into a trance again.

Leaving these fish, I swam on, gazing enthralled at the sandy bottom, barred with broad stripes of gold by the sun and these, by some optical alchemy, spangled all over with golden, trembling rings. Then, looming up ahead of me, I saw a shape, a dim blur which materialized into a massive rock some nine feet by three, shaped like the dome of St Paul's Cathedral. As I got closer, I saw that the whole rock was encrusted with pink, white and greenish corals and on top of it there were four huge, pale bronze sea anemones, attached like flowers to a monstrous, multi-coloured bonnet.

I swam over this fascinating rock and anchored myself against the slow pull of the tide by catching hold of a projecting piece of coral, having first examined it carefully to make sure that there was nothing harmful lurking on, or under, or in it. That this was a wise precaution, I soon realized for as soon as my eyes got focused, I saw lurking, almost invisible, in the coral-and reed-encrusted grotto, a foot or so away from my hand, a large and beautifully coloured Scorpion fish; whose dorsal spines can cause you agony and even, in rare cases, death, should you unwittingly touch it and it jabs them into you. He was some seven inches long, with a jowly, pouting face and huge, scarlet eyes. His predominant colour was pink and orange, with black bars and stripes and specklings. His pectoral fins were greatly elongated so he looked as though he had two pink hands growing out from under his gills, with attenuated fingers. Along his back was the row of scarlet spines that could prove so lethal. Altogether, he was a most flamboyant fish and, once you had spotted him, he glowed like a great jewel; yet until I had noticed a slight movement from him, he had, with his striped and spotted livery, melted into the background. Now, realizing he had been spotted, he moved his great trailing fins gently and gradually edged his way round and down the rock away from me. Beautiful though he was, I was relieved not to have him at quite such close quarters.

Living in and around the anemones, were some handsome clown fish, about three inches long, a bright orange colour, banded with broad stripes of snow-white. These pretty little fish have a symbiotic relationship with the anemones. They live among the stinging tentacles which would kill other fish, and so the anemone becomes their home; a formidable fortress in which the clown fish takes refuge in moments of danger. In return for this protection, the fish, of course, drops some of its food which then becomes the anemone's lunch. Why, or how, this curious relationship came about, is a mystery. Anemones can hardly be described as having scintillating intellects, and how they managed to work out the usefulness of the clown fish and refrain from stinging them, is a puzzle.

Wedged deep into the coral here and there were a number of large clams. All that could be seen of them were the rims of their scalloped shells, over which the edge of their mantle protruded, so they appeared to be grinning at you with thick, blue and iridescent green lips. These, each about the size of a coconut, were, of course, relatives of the famous giant clam found further out on the reef – a monstrous shell that could weigh up to two hundred pounds and measure three feet. Many blood-curdling stories have been written about unfortunate divers who by chance have put their foot into one of these shells, which immediately slammed shut like a man-trap (as all clams do in moments of stress) thus consigning the diver to death by drowning. There does not appear to be an authenticated record of this ever having happened, although of course it is perfectly possible, for the shell could snap shut and unless the diver had a knife with which to cut the massive muscle that acts as both hinge and lock on the two halves of the shell, it would be as immovable and unopenable as a castle door. Again, in the case of these highly coloured clams, there is a curious symbiotic relationship, for in the brilliant mantle there are a number of small, unicellular algae, called by the rather attractive name of Zooxanthelae. These minute creatures obtain their sustenance from the food the clam sucks in, and in payment they give the clam an additional supply of oxygen. It is rather like paying for your daily bread with air, a thing most of us would like to do.

I shifted my vantage point to the other side of the rock, making sure of the whereabouts of the Scorpion fish, and came upon yet another symbiotic relationship. There was a small shoal of various multi-coloured fish, which included a Box fish and three canary-yellow Surgeon fish. The Box fish was quite incredible. He was only three inches long, vivid orange with black polka-dots over him; but it was not the colouration so much as the bizarre shape of the creature which amazed me, for the whole body is like a square box of bone and through holes in this protrude the creature's fins, vent, eyes and mouth. This means that the tail has to wave around like the propeller of an outboard engine. This mode of locomotion, coupled with the fish's big, round, perpetually surprised-looking pop eyes, its square shape and polka-dot suiting, combine to make it one of the most curious inhabitants of the reef.

The Surgeon fish were quite different. Their yellow bodies were roughly moon-shaped, they had high domed foreheads and their mouths protruded, almost like the snout of a pig. They get their name from the two sharp, scalpel-like knives set just behind the tail. These dangerous weapons can fold back like the blade of a pocket knife into a hidden groove.

But, fascinating though these two species of fish were, it was what was happening to them that was so curious. The two Surgeon fish were close to the rock, hanging in a trance-like state while the Box fish puttered to and fro like some weird, orange boat, occasionally coming to a standstill. Among them darted three lithe little fish, small gobies with bright prussian-blue and sky-blue markings. They were cleaner fish and they worked assiduously on their three customers, zooming in to suck the parasites off their skin and then, as it were, standing back to admire their handiwork before dashing in again, rather like effeminate hairdressers admiring the creation of a new hairstyle. Later on, on the big main reef, I sometimes saw queues of fish waiting their turn at the barber's shop, where the little blue barbers worked in a frenzy to keep up with their customers.

So captivated had I become by all I had seen, for every inch of what we came affectionately to call 'St Paul's' was covered with tiny anemones, sea fans, feather worms, shrimps, crabs and a host of other things, that I discovered I had spent over an hour suspended in one spot and even then, had been unable to take it all in. Here, on this one rock, was a myriad of life which would require a naturalist to spend a dozen lifetimes even to start to unravel it. What, I wondered, as I swam slowly back to breakfast, was the real reef going to be like? I was soon to know. It was overwhelming.

FROM HOW TO SHOOT AN AMATEUR NATURALIST:

On our second day [in Panama] we came to a clearing in the forest that had been created by the death of one of the giant trees. Growing on a slope, torrential rains had undermined its roots' tenuous hold on the topsoil and a gust of wind had then torn it free, as easily as a dentist wrenches a tooth from a jaw. It showed clearly why the tropical forest is so fragile. The topsoil is only a thin layer, so thin that the trees have to grow these giant buttress roots in order to keep upright. These huge trees, in fact, are feeding on themselves, for the moment their leaves fall they decay and become the humus on which the trees feed. So rapid is this process that only a thin topsoil is able to form. So the felling of the forest – as is happening at a horrifying rate throughout the world – exposes this thin layer, which only lasts a short time as agricultural or grazing land. Then it disappears and leaves erosion in its place. However, a natural tree-fall such as the one we found is a boon to the forest. As the giant crashes to earth, it splinters and fells smaller trees in its line of fall and tears a rent in the thick forest canopy. The sun floods in and the shrubs, creepers and baby trees, who have all been struggling in the gloom of the forest floor, shoot upwards in it. Seeds, which have been lying dormant in the humus for perhaps many years, waiting patiently for such an event, now sprout and start to rocket upwards towards the blue sky before the gap is closed by other plants. Thus the death of one of these forest mammoths is a signal for new life and growth around its huge carcass.

On the slopes above the fallen tree we heard a series of squeaks, chatterings and rustlings in the trees. Leaving the path to investigate, we found a group of spider monkeys disporting themselves low down among the trees, feeding on some pink buds. They are aptly named, for with their long, furry, dark limbs and their long tails (so prehensile that they use them as skilfully and as casually as if they were another limb) they did look rather like some strange giant spiders spinning webs among the branches . . . [They] seemed captivated by us and swung on their wonderful tails closer and closer and lower and lower. One in particular seemed specially fascinated by Lee, for she had just started to eat an orange to quench her thirst. He swung himself down from branch to branch until he was within fifteen feet of her, peering at her with all the dedicated interest of an anthropologist watching the feeding habits of an aborigine. Lee broke off a small piece of orange and held it out to him and, to our astonishment, without hesitation he swung down, grabbed the fruit and stuffed it into his mouth. After that, they followed us through the trees gazing at us wistfully and only going their own way when it became apparent that there were no more oranges forthcoming.

Alastair [the director] had arranged with one of the hunters attached to the station that he would comb the forest for suitable subjects for us to film, and the next day he came in with the first specimen, one of my favourite animals, the two-toed sloth. They really are enchanting creatures, their small heads, their shaggy bodies, their round, slightly protuberant golden eyes, and their mouths set in a perpetual, dreamy, benevolent smile. Slow and gentle, they will suffer you to hang them wherever you like, as though they were an old coat, and only after half an hour or so of deep meditation will they move perhaps six feet and that in slow motion. Sloths are really fantastic creatures. They are so beautifully adapted for their strange, topsy-turvy life in the tree-tops and, because they spend most of their lives upside-down, and because their diet is highly indigestible leaves, their internal organs are unlike those of any other mammal. Their whole metabolism is as slow as their movements, as slow as bureaucracy. They may go for a week without urinating, for example.

The sloth's fur, of course, grows differently from that of other animals. In other mammals the hair grows from the backbone towards the ground, so the parting, so to speak, is on the backbone. In the sloth, it lies along the side of the belly and the rest of the hair grows towards the backbone, so when the sloth is upside-down the rain runs off the fall of the fur more easily. They have a very strange adaptation of their fur – thin layers of cells which lie diagonally across the hairs forming ridges in which two species of blue-green algae flourish. This gives the animal's fur a greenish tinge, which acts as a camouflage among the leaves, so the sloth is, in effect, a sort of hanging garden.

Even more curious than this, there are several species of beetle and mite which have taken up residence in the sloth's fur, as well as a strange species of moth called the snout moth. There are approximately twelve thousand different species of this sort of moth scattered around the world and many of them are very curious. For example, some have what is called a tympanal organ on the base of the abdomen. This hearing organ can detect the ultrasonic cries of bats (developed to capture prey) and thus allow the moths to escape this predator. Some of the snout moths' caterpillars live on or in aquatic plants and in many cases become really aquatic, one species of caterpillar even developing gills. The species has a curious relationship with the sloth. It lays its eggs on the sloth's fur and when these hatch out the larvae feed on the algae which exist in the grooves and possibly on the fur as well, so as well as being a sort of hanging garden the sloth is also a sort of perambulating furry hotel for all these insects.

The next film star that was brought from the forest to appear in front of the cameras was a fascinating little creature that I have not seen since I obtained some in Guiana many years ago. It was a pygmy anteater, the smallest of the anteaters, a beast that, fully grown, would fit comfortably into your cupped hand with room to spare. Like the sloth, this diminutive creature is perfectly adapted to its arboreal life. Its fur is short, dense and silky, an amber brown in colour. Its prehensile tail is naked at the end, which enables the creature to get a firmer grip with it, when it is wound round a branch. It has a short, tube-like snout, slightly curved, and tiny eyes and ears hidden in its thick fur. It is the feet of this little beast which are so extraordinary. Its hands are fat, pink pads armed with three long, slender, sharp claws, the middle one being the biggest. These claws can fold back into the palm of the hand like the blade of a pocket-knife. On the hind feet (the heel of the foot, so to speak) is a muscular pad shaped like a cup, which enables it to fit snugly round a branch. The toes on these feet end in sharp claws and have pads at their base so these, together with the suction-cup effect, help to form a prodigious clasping mechanism, without actually involving the claws. When in danger, the pygmy anteater lashes its tail round a branch, attaches its hind feet firmly (thus forming a triangle with the two feet and the tail), raises its arms above its head and, when its adversary is within range, falls forward, slashing downwards with its razor-sharp front claws. Unlike the sloth, who has blunt, peg-like teeth with no enamel that go on growing throughout its life, this anteater has no teeth, merely a long, sticky tongue and a very muscular gizzard in its stomach, which pulverizes the tree ants on which it lives.

Our specimen behaved with great fortitude during the filming and soon became so inured to us that, between takes, he sat quietly clinging on to Lee's forefinger, his tail carefully wound round her thumb or wrist. When the time came to release him, he was reluctant to leave Lee's hand and sat for a long time in the bushes, peering at us pensively, before moving away into the forest.

Although we had miles of film of the leaf-cutting ants going about their business of defoliating the forest, carrying their leaves back to their nest, cleaning out the nest and creating huge garbage-heaps, we had to part company with them when they vanished underground. This irked Alastair.

'I want . . . you know . . . I think . . . well, gardens,' he said, with his head on one side, revolving slowly, looking like a beaming, benevolent corpse on a gibbet. 'Mushroom-beds, you know . . . underground?'

'The only way you'll get them, honey, is by digging the guys out,' said Paula [the producer] practically.

'Yes,' said Alastair musingly, moving top-like on the nest he was standing on, which covered an area approximately the size of a small ballroom.

'Is possible?' asked Roger [the cameraman]. 'Is not too deep?'

'Well, sometimes the mushroom-beds lie quite close to the surface,' I said, 'but the ants won't take too kindly to it.'

'Paula, you get some spades and we dig, eh?' said Roger enthusiastically. 'Dig out ze little *jardins des champignons*, yes?'

'Yes . . . spades,' said Alastair, struck by the novel idea. 'Get some spades.'

So Paula traipsed back through the forest to the research station and eventually reappeared with a bundle of spades. The word 'producer' means exactly that. They are expected to produce – at the drop of a hat – anything from a four-wheel-drive truck to a square meal, a motor-launch to a bottle of whisky.

'Just the job,' said Alastair.

He and Roger seized spades and started to dig. Having had some experience of leaf-cutting ants, I took Lee and Paula by the arm and led them away from the scene of operations. Leaf-cutters, as a species, are highly successful creatures. The whole colony is founded by the queen, who, on her nuptial flight, carries (in a sort of pouch) a cluster of fungus threads which constitute the food for the future colony, in much the same way that the American pioneers used to take sacks of grain to plant when they eventually settled. When the wedding flight is over, the queen plants the fungus in a brood chamber and looks after it with all the dedication of a horticulturist, manuring it with her excrement. If the fungus dies, the colony fails; when it is successful, the colony expands and grows in proportion to the fungus gardens and may eventually have more than a million individuals to a nest. I had just explained this to Paula when approximately half the million inhabitants of this nest decided that the activities of Roger and Alastair were inimical to their well-being, so they poured forth to remonstrate. One minute Alastair and Roger looked like two earnest gardeners turning over their asparagus-beds in preparation for a new crop and the next minute they were executing leaps and twists and *pas de deux* that would have been the envy of the Moscow Ballet. This was accompanied by wild, tremulous screams of agony, interspersed in equal parts with blasphemy and procreative oaths.

'Christ,' shrieked Alastair, waltzing around, now of necessity. 'Ouch, ouch, they're biting. Oh, the bloody things!'

'Ouch, ouch, *merde alors!*' screamed Roger, waltzing, too, and slapping his trousers. 'Zey is biting.'

The chief problem was that Alastair was wearing shorts and an ancient pair of baseball boots, and this did not give his legs any protection, so the ants swarmed up him as though he were a tree, attempting to tear him to pieces. Roger, if anything, was in worse case, for he was wearing elegant, fairly tight-fitting trousers, up which the ants flowed with speed and precision. Those on the outside bit right through the thin cloth and into his flesh. Those on the inside concentrated on getting as high as possible before beginning their assault, so that Roger was being bitten in the most intimate and tender parts of his anatomy. The ants' jaws, powerful enough to chop up tough leaves, made short work of the thin trouser material and Roger's legs were patched with bloodstains as were Alastair's legs. We got them both away from the immediate scene of battle and de-anted them. Paula then practised first aid with antibiotics, but it was a considerable time before we got all of the ants off them.

'Did you see that?' panted Alastair, his spectacles misted over with emotion. 'The buggers were trying to defoliate me.'

'What about me?' said Roger. 'Me they go for the private parts. Me they try to make eunuch.'

Later on, wrapped in so many layers of clothing that they looked like Tweedledum and Tweedledee clad for battle, they succeeded in unearthing a small section of the mushroom-garden and filming it, to the ants' fury.

One of the most fantastic pieces of natural history in the forest, one that was in its own way just as difficult to obtain on film as the ants' fungus-garden, was the extraordinary story of the giant fig tree and the minute fig wasp. This strange relationship only recently became unravelled, and it shows part of the enormous complexity of the tropical forest and how any plant or creature is only part of the whole intricate ecosystem, for without the great fig trees the fig wasp would perish and without the fig wasp the fig tree would never reproduce its kind, and its numbers would dwindle and it would eventually become extinct.

All figs have a very curious flower structure, resembling, in fact, that of a fruit more than that of a flower. A host of tiny flowers lie inside the fig, which is attached to the tree by a stalk at one end; at the other there is a minute opening almost obscured by scales. Figs have male and female flowers and the way the pollen is ferried from one to the other is as enchanting as it is awe-inspiring. This is what happens:

In the fig the first to mature are the female flowers, and their scent attracts female fig wasps, who are carrying pollen from other fig trees in the forest. To get at the blooms, the wasp must climb inside the fig using the opening at one end, shouldering the scale 'door' open. This is not an easy process for the door is stiff, and the female wasp is fragile and often loses her wings and antennae when entering the fig.

Once she (and other females) has successfully broached the fig, she proceeds to bore down through the styles of the female flowers using her long ovipositor, like someone drilling for oil. The flowers are of two sorts, one with short styles and one with long styles. This design is such that the ovipositor of the wasp can only reach the ovules of the short styled variety to lay the eggs. The long styled ones are only probed, but while being probed they receive the pollen carried by the wasp. So, by this process, the short styled fig flowers produce fig wasp larvae, whilst the long styled flowers produce seed. This is extraordinary enough, but the story gets even more bizarre and magical.

The next thing is that the larval wasps develop and then pupate. At this stage they apparently produce a substance that prevents the fig from maturing, for if it were to ripen while the wasps were pupating, their nursery might be eaten with them inside. At last the pupae mature. The males are the first to hatch; they go the rounds of the as yet unhatched females to fertilize them. Up to this point, to all intents and purposes, the fig is completely sealed so that the atmosphere inside it contains up to ten per cent carbon dioxide (as opposed to .03 per cent outside it), but this does not seem to worry the males. However, after mating the male wasps tunnel through the sides of their nursery and the carbon dioxide level falls dramatically. This in some way accelerates both the hatching of the female wasps and the emergence of male flowers, and the females get coated with pollen from them. Both the male and female wasps, working as a team, bite away the scales at the end of the fig, and the females fly off, carrying fertilizing pollen and stored sperm to found a new colony in another fig tree at the female stage. The males, being wingless, cannot leave the fig and so they die, their life's work done.

When you think that the fig wasp story is only one of the many fantastic things that are being discovered in the tropical forests everywhere, it makes you realize what a complex world we live in and how our ham-handed tinkering can cause havoc with the delicate balance of the ecosystems.

The tropical forests of the world are one of man's greatest bounties and yet the way we are treating them you would think that they are dangerous to us, instead of being an enormous self-generating storehouse of medicines, foodstuffs, timbers, dyes, spices and a host of other things. We do not as yet know the full benefit of the tropical forests to mankind, yet we are destroying the forests so fast that species of plant and animal are becoming extinct even before they are scientifically described. It is estimated that this wild suicidal attack on the tropical forests of the world is resulting in 110,000 square kilometres – 43,000 square miles – of trees being felled and burnt each year. Cheerful prediction is that at this rate all this kind of forest will have disappeared in eighty-five years. If this happens – and there is no indication that mankind is suddenly going to give up stupidity and behave sensibly – the alteration to the climate may well be catastrophic, for forests control the weather and without them you can turn rich areas into deserts in a very short time. This is to say nothing of the benefits to us that we have already discovered in the forests and the ones that await discovery. We have only touched the fringe of knowledge when it comes to that enormous ecosystem known as the rainforest or jungle. What inestimable benefit for mankind may lurk among the trees we have no idea, and yet in a profligacy that is almost maniacal we are destroying something that can never be re-created, something of tremendous value to mankind; something, moreover, which is self-renewing if it is husbanded and exploited with care. However, at the rate we are going, it is probable that in less than a hundred years with millions more mouths to feed we will be faced with deserts on which to grow food, simply because we are behaving in a greedy, malicious and totally selfish way, and this goes for everyone, regardless of colour, creed or political persuasion, for unless we move and move fast our children will never have the chance to see that most fascinating and important biological region of the planet, the tropical forest, or to benefit from it.

FROM DURRELL IN RUSSIA:

We dragged ourselves out of bed to find it was snowing, although the temperature had risen in the night. Five skidoos (rather like a motorbike with tank tracks on it, noisy, smelly, but fast) had been assembled. One of them dragged a flat sledge with some of the equipment while another pulled a sledge that looked like a cross between a giant infant's crib and the sort of sleigh Father Christmas is wont to use. The back of this monster construction had been filled with hay and lambskin rugs and into it Lee and I were installed (like Tsar and Tsarina), together with the more delicate equipment. We set off through the fine, driving snow and in the pale yellow and purple dawn light the lake looked immense, with the rim of forest crouched black and malevolent-looking on the further shore. After a couple of hours' travel, it became patently obvious that we were not going to be able to keep our rendezvous with the bear. Rising temperature had softened the layer of snow so that, instead of gliding over it, both skidoos and sledges were constantly breaking through the crust of snow and sticking. However, a mile or two further on, we were assured, there was a remote forester's house where we could have some breakfast and review the situation.

It was at this point that the raccoon dog entered our lives. Vasily, who had got increasingly depressed at the non co-operation of bears and the disinclination of the weather to obey him, suddenly, like a conjurer, whipped open the boot of his skidoo and produced from it a half-grown raccoon dog, which he dumped into my lap with a flourish. It crouched there with the same expression of shock on its face that I must have been wearing, for the last raccoon dog I had been on intimate terms with was one that I looked after when I was a student keeper at Whipsnade, some forty years ago. These attractive creatures are extremely interesting canines and their introduction and consequent spread throughout Europe is a perfect example of man's stupidity and unnecessary tinkering with nature. These animals, with their short legs, look like very hairy corgis with a raccoon-like face. They were once confined to Japan and eastern Asia and then somebody had the bright idea that if they were introduced into the forest areas of western Russia they would be a valuable fur-bearing creature. So they were introduced and, being an omnivore with a penchant for survival, soon spread over the whole of middle Europe and became a pest. To add insult to injury, it was then discovered that their skin was useless, so Europe had acquired a large pest to the detriment of its natural fauna, in the same way that it had acquired the South American coypu or nutria. Man is forever meddling with nature in a stupid fashion.

The raccoon dog lay in my lap and allowed me to stroke it, appearing to be perfectly content, but then Vasily appeared with a large dog collar and leash and attempted to put them on the animal. The raccoon dog decided that this was too much of an indignity. With a quick wriggle and a jump, it rocketed out of my lap and over the side of the sledge. Once on the ice, its furry feet gave it terrific purchase and it set off across the lake at a smart, determined trot that soon had it about a hundred yards away. Everyone set off in pursuit, but they were not nearly as agile as the raccoon dog and soon the ice was littered with fallen bodies. In the end they had to return to the skidoos and, mounting them, used them to surround and recapture our raccoon dog. He was bundled back into the boot to be filmed on the following day, for the sky was now so overcast and the snowfall so heavy that it precluded all thoughts of filming. I noticed a curious thing: the snowflakes that were falling (each one about three times the size of a pinhead) were shaped like tiny flowers with five petals, each petal filigreed in the most minute and intricate fashion so that the flowers looked as though they were made out of lace. Very soon, the dark sheepskin rug over our laps was covered in these tiny snowflakes so it looked like a field of miniature daisies.

We eventually reached the forester's house, where we had a most welcome meal and drank gallons of sustaining tea. After this, we decided to return home, for the weather was getting worse and worse and so our chances of filming a bear, even if we saw one, were nil. We had progressed a few miles on our homeward journey when the skidoo that was pulling us rounded a snow bank at too acute an angle, whereupon our massive Father Christmas sledge turned turtle, precipitating me, Lee and all our delicate equipment out on to the ice in a welter of sheepskin rugs and hay. Fortunately, neither we nor our equipment were hurt, but the poor forester who was driving us was chagrined and ashamed of himself, and it took a lot of hugging and kissing to persuade him not to commit suicide out of mortification.

The following day was a disaster. The raccoon dog had escaped and the crew tried to film wild capercaillie with no success. Then in the afternoon

I had promised to give a talk to the assembled foresters and their families about our work. As this is a reserve called after Charles Darwin, there was naturally a large, heavily framed portrait of that distinguished scientist hanging on the wall opposite me in the room where I gave my talk. I had just been asked if I thought there should be more captive breeding centres in the world like the one I had set up in Jersey and I was launching enthusiastically into my reply, when the massive portrait fell off the wall with a crash that shook the building and filled everybody with alarm and consternation.

Darvinsky, though a fascinating place, was not one of our more successful shoots.

PART FOUR

1985–1995

Reflections and Reflexes

In the last ten years of his life Gerry occasionally reflected on what his efforts and those of his now considerable team had achieved after the quarter of a century since he had started his zoo from scratch. But even more often he thought about what we should and could be achieving on behalf of the animal kingdom, where to do it and how a book and a film could promote it – in other words, he was always planning expeditions, or at least short trips to far-away places to see new creatures or old animal friends and to talk to the people who were trying to save them. Just a few months before he died we sat in his hospital room and seriously discussed going to Australia. He wanted to show me this zoological wonder of the world, for I had never been.

Gerry sometimes startled people by saying that what he wanted most in the world was to be able to close down his precious zoo because there was no longer a need for it. The crowning achievements of his lifetime were not, in his view, the successful capture and breeding of endangered animals, nor the acquisition of knowledge through research on a rare species, nor the education and training of laymen and professionals in matters of conservation – although he and his team did all these things, and he viewed them as vitally important means to an end. His greatest aim was the return of wild animals from captive sanctuaries back to the wild where they would thrive, no longer under the shadow of extinction. The following extract from The Ark's Anniversary, *a chapter entitled 'Return to the Wild', shows just how much easier said than done this process is. Gerry wrote the piece towards the end of the eighties when re-introduction was more of an art or an alchemy than a science and, although much progress has been made since then, it is still in its infancy.*

Gerry's last expedition was to Madagascar, that ravishing and ravaged island, the naturalist's paradise. He was seduced by the animal he writes about so beautifully in the last selection, the aye-aye, and, like a knee-jerk reflex, he decided that he must try to save it from extinction, in spite of his own failing health.

A good many years ago, when we had just started the Trust, I would try to point out to people the point and purpose of captive breeding. Their inevitable question was 'What have you put back?' as if the whole exercise consisted merely in breeding a few specimens, bundling them into crates, shipping them back to their country of origin and flinging them out into the nearest bit of forest. Nothing could be further from the truth.

The whole business of captive breeding for conservation is one beset with problems, but once overcome, i.e. getting successfully through stages one and two of our multifaceted approach, you can begin in earnest on stage three, which is to put captive-bred stock back in the wild, in places where the species has become extinct, in new areas within or near the species' natural range which have suitable habitat, or in areas where an endemic wild population needs an infusion of new animals. Stage three is the trickiest part of all.

The tricky thing about returning captive-bred animals to the wild is that it is a wholly new concept, a wholly new art if you like, and we are learning as we go. To begin with, no two species are alike in their demands, and the wants of each have to be learnt as a vital preliminary. Second, you cannot take an animal which may be the third or fourth generation born in captivity and simply push it back into the wild. Surrounded by food it would in all probability perish, for it would be used to having its fruit or whatever cut up and served in bowls. It would be the same as taking a millionaire of long standing out of the Ritz and making him sleep on a park bench covered with newspapers and forage for his food in dustbins. It would take time to indoctrinate him.

The methods so far evolved are fairly straightforward but, as I say, the whole process has to be adapted to the individual animal and, for that matter, to the individual place. Our first attempt at returning the Pink pigeon to the wild in Mauritius was an example of how easily things can go wrong. We had decided to do our first release of the birds into a sort of 'halfway house' in the botanical garden of Pamplemousses. In this vast area there was a plentiful supply of leaves and fruit and, because there were plenty of access roads criss-crossing the gardens, it would be possible to monitor closely the birds' movements and reactions. So we constructed a special release aviary, one side of which would hold two pigeons to be released and the other two more which we hoped would serve as 'decoys' to encourage the freed birds to stay in the gardens.

The first birds were carefully chosen from the breeding centre at Black River, the complex of aviaries and enclosures built and staffed by the Mauritian government and operationally funded in great part by our Trust. Once they had settled down and adapted to their new home the great day of the release came. I was in Mauritius for this auspicious occasion and I was to release the birds. The idea was that once the birds were freed – or at least had access to freedom – they could still use the aviaries as sanctuary and a constant food supply would be kept there until such time as they decided that they were self-sufficient. I went along on the appointed day and with a great flourish – for it was an important occasion – I pulled the string to raise the flaps which would allow the pigeons their freedom.

The string broke.

There was an embarrassing pause while someone was dispatched for more string. At that moment I sympathized deeply with those ladies, dressed in their best, who keep banging bottles of champagne against the bosom of new ocean liners without effect. Eventually, string was procured and the flaps duly raised. The pigeons behaved beautifully and flew out and sat on top of the aviaries. We then expected them to take advantage of their freedom and fly off into the trees. Not a bit of it. They sat stolidly on top of the aviaries without blinking an eye, looking like mentally retarded examples of an amateur taxidermist's work. How I wish all the idiotic people who prate about the cruelty of captivity and the joys of freedom could have seen those birds.

It was unfortunate – in hindsight – that the authorities wanted this, the first release, to receive no publicity, and at the time it seemed a sensible enough request. We released eleven birds altogether into Pamplemousses, and they eventually plucked up courage and began to sample their new-found freedom by investigating all areas of the extensive gardens. They soon had a new hazard to face. Small boys with slingshots patrolled the grounds endeavouring to get specimens of the Common dove for their tea. They could not be expected to tell the difference between a Pink pigeon and a dove, except that one was fatter and therefore more desirable (in fact, the flesh of the Pink pigeon has an unpleasant taste and is therefore inedible).

This, combined with the Pink pigeon's trusting – almost imbecile – nature was fatal. Several of the pigeons fell to the young hunters' deadly weapons. One wonders, as I say, whether a big publicity campaign would have made any difference. Are small boys with slingshots affected by publicity campaigns? No one can be certain. But in spite of the small boys, some of the birds paired up and produced babies, although they deserted them at the nestling stage, probably as a result of human disturbance.

Suffice it to say that this our first release was not a resounding success, and so we caught the birds and took them back to Black River. Still, we had learnt a lot from this 'practice' release. The birds did not immediately fly off into the wild blue yonder, but stayed near the release site, where they could be fed until they got used to their surroundings. Then they began feeding on the leaves and fruits of exotic as well as native plants, an important observation because exotic plants have invaded the Mauritian forests to which the birds would one day be returned. Finally, we had proved that captive-bred birds could and would reproduce outside of captivity.

So with great confidence we planned the next step: a real release to the wild in a remote part of Mauritius known as the Macchabe Forest. Again we built aviaries and established the birds in them. This time, before release, some of the pigeons were fitted with tiny radio transmitters, so that we could track them, for it was one thing to find a bird in the botanical gardens and quite another to find it in the thick forests and deep valleys of Macchabe. A few days after release, the birds followed no set pattern. Some flew off beyond the range of their transmitters and disappeared for weeks at a time, only to reappear mysteriously. Others flew into the forest but reappeared at their aviaries every day for supplementary feeding. Others flew only a few hundred feet from the aviaries and remained there for months. Gradually, it became apparent that the birds were getting acclimatized to the wild state and were becoming daily more self-sufficient, choosing the leaves and fruit that took their fancy. Nevertheless, we kept up the supplementary feed as a precaution, for we did not want a wild source of seasonal food to disappear suddenly and the birds to starve in consequence. At the time of writing, two of the released pigeons have appeared back at the feeding platform each with a youngster in tow. So far we can say, cautiously, that this new release has been a success.

This is excellent for two reasons. It now proves that birds several generations born in captivity can re-adapt to the wild state, and, probably more importantly, we have established the bird outside what we have always called the Pigeon Wood. This is a valley set deep in the mountain forests, consisting of a small stand of exotic cryptomeria trees. The entire wild population of pigeons (probably fewer than twenty-five in 1978) nest in these. To have all the birds nesting in an area covering a few acres was, of course, dangerous in the extreme, for a happy band of the introduced monkeys or an equally happy primate – a man with a shotgun – or a really bad cyclone could have wiped out the Pink pigeon for ever. Yet stubbornly the wild birds would nest nowhere else. It was a case of having all your eggs in one basket with a vengeance, but, by establishing a new colony in Macchabe we hope that the birds will get fixated on this new area and thus found a new colony. Having done this, we can continue to found other colonies in suitable patches of habitat throughout Mauritius so that should anything untoward happen to the original wild colony we have not lost the species.

*   *   *

... a few years ago, just after we had begun the pigeon release, we were ready to go ahead with another species, this time a mammal, a creature called the Jamaican hutia. This had all the hallmarks of success, but what happened shows how a project which on the surface seems simple and straightforward can develop unsuspected pitfalls if you are unwary.

Hutias are a group of rodents confined to the Caribbean Islands. There are different species in the Bahamas, Cuba and Jamaica. The Jamaican species, locally called a 'coney', is a browny-green animal, about the size of a miniature poodle and looks not unlike an enlarged guinea pig. They are the only large indigenous surviving mammal found on the island, although at one time they were abundant and provided a major food source for the original inhabitants as well as for the indigenous Jamaican boa constrictor. However, excessive hunting with modern weapons and destruction of the forests in which they live put them in peril. The Trust received its first hutias in 1972 – two males and a female captured in the John Crow Mountains – through the good offices of a Trust member, and eight more were acquired in 1975. From these came the first captive birth ever recorded, and during the next ten years sixty-one litters comprising ninety-five young were produced. Of these, acting on our principle of never having all your eggs in one basket, nineteen were sent on breeding loan to six other collections in four different countries.

Back in 1972, just as our splendid new hutia accommodation was nearing completion, I got a telephone call from Fleur Cowles, one of our trustees. She told me that the Hollywood star, Jimmy Stewart, and his wife Gloria were going to visit her and that she was going to bring them over to Jersey. Always with an eye to the main chance, I asked if Mr Stewart would like to open our new hutia breeding unit to provide some publicity for the Trust. Back came the answer that he would be delighted.

On the appointed day I went down to the airport to meet them. Stewart was unassumingly himself, walking with a slight cowboy slouch, drawling sentences in his lovely husky voice. Gloria was a handsome woman, immaculately groomed as only a wealthy American can be, with immense charm but a slight glitter in her eyes which told me she could easily resemble one of Mr Wodehouse's famous aunts if things did not turn out to her satisfaction. She was the sort of spirited person to whom *maîtres d'hôtel* give instant allegiance and servility, in case worse than their wildest nightmares should ensue. As we waited outside the airport for John to bring the car round, talking about this and that, James Stewart suddenly disappeared. One minute he was there – tall, gangling, a gentle smile on his face – the next he had softly and silently vanished like a puff of smoke. One would have thought it impossible for such a big man (in every sense of the word) to eclipse himself so deftly without anyone noticing.

'Where is Jimmy?' Gloria asked suddenly and accusingly, as if we were concealing him from her. We all looked around vacantly.

'Perhaps he has gone to the comfort station,' I said, using an American euphemism I adore.

'He did that on the plane,' said Gloria. 'Where on earth is he?'

Having eliminated the comfort station as a possible hiding place, I could not think for the life of me where he could have gone. Gloria's increasing agitation infected me with a sense of unease. Had he been kidnapped? I could see the world headlines in the illiterate press: 'James Stewart snatched at hutia party – famous actor becomes as extinct as the animals he went to visit.' This was not the sort of publicity I was seeking for the Trust.

At that moment, John rolled up in the car. 'Shall I go and tell Mr Stewart the car's here?' he asked.

'Where is he?' everyone asked in unison.

'He's out there on the tarmac looking at a plane,' said John.

'Go and get him, please,' said Gloria. 'He can't keep his hands off planes.'

'How did he get out there?' I asked, for airport security is very tight in Jersey.

'Can you imagine anyone stopping him, seeing who he is?' asked John.

Presently, the truant loped back into our midst.

'Er . . . kinda nice little plane out there,' he explained. 'Yeah, sorta little job, very neat. Kinda cosy, you know. Neat. Hadn't seen one before.'

'Get into the car, Jimmy,' said Gloria, 'you're holding everyone up.'

'Yeah, yeah,' said Jimmy, either unrepentant or not listening. 'I'm glad I saw that. Kinda neat.'

After we had lunched he opened our hutia nursery with great charm, saying that he had always liked Hoot Ears ever since he first met them, which was about five minutes ago. This ordeal over, we took them out to dinner at a friend's house.

Over drinks in the conservatory and the excellent meal that followed it, Jimmy seemed preoccupied. I think he was suffering from jetlag, which has a stultifying effect on anyone. The meal over, we repaired to the drawing-room where Jimmy carefully lowered his gangling shape into the bosom of an enormous sofa. His eyes wandered vaguely round the room and suddenly focused on something that interested him.

'Gee, it's a piana,' he said, his eyes fixed longingly on the baby grand that crouched in the corner.

'Jimmy, no,' said Gloria Stewart, warningly.

'Yes sir, a piana,' said Jimmy, with the delight of one making the discovery of the century, 'a kinda little baby piana.'

'Jimmy, you're not to,' said Gloria.

'A little toon . . .' said Stewart musingly, starting to unravel his length from the sofa, a fanatical gleam in his eye, 'a toon – what's that toon I like?'

'Please Jimmy, don't play the piano,' said Gloria desperately.

'Oh, I know . . . "Ragtime Cowboy Joe" . . .' said Jimmy approaching the instrument, 'Yes siree, "Ragtime Cowboy Joe".'

'Jimmy, I beseech you,' said Gloria, her voice breaking.

'Yes, a kinda nice, swinging toon, that.' Jimmy seated himself on the piano stool. He lifted the lid and the baby grand grinned at him like a crocodile.

'Now – er – let's see – er, how did it go,' said Jimmy, plonking his long fingers on the keys. We were immediately apprised of two facts. The first was that Jimmy Stewart was tone deaf and the other that he could not play the piano. In addition, he had forgotten all the lyrics except the basic one of the title. In all the years I had watched his impeccable performances on the screen, I had never seen him do anything like this. He played all the wrong notes and sang out of tune, trying to make the two match. In his husky, croaking voice he sang the title of the song over and over again, going back to the beginning when he thought he had missed something out. It was like watching an armless man try to swim the English Channel and yet it was excruciatingly funny, but you did not dare laugh as he was taking such pride in his performance. In the end, he exterminated 'Ragtime Cowboy Joe' to his satisfaction and then turned to us, happy in his achievement.

'Would anyone like to hear some other toons?' he inquired generously. I was tempted to ask for the 'Star Spangled Banner', but it was not to be.

'Jimmy, we must go.' said Gloria.

And go they did.

To have been given a performance like this by the great James Stewart was an honour, but I was sure his wife did not agree.

It is always exciting when a new animal arrives at the Trust's collection, is released into its new quarters and you can watch it settle down. The Hoot Ears, as christened by Jimmy Stewart, however, proved to be the exception rather than the rule. Handsome, portly animals though they were, with heavy hindquarters which made them look as if they were wearing trousers several sizes too large for them, they lacked the scintillating personality one might have hoped for. They displayed all the *joie de vivre* of a bevy of churchwardens attending the funeral of one of their number. There was only one thing they did which could possibly be described as eccentric. Like most creatures, they had not read the textbook description of their behaviour and so they did not know that they were supposed to be strictly terrestrial. Ponderously, and with total lack of expression, they would climb up the branches in their cages and perch near the ceiling – one supposed imagining themselves to be flocks of flightless birds. True, I did see the young ones frequently indulge in what could be described as 'catch-as-catch-can' games, but they were of a very staid variety and one was reminded of overweight

Victorian children indulging because their elders expected it of them.

When the numbers of young we had bred were sufficiently high, we started thinking in terms of re-introduction. Our then Research Assistant, William Oliver, went out to Jamaica to fix up all the preliminaries, which included the selection of a suitable site (a place that seemed satisfactory from the hutias' point of view, particularly freedom from hunting pressure) and the involvement of Hope Zoo in Kingston in the venture. A total of forty-four of our Jersy-bred hutias were sent out in 1985–6, and settled in their family groups in specially built cages at the Hope Zoo. Meanwhile, an extensive vegetation survey was done on the chosen site to make sure that the hutias would lack for nothing in terms of foodstuffs. Then they were transferred to the release site, each family group into a temporary enclosure surrounding a specially constructed, semi-artificial rock warren or 'coney' hole. After a week or two, when the animals seemed to be used to their new situation, the fence was removed and the progress of each group was monitored for up to three months.

Early reports were most encouraging. Only three animals disappeared during this initial monitoring period, but the rest of them rapidly became self-sufficient and remained in good condition. Our hopes were high that the re-introduction was going to be a great success. However, when the site was re-investigated later in the year only eight hutias could be located. These animals, which included two conceived and born on the site, were all in excellent condition. However, no others were found during a six-week search. In the following year only two animals were found, one a Jersey-bred specimen and the other thought to be wild born. Both were in good condition, but the whereabouts of the rest of the specimens was, and remains, a mystery. The animals that had been released had, early on, adapted to the wild excellently and behaved as normal wild hutias do. This site seemed eminently suitable with a plentiful food supply and freedom from hunting pressure. We had to conclude, therefore, that the disappearance was due to illness or to predation by feral dogs and cats. However, we haven't given up hope – literally – because we are now working with the Hope Zoo to establish a sufficiently large breeding colony there from which a second re-introduction, with the help of students from the University of the West Indies, will be attempted.

All the frustrations involved in releasing animals to the wild are more than made up for when you join forces with people and meet with success, as in the case of the Golden lion tamarins. These enchanting creatures, smallest of the primates, along with their close relatives, the marmosets, live in the coastal rainforest of Brazil. Unfortunately, this special rainforest has been ruthlessly and thoughtlessly destroyed and all that is left are pockets of trees, some not even connected with one another, so that the animals of each of these pockets are isolated and cannot renew their species' genetic resources by mixing and mating with others of their kind, even if they are only a few miles away. At one time, the Atlantic coastal rainforest covered an area of 135,000 square miles. Now less than five per cent remains and this is being steadily whittled down by axe, fire and bulldozer. As this forest is stripped, it not only drives to extinction – or its brink – the tamarins, but the myriad other creatures and plants that go to make up this extraordinary ecosystem. When you fell a tropical tree you are doing the equivalent of destroying a huge city, because of the thousands of creatures that live in, on and around it.

The Golden lion tamarin is probably one of the most beautiful of all mammals. A little bigger than a newly born kitten, it has incredibly long 'artistic' fingers and its long fur looks, quite literally as if it is spun gold. This amazing glittering pelt stands away from its face in a sort of semi-recumbent mane which gives it a lion-like look. Like all the marmosets and tamarins, their movements are incredibly quick and sometimes they move with such speed it is impossible to follow the movement with your eye. They are omnivorous, the bulk of their food being fruit and insects, but they will eat tree frogs with relish and will even (it has recently been discovered) go into hollow trees in the daytime to hunt for roosting bats to add to their diet. Their vocalizations are very bird-like as they communicate in a series of trills, sharp squeaks and chatterings.

In addition to the destruction of the forest, these beautiful little animals had been popular with the pet trade and for biomedical research, so by the late sixties and early seventies it was apparent that the species was in serious danger. It was estimated then that no more than 150 individuals were still living in the fragmented forest blocks which remained. This alarming state of affairs was highlighted by the brilliant work carried out by Dr Adelmar F. Coimbra-Filho, now director of the Rio de Janeiro Primate Centre. In 1972 a conference was held, during which the plight of these animals was discussed and an attempt made to assess both wild and captive populations. It was obviously of the greatest importance that self-sustaining captive populations were established while, at the same time, trying to address the problem in the wild. It is mainly due to the dedicated work of Dr Devra Kleiman that this has been so successful. Between 1972 and 1980 very few zoos had Golden lions and these were mostly American. These zoos carefully expanded their small populations, and the result was spectacular. The captive population sprang from 153 to 330 – about double the wild population – within five years. Fifty to sixty Golden lions were being born every year and so there was now a sufficiently large and stable population to start thinking about putting some captive-bred specimens back into the wild. The success of this project was due to the formation of a consortium of zoos for the management of this species.

In 1978 we received our first pair of Golden lions and also joined the consortium. The arrival of our Golden lions caused quite a sensation. It is one thing to see a painting or colour photograph of a creature, quite another to see the animal in the flesh. These tiny primates, glittering like doubloons, raced about their cage at such speed they looked like ingots being thrown about. As they whisked about exploring their new domain, they kept up a chorus of chirrups, squeaks and chitters as if each were a miniature tour guide telling the other where it was and what to look at.

Finally, when they had settled down, they became the centre of attraction in our marmoset range for they were by far the most striking and attractive of this enchanting group of primates. Finally, came the day when the female successfully gave birth to twins (the normal complement), two minuscule little gold nuggets which could each easily have fitted into a small coffee cup. At first, clinging to the dense fur of their parents and matching it so beautifully, they were extraordinarily difficult to see, for their little faces were smaller than a fifty-pence piece. As they grew older they grew bolder and would leave the security of their parent's body to explore the cage on their own, though always ready to fly back to the security of the parent's fur at any imagined danger. To see them in the sunshine chasing butterflies unwary enough to drift through the wire mesh was an entrancing sight. Not only was it an incredible, dainty ballet as they twisted and turned, leapt and scuttled after the pirouetting insects, but as the light caught them their coats sparkled in myriad colours from sandstone red to the colour of the palest wedding ring. For some reason my suggestion that the babies be christened Fort and Knox respectively met with such antagonism from all quarters that, outnumbered, I was forced to relinquish the idea.

Meanwhile the plans for release into the wild of captive-bred lions were moving ahead. Naturally, a plan of this magnitude had to be approached with great caution and attention to detail. An ecological survey had to be done to assess the wild population of Golden lions and, this done, to locate an area of forest uninhabited by a wild population but suitable for the release of the captive-bred specimens. Meanwhile, fifteen animals from five US zoos were chosen and sent to the Rio Primate Centre for training. An animal which is perhaps the third generation born in captivity is used to set mealtimes and never has to go out and search for its food. Most important of all in the cushioned world of captivity, there are no predators in the shape of snakes and hawks, and even *Homo sapiens* is considered an obliging gift-giving friend. So the animals have to be introduced slowly to the stern realities of life in the forest if they are to survive. At one point it was discovered that they were alarmed and daunted by tree branches which bent. In the well-conducted zoos they came from the branches were rigidly nailed into place, so a branch which gave under your weight was an alarming experience until you learnt how to cope with it. They had to learn how to incorporate into their diets wild fruit they had never seen before and here it was discovered, fascinatingly enough, that the younger animals were quicker at learning this and were showing the older ones what to do.

The initial releases got off to a slow start, but as the animals *and* the people in charge of the project learnt more and more they were finally successful. One photograph shows a captive-bred specimen eating a frog, an item never included in her diet in Washington, and proof that the animals had settled down in their environment. The next phase involved releasing captive-bred animals with wild ones, and it was a great day when twins were produced by a female born in captivity but who had mated with a male born in the wild. By this time we had bred over twenty-five Golden lions in Jersey and so were able to take part in the venture by donating five of our animals. These were released a family group in a patch of forest with no wild tamarins present, and we're very proud to say that our group was the first in the project to produce offspring from parents which had *both* been born and raised in captivity. This is proof, if proof were needed, that if all the various disciplines involved work in harmony towards a common goal, captive breeding can and does work, and with it we should be able to pull back innumerable species from the brink of extinction.

I always remember having a delightful picnic lunch with Roger Payne and his family on my second visit to America. It is Roger, of course, who has done so much wonderful whale research and is responsible for those mournfully beautiful whale songs to which one listens enraptured, longing to know what these huge and extraordinary animals are saying to each other. However, during the course of the picnic, Roger asked me what the Trust was all about and I endeavoured to explain our aims and objectives.

Finally, Roger said, 'I think I see what you mean – you're breeding them to put back *there*, providing there is a *there* to put them back into.' Thus, in one pithy sentence, he highlighted one of captive breeding's great problems: call it the 'There Syndrome' for want of a better description . . .

*   *   *

When John Hartley and I were in Mauritius setting up the breeding project for the Pink pigeon, my attention was drawn to the problems facing Round Island, a volcanic cone some 350 acres in extent, lying thirteen miles northeast of Mauritius. The extraordinary thing about it is that on this small scrap of earth live no less than two lizard and two snake species and several plant species found nowhere else in the world. Furthermore, it is one of the very few elevated tropical islands in the world free of rats and mice, and it is an important breeding station for various seabirds. Many years ago Round Island resembled Mauritius in miniature: that is to say the high parts of the island were thickly forested with hardwood trees including ebony, while on the lower slopes lay an apron of palm savannah. Then sometime in the 1800s some fool released some goats and rabbits on the island, of all animals the most destructive. The result was like shutting a Sabre-toothed tiger in a sheepfold. What the goats did not eat the rabbits did, and soon the hardwood forest had disappeared altogether, the palm savannah was fighting a rearguard action and the rapidly eroding island was slowly but surely starting to slip into the sea. On my first visit it was looking like the raddled, seamed death mask of a centenarian Red Indian, with only a scattering of palms, a few pandanus and some scant low growth left. It was obvious that something had to be done very quickly about the reptiles, for their habitat was being munched away as it grew. John and I paid two visits to the island, for the Mauritius government was in complete agreement that a nucleus of the reptiles should be captured for a captive-breeding initiative first in Jersey and later, perhaps, in Mauritius. A method for dealing with the rabbit and goat situation was, we were informed, in hand.

I have collected animals in a great many parts of the world and none of the captures has been easy. However, on Round Island the reptiles went out of their way to be co-operative to an extraordinary degree. Of the lizards, the Telfair's skinks were so tame that when we squatted down to have a picnic in what little shade was provided by a pandanus' green hand-like leaves, they joined us with whole-hearted enthusiasm. Large smooth-scaled reptiles, a sort of greyish caramel colour which was iridescent as a rainbow when the sun caught them, they had pointed, intelligent faces and thick black tongues. They clustered around us, climbing into our laps and partaking of hard-boiled eggs, tomatoes and passion fruit in the most genteel way and sipping beer and Coca-Cola out of our glasses with all the decorum of a group of village ladies at a vicarage tea party. We felt like cads and bounders when, at the end of the repast, we simply picked up our well-behaved guests and bundled them head first into soft cloth bags, rather as the Mad Hatter and the March Hare bundled the Dormouse into the teapot in *Alice*.

Our next objective was the capture of the Gunther's gecko, an eight-inch plump lizard with huge golden eyes, fan-shaped suckers on its toes and a mottled black and ash-grey skin as soft as velvet. They were not as convivial as the skinks and preferred to live in the remaining palm savannah, clinging to the trunks of the trees about halfway up. We had to use a more complex method of capture; we had to fish for them. We had brought bamboo poles with us and we attached slip knots of fine nylon to these. The geckos were most co-operative, staying quite still until we had the noose over their heads and round their fat necks. Then it was merely a question of chivvying them down the trunk and into a bag. This had to be done very gently and with great care, for should the lizard suddenly panic and pull against the noose there was a danger of the nylon cutting into the tissue-paper-soft skin of the neck. We were successful, however, and we now had twenty skinks and sixteen geckos in the bag – quite literally.

Next came the snakes. The two species found on Round Island are non-poisonous and distantly related to the family of snakes which includes the boa constrictors of tropical America, but are now considered to comprise a family on their own. One of them is an olive-coloured snake with lighter markings, about three and a half feet long. During the day it rests in the skirt of dead fronds which hang down bases of the Latania palms, of which there are quite a few left in the savannah area. These snakes were easy enough to catch since they just lay there and let you pluck them out of the fronds, but the difficulty was that they lay so still they were difficult to spot. With the other species of snake, we had no success at all. It is subterranean and so much more difficult to locate. The last one had been seen in 1975; since then there had been no reports of it, and it was feared extinct. Though we hunted high and low, we could find no trace of it and regretfully decided that it must be so.

When we returned to Mauritius, we found that all hell had broken loose over the rabbit and goat extermination plans for Round Island. The authorities had been advised that poisoning was the only solution since the terrain was too difficult to employ any other method, and so strychnine had been chosen. This is an unpleasant poison but, unfortunately, the only one apparently available at the time which could be left out in the blistering sun for days on end without losing its potency. In hindsight, of course, the choice of strychnine was even more unfortunate, for it was discovered later that it could have poisoned some of the reptiles, as well as the target goats and rabbits. However, strychnine was thought the best choice at the time, and it was imperative that Round Island be cleared of the offensive herbivores as soon as possible. Then someone connected with the project gave a press interview in which he blandly outlined the plan and pandemonium erupted.

Various animal protection societies in the UK took up the cause, baying like hysterical hounds, one of their representatives even going so far as to say to Sir Peter Scott (who was attempting to mediate) that he would rather see all the species on Round Island become extinct than one rabbit killed. The local Society for the Prevention of Cruelty to Animals in Mauritius who up till then had been most helpful and had agreed to the poisoning campaign now got cold feet, back-pedalled madly, and said it would be rank cruelty to poison the rabbits and goats and they would certainly do everything to stop it. In vain did we plead that at this rate the rabbits and goats would eradicate their food supply and thus die a slow death by starvation, surely worse than a quick one by poisoning. One English society for the welfare of animals did send out a marksman who spent some time on the island trying to eliminate the goats with the aid of a rifle and, to our considerable surprise, succeeded. I say to our surprise, for the animals were extremely wary and had made their headquarters at the lip of the volcano crater, the most difficult and dangerous terrain on the whole island. But this still left the insidious munching rabbits, and so matters rested.

It was during this extremely worrying time that an amusing incident occurred which lightened our load a little. The man in England who was causing the most trouble over the whole business of rabbit eradication was a certain Dr Glenfiddis Balmoral. This is obviously not his real name, but his name was sufficiently unusual to make it memorable. John Hartley and I, together with my friend Wahab Owadally, Chief Conservator of Forests for Mauritius, were attending a conference at London Zoo and, glancing casually through the list of participants, I saw the dreaded doctor was going to take part. I felt sure that if the three of us could get him somewhere privately we stood a chance of talking some sense into him. We planned our kidnap with great care. Firstly, I asked Michael Brambell, then Curator of Mammals at London Zoo, if we could borrow his house, which stood on the banks of the Regent's Park Canal, not far from the conference hall. Then I got an exalted personage to introduce me to the doctor. He seemed a nice, sensible man and I was amazed that he was taking such an extreme view over the so-called Bunny Blood Bath. I said there was something I and my colleagues would like to discuss with him and would he join us during a break in the conference to have a drink at Michael's house; he agreed with alacrity. Unfortunately he chose the moment when someone was giving a paper on breeding manatees, animals for which I have a passion, but I felt I would have to forgo it as Round Island was so important. It is one of the many sacrifices I have made in the name of conservation.

Anyway, we dragged the good doctor off to Michael's house, raided the drinks cabinet and soon had our victim mellowing under the influence of a huge gin and tonic. I started in on the Round Island problem and its global importance. The good doctor listened, nodding wisely. When I flagged, Wahab took up the reins and explained how the rabbits were doomed to slow death by starvation. He painted such a horrific picture that there were tears in all our eyes. Then John leapt into the fray and explained eruditely why Round Island was of such biological significance that to let it be destroyed by rabbits would be criminal. Throughout this, the good doctor had nodded agreement and said encouraging things like 'Quite right – I agree – yes, very true', so it came as something of a shock finally, when we had run out of steam, to hear him say, 'But I don't really see how I can help you.'

I looked at him blankly.

'But you're Dr Glenfiddis Balmoral, aren't you?'

'Yes,' he said, puzzled.

'Of the Society for the Greater Protection of Fur and Feather?'

'No, no,' he corrected, 'of the Society for the Preservation and Better Understanding of the Coleoptera.'

It was the wrong doctor. But who would have thought there could be two doctors with the same unusual name? The really bitter part of it was that I had missed my manatee paper.

In the meantime, seeds from the rare Round Island palms had been collected and successfully reared at the Botanical Gardens in Mauritius and we were having spectacular success in breeding all the reptile species we had brought back to Jersey. Of the Gunther's gecko we have bred 235, of the friendly Telfair's skink 327 and – probably our greatest achievement – thirty-one Round Island boas. We have sent specimens of the skinks and geckos on breeding loan to the USA, Germany, France, the UK, Holland and Canada, thus making sure that they were well established in captivity. Some of the boas we sent, appropriately enough, to Canada, to the Reptile Breeding Foundation belonging to Geoff Gaherty, whose enormous gift enabled us to build our own Reptile House.

We now had both palms and reptiles that could be returned to Round Island and all that stood in the way was this bunch of unattractive invaders. We had the 'there' to put native plants and animals back into, but the 'there' was not as yet suitable.

Ever since I visited New Zealand many years ago, I have kept in touch with the New Zealand Wildlife Service, probably the best in the world. In one of my letters, I mentioned the problems we were having with Round Island and asked if they had any suggestions, for I knew they had had terrible problems with rats and feral cats on their offshore islands. Back came the answer from Don Merton who said he thought could solve our problem for us. They had evolved a new form of poison which was specific to mammals and painless, unlike strychnine, and which moreover remained stable in extremes of temperature. In addition, said Don, he felt sure that if we approached the Wildlife Service he had some colleagues would be given leave of absence and would be delighted to place their expertise at our disposal and do the job for us. This seemed almost too good to be true, but in due course Don and his friends arrived in Mauritius carrying goodness knows how many hundredweight of deadly poison in their luggage, as well as tents, tarpaulins and other vital equipment. It was going to be a long job, we knew, for the task of poisoning all the rabbits in 350 acres of terrain which resembled the surface of the moon was not going to be easy. All this heavy equipment would have to be carried to Round Island by helicopter, since it would be impossible to land it all from boats and then carry it up almost perpendicular cliffs. Just as they were all packed up and ready to go on their vital mission, the government helicopter we were relying on broke down. We were in despair at the thought that we might have to put it off for yet another time, but a kindly Fate stepped in to our rescue. A destroyer of the Australian Navy was paying a courtesy call to Mauritius and had on board a spanking new helicopter. Frantic phone calls to the Australian Ambassador met with a kindly response and the Australian Navy was pressed into service to help us. Don and his team, plus their gear and poison, plus a six weeks' water supply (for there was none on the island), were taken by HMAS *Canberra* to Round Island and there the helicopter lifted the whole cargo, both human and inanimate, on to the only bit of Round Island that, could be called flat. Here Don and his team made camp and started work.

They did the most wonderful job under the most trying conditions and within six weeks Don reckoned that they had eliminated all the rabbits. However, to make absolutely sure, he and his team paid a return visit a year later. The reason we had to make sure of course was that if there were half a dozen rabbits of both sexes left, the poisoning would have merely acted like a cull, the surviving rabbits would have undergone a population explosion and we would be back to square one. However, there was not a trace of a rabbit and Don sent me some exciting photographs that showed the caruncated, desiccated, eroded surface of Round Island already wearing a green haze of new growth. The island was having its second chance to survive. The work does not stop there, of course, for palms and, we hope, hardwoods will be planted. But we also hope that in fifty years' time the island will closely resemble what it was some two hundred years ago, and offer a safe habitat for its strange and unique denizens.

Just recently, we had a visit from the distinguished author, Richard Adams, who wrote that extraordinary best-selling book about rabbits called *Watership Down*. Jeremy was showing him around the collection and, as Jeremy always does, was getting more and more enthusiastic about our work and particularly about the far-reaching ramifications of it. He was busily telling Mr Adams probably more than he wanted to know about our work on Round Island when he made a mistake.

'Yes,' said Jeremy with enthusiasm, 'and after the goats were eradicated, we managed to get rid of three thousand rab ... rab ... rab ...' Jeremy's voice faltered and came to a stop. How could you tell the man who had written *Watership Down* that you had exterminated 3,000 rabbits, without earning a certain amount of displeasure?

They looked at each other in silence for a moment. Jeremy got redder and redder.

'It's quite all right,' said Richard Adams, placidly. 'I don't know why everybody thinks I like rabbits so much just because I wrote a book about them.'

So, in collaboration with the Mauritius government and with the aid of the New Zealand Wildlife Service and the Australian Navy, the Trust had saved Round Island. We had, as I wrote to Roger Payne, saved a 'there' to put 'them' back into. But more than that, I believe that by this achievement we have taken the conception of a 'zoo', as it is popularly thought of, a stage further. Not only have we demonstrated that captive breeding, be it in Jersey or the country of origin of the species, is of vital importance, but we have shown how a 'zoo' can help in the resurrection and protection of the habitat of the animals it deals with.

What we have done for Round Island will, I am convinced, be used as a model for many parts of the world where fragile ecosystems exist and are under the same threat. So we hope we have shown that the zoological garden will have progressed from being the sterile Victorian menagerie (of which there are still far too many examples), to being a vital force in the conservation of the other forms of animal life which share the world with us. We feel this is what all zoos, especially the ones in richer countries, should be doing, and if for financial reasons they cannot venture as far as the Mascarenes they will, if they look, inevitably find on their doorstep a Round Island they can help, such is the urgent need for conservation in the world today.

FROM THE AYE-AYE AND I:

In the gloom it came along the branches towards me, its round, hypnotic eyes blazing, its spoon-like ears turning to and fro independently like radar dishes, its white whiskers twitching and moving like sensors; its black hands, with their thin, attenuated fingers, the third seeming prodigiously elongated, tapping delicately on the branches as it moved along, like those of a pianist playing a complicated piece by Chopin. It looked like a Walt Disney witch's black cat with a touch of E. T. thrown in for good measure. If ever a flying saucer came from Mars, you felt that this is what would emerge from it. It was Lewis Carroll's Jabberwocky come to life, wiffling through its tulgey wood.

It lowered itself on to my shoulder, gazed into my face with its huge, hypnotic eyes and ran slender fingers through my beard and hair as gently as any barber. In its underslung jaw, I could see giant chisel-like teeth, teeth which grow constantly, and I sat quite still. It uttered a small, snorting noise like 'humph' and descended to my lap. Here, it inspected my walking-stick. Its black fingers played along its length as if the stick were a flute. Then it leant forward and, with alarming accuracy, almost bisected my stick with two bites from its enormous teeth. To its obvious chagrin, it found no beetle larvae there and so it returned to my shoulder. Again, it combed my beard and hair, gentle as a baby breeze.

Then, to my alarm, it discovered my ear. 'Here,' it seemed to say to itself, 'must lurk a beetle larva of royal proportions and of the utmost succulence.' It fondled my ear as a gourmet fondles a menu and then, with great care, it inserted its thin finger. I resigned myself to deafness – move over, Beethoven, I said to myself, here I come. To my astonishment, I could hardly feel the finger as it searched my ear like a radar probe for hidden delicacies. Finding my ear bereft of tasty and fragrant grubs, it uttered another faint 'humph' of annoyance and climbed up into the branches again.

I had had my first encounter with an Aye-aye and I decided that this was one of the most incredible creatures I had ever been privileged to meet. Since it needed help, help it we must. To allow such an astonishing and complex creature to become extinct was as unthinkable as burning a Rembrandt, turning the Sistine Chapel into a disco, or pulling down the

Acropolis to make way for a Hilton. Yet the Aye-aye, this strange creature that has attained near-mythical status on the island of Madagascar, *is* in danger of vanishing. It is a magical animal, not only biologically speaking, but in the minds of the Malagasy people amongst whom it lives and, unfortunately, perishes.

When this strange beast was first described in 1782, it had such an anatomical jumble of various qualities that for many years scientists could not make up their minds what it was. Obviously, it was not a common or garden lemur and was thought, for a time, to be a rodent, because of its massive teeth. Finally, it was decided that an Aye-aye was an Aye-aye, one of the lemurs, but a unique inhabitant of the planet, like no other creature. It was dignified with a family of its own and christened with the euphonious name of *Daubentonia madagascariensis*.

Madagascar is an island filled with magic and many taboos, or *fadys* as they are called, which vary from place to place, so it is not surprising that such a weird product of evolution as the Aye-aye should be credited with magical powers that vary from village to village, from tribe to tribe. In places, if it is found near a village, it is thought to be a harbinger of death and so must be killed. If it is a small one, then an infant in the village might die. If it is a large, whitish animal, a pale-skinned adult will be in danger and if it is a dark animal, a dark-complexioned human will be in danger.

In other parts of the island, if a villager finds and kills an Aye-aye near his house, he thoughtfully removes the bad luck from himself by putting the corpse in his neighbour's back garden. The neighbour, finding this somewhat doubtful gift, makes haste to put it in *his* neighbour's back garden. So the Aye-aye corpse progresses through the village until thrown out on to the road to the alarm of passers-by. It is an Aye-aye chain letter: pass this on, or something awful will befall you. In other areas, the animal is killed, its hands and feet bound in raffia and it is hung at the entrance to the village until the corpse starts to rot, when it is fed to the dogs. In other places, its slim third finger is dried and used by the village sorcerer as a magic charm for good or for evil. So the Aye-aye, through a quirk of evolution, has become possessed of a magic finger.

As the Malagasy people continue with their relentless and suicidal policy of 'slash and burn' agriculture, cutting down the forests which are the life-blood of the island, the Aye-aye and many other unique creatures are threatened with extinction. At one time, the Aye-aye was thought to *be* extinct, but then it was found that this curious animal was still clinging on in isolated pockets, nearly all of which were threatened by forest destruction.

The Aye-aye had used its magic to become a survivor of a sort. As its natural habitat diminished, it took to invading what man had replaced it with – coconut plantations, sugar-cane groves and orchards of cloves. With its huge teeth, it trepanned the green coconuts, drank the juice and extracted the jelly-like, unripe fruit by using its thin middle finger like a hook. It disembowelled the sugar cane, leaving the stems looking like some strange, medieval musical instrument. It bisected the clove trees in search of beetle grubs. If you are a villager whose whole livelihood depends on, perhaps, five coconut trees, a tiny patch of sugar cane, and half a dozen clove trees, then the Aye-aye becomes not a magical menace but a creature that can ruin your income for ever. Therefore, you kill it or starve.

As forest decimation continues unabated, these isolated pockets of Aye-aye, leading a bandit-like existence, are doomed. It is to be hoped that new, more intelligent agricultural methods will be soon introduced to replace the destruction. In the meantime, for the sake of the Aye-aye, some must be established in captivity to maintain the species: if they vanish in the wild, we will have at least some animals to return to the natural habitat (if, of course, their natural habitat still exists). At present, there are eight Aye-aye at Duke University's Primate Center in the USA, and one at Vincennes Zoo in Paris. It was essential that more were brought into captivity to build up viable breeding colonies. So the Jersey Wildlife Preservation Trust decided to undertake a rescue expedition to accomplish just that.

Envoi

This last selection for The Best of Gerry *really chose itself. It is his most powerful and emotive call for conservation, the last chapter of the account of the mid sixties expedition to Sierra Leone, a plea well ahead of its time.*

FROM CATCH ME A COLOBUS:

When man continues to destroy nature, he saws off the very branch on which he sits since the rational protection of nature is at the same time the protection of mankind.

Extinct and Vanishing Animals

On the bookshelves that line my office there are two squat, fat, red books that glower at me continuously. They are the first things that catch my eye in the morning and the last things that catch my eye as I close the office door at night. They act as a constant reminder. These are *The Red Data Books* produced by the International Union for the Conservation of Nature. One deals with mammals, the other with birds, and they list the mammals and birds in the world today that are faced with extinction – in most cases directly or indirectly through the interference of mankind. As yet there are only these two volumes, but there are more to come, and they will make a depressing line when they eventually arrive, for there is a further one on reptiles and amphibians, another on fishes, and yet another on trees and plants and shrubs.

I was once interviewed by a reporter from some newspaper or other, who said:

'Tell me, Mr Durrell, how many species of animals are actually endangered?'

I went to the bookshelf, I took down the two fat, red volumes, and I plonked them in his lap.

'I'm not sure,' I said. 'I haven't had the courage to count them.'

He glanced down at the two volumes and then looked up at me with real horror on his face.

'Good God!' he said. 'You don't meant to say that *all* these are threatened?'

'Oh, those are only half of them,' I explained. 'Those only deal with the birds and the mammals.'

He was visibly shaken by this, because even today the majority of people do not realize the extent to which we are destroying the world we live in. We are like a set of idiot children, let loose with poison, saw, sickle, shotgun and rifle, in a complex and beautiful garden that we are slowly but surely turning into a barren and infertile desert. It is quite possible that in the last few weeks or so, one mammal, one bird, one reptile, and one plant or tree, have become extinct. I hope not but I know for certain that in the same time one mammal, bird, reptile, and plant or tree, have been driven just that much nearer to oblivion.

The world is as delicate and as complicated as a spider's web, and like a spider's web, if you touch one thread, you send shudders running through all the other threads that make up the web. But we're not just touching the web, we're tearing great holes in it; we're waging a sort of biological war on the world around us. We are felling forests quite unnecessarily and creating dust bowls, and thereby even altering the climate. We are clogging our rivers with industrial filth, and we are now polluting the sea and the air.

When you start talking about conservation, people immediately leap to the conclusion that, as you are an ardent animal lover, what you mean is that you just want to protect the fluffy koala bear or something similar. But conservation doesn't mean this at all. Conservation means preserving the life of the whole world, be it trees or plants, be it even man himself. It is to be remembered that some tribes have been exterminated very successfully in the last few hundred years and that others are being harried to extinction today – the Patagonian Indians, the Eskimos, and so on. By our thoughtlessness, our greed and our stupidity we will have created, within the next fifty years or perhaps even less, a biological situation whereby we will find it difficult to live in the world at all. We are breeding like rats and this population explosion must be halted in some way. All religious factions, all political factions, the governments of the world, must face facts, for if we persist in ignoring them then, breeding like rats, we will have to die like them also.

Now, though my primary concern is with the conservation of animal life, I am fully aware that you must also conserve the places in which they live, for you can exterminate an animal just as successfully by destroying its environment as with gun or trap or poison. When asked, as I frequently am, why I should concern myself so deeply, I reply that I think the reason is that I have been a very lucky man and throughout my life the world has given me the most enormous pleasure. I feel indebted to it, and I would like to try and do something to repay the debt. People always look at you in a rather embarrassed sort of way when you talk like this, as though you had said something obscene, but I only wish that more people felt that they owed the world a debt and were prepared to do something about it.

Among the numerous letters I get every day there are always those from people who ask me about conservation. They ask whether it is really necessary. Well, as I have just explained, I think it is; I think it is one of the most necessary things in a world full of unnecessary activities, and conservationists are not just making a fuss about nothing. Then I get letters from people who have never, apparently, used their eyes in looking at the world around them. The only thing they understand is figures, because actual figures on paper mean something to them. To this type of person I give figures. And for this purpose the North American continent provides two very good examples of the wastefulness of man.

North America, when it was first discovered by the Europeans, contained two species of creature which were the largest conglomerations of animals that man has known on earth. One of these was the North American buffalo. At first it was killed in order to provide meat. Then it was killed as a deliberate act of policy, in order to try to starve the Indian to death, for it was one of the commodities that he could not do without. The buffalo meant everything to him – even the bones and the hide were of importance to his existence. The much-lauded 'Buffalo Bill' Cody once killed 250 buffalo in one day. Passengers travelling in trains through buffalo country had to close the windows for the stench of rotting carcasses because by that time buffaloes were being killed merely for their tongues which were considered a delicacy, and the bodies were left where they fell. Mercifully, the buffalo was saved just in time, but even now we have only a minute remnant of the millions of animals that used to thunder magnificently over the North American prairies.

The second species was the Passenger pigeon, and it was probably the most numerous species of bird that has ever been or ever will be in existence in the world. Flocks of them estimated at two billion used to darken the skies. The weight of their numbers perching in trees could break off quite large branches. It was impossible, everyone thought, that the Passenger pigeon (so delicious to eat and so plentiful) could ever be exterminated. And so they killed and killed; they shot the parent birds, they robbed the nests of the eggs and young. In 1869, seven and a half million birds were captured in one spot. In 1879 a *billion* birds were captured in the state of Michigan. This was because it was 'impossible' to exterminate the Passenger pigeon. It was too numerous. It bred too well.

The last Passenger pigeon in the world died in the Cincinnati zoo in 1914 . . .

Man is clever enough to obliterate a species but he has not, as yet, found a way of re-creating one that he has destroyed. This fact, however, doesn't seem to worry the majority of people. There are even some so-called zoological pundits who say that this is a natural part of evolution and that the animal would have become extinct anyway, with or without our help. I couldn't disagree more violently. To say that it is part of natural evolution is nonsense. It is just begging the question. It is like a man owning a blood bank and saying to somebody who is bleeding to death: 'Oh, we've got plenty of blood, old boy, but we can't give you a transfusion because it's in the scheme of things that you should die now.'

'Ah, but,' people say, 'that's what happened in the old days; it doesn't happen now. You've got reserves and so forth where the animals are safe. We don't do that sort of thing nowadays.' To people who believe this I can only quote a few more up-to-date figures to make the picture a little clearer. Every year they 'harvest' – as they call it – between sixty and seventy thousand whales. Although scientists have warned that this exploitation will very shortly make several species of whale extinct and will probably put an end to the whaling industry once and for all, they still continue to do it. It seems that the motto of the whaling industry is: 'Get rich today, and to hell with tomorrow.'

There are many different ways in which an animal can be exterminated and not all of them are simply killing for the sake of clothing or food or because they are considered to be pests. The various species of rhinoceros that were found in the east have been hunted until their numbers are at such a low level that now most of them are only represented by a couple of hundred animals at the most, and the reason for this is the quite stupid belief that the horn, powdered and taken, would act as an aphrodisiac, making the old men virile and attractive to young girls – and this in one of the many parts of the world that is so heavily over-populated that a contraceptive would be more appropriate than an aphrodisiac. Having exterminated practically all the rhinos that were found in India, Sumatra, and Java, they have now turned their attention to the African and, I presume, these will be the next on the list to go down the slippery slopes to extinction.

Let us take the case of the Pacific walrus. When the Eskimos used them simply as a source of food they utilized the massive tusks to do the most intricate and beautiful carvings. When Eskimo art was 'discovered' by the intelligentsia it became all the rage, and so now the walrus is hunted for its tusks alone and, in fact, is being massacred to such an extent that it will probably shortly be extinct. It is already on the danger list.

Let us take another example of the clever thinking of sections of mankind, who have no knowledge of nature. In Africa it was decided that the wild-living animals were hosts for the organism that causes Sleeping Sickness. So a brilliant decision was taken: in order to protect man and coddle his scrawny cattle (which were – and are – rapidly eating up all the undergrowth and turning vast areas into dust bowls) it was decided to kill off all the wild animals. Half a million zebras, antelopes, gazelles, and other animals were destroyed before it was discovered that all the smaller animals could also carry the disease. The extermination of this vast quantity of beautiful wildlife had therefore been utterly useless.

People get worked up when a couple of thousand human beings per annum are killed on the roads of Great Britain. That is a tragedy of course – but few people know that two million wild birds are killed per annum on the roads, or that in a small area studied by a Danish scientist the number of road deaths were: hares 3,014; hedgehogs 5,377; rats 11,557; various small mammals 27,834; birds 111,728; amphibians 32,820. These, of course, are only figures for the main roads; if you included the figures for the side roads they would probably be trebled. Now, if human beings were knocked down to that extent in any country in the world there would be such a shriek of protest, such an outcry, such a lamentation, that any government in power would be forced to make us give up the motor car as a means of locomotion and go back to the horse and cart. Not that I'm against the motor car *per se*, but you do see my point?

What is not generally realized is that if you look at a map of the world and see the areas that have been set aside for reserves for wildlife, it makes an infinitesimal pinprick on the map; the rest is all a gigantic reserve for mankind. And even if you have reserves, you have to have adequate resources to run them properly. Most governments are reluctant to pay out money for the preservation of habitat or fauna (unless there is some great public outcry and the animal in question happens to be particularly attractive), and many others do not have the necessary resources.

Do not think, for one moment, that I am painting too gloomy a picture. I could go on reeling out these breath-taking statistics for the whole length of this book, and it would only go to prove that, of all the creatures that have ever lived on earth – whether the giant carnivorous reptiles of past ages or the creatures of today – the most rapacious, thoughtless, and blood-thirsty predator is man. And, moreover, he is doing himself irreparable harm by behaving like this. It is suicide; an extraordinary form of Roman death whereby, in bleeding the world white, you kill yourself.

Now, as I said earlier, there are parks and game reserves and so on, but if I may quote from the very excellent book, a quotation from which appears as a heading for this chapter: 'Government protective regulations are meaningful only when resources for their effective execution are provided.' We can, perhaps, forgive our ancestors their sins, saying 'They knew not what they did,' but can we – in this technological age that we are so proud of – forgive ourselves for the things we are doing now, and continue to do in the face of opposition from all thinking people whether they be professional zoologists, ecologists, conservationists, or merely thoughtful and perceptive human beings? We have now landed on the moon, and that is a remarkable achievement. But have we gone there just for a few extra minerals, or is the moon to be a great white stepping-stone to other planets, some of which may well harbour their own forms of life? If we are going to go from planet to planet creating the same mess that we have made on our own, then I think it would be a happier thing if the vast sums of money that were spent on space projects were used to try and cure some of the ills that we have inflicted on earth.

The problem of trying to preserve wildlife and habitat (both for our own sakes and for the sake of those who will follow us) is a gigantic one, and complicated indeed. There are a great number of countries in the world which, as I have said, give 'paper protection' only to an animal, because the government concerned will pass a law to protect a certain creature but will not allow sufficient funds for reserves to be made; nor do they make funds available so that the reserves – even when they *are* created – are properly controlled and adequately run. In one country I visited I asked what reserves they had, and the man in charge of fauna conservation unrolled an enormous wall map which was covered with green blotches. These, he explained to me proudly, were all reserves. Had they, I inquired in a casual sort of way, been investigated by zoologists or ecologists or biologists, who could tell whether they were, in fact, the most important areas that could be turned into reserves? Oh no, he said, they couldn't afford to do that. Then had investigations been done on these areas, these great green blobs, to find out whether there were, in fact, any animals in them and whether they were suitable as reserves? No, he said, that hadn't been done either, because they lacked the resources to employ the proper people ... Were they, I asked, patrolled in any way? No, he said, they hadn't got the money to have guards or wardens ... So there was this very fine map, covered in green blotches, which meant nothing at all.

This, as I say, is a common complaint in nearly every country in the world that has any sort of regulations for the preservation of habitat and fauna, and, of course, there are many other countries which have no legislation at all. This is widely recognized by conservationists and they are doing their best to put the matter right, but it is a slow process. Before we reach the day when the conservation and protection laws are implemented, I'm afraid many species will have vanished for ever from the face of the earth.

In most literate countries there are a vast number of clubs, study groups and societies, be they for the ornithologist or for the general naturalist, all trying desperately to do what they can to save their local fauna. On a wider scale you have organizations like the International Union for the Conservation of Nature, the World Wildlife Fund, and so on. In many instances, I'm delighted to say, they have been successful. They have saved, for example, an enormous area of Spain, the Guadalquivir of 625,000 acres. In Australia they rediscovered the Noisy Scrub Bird which had been thought to be extinct. Unfortunately its nesting ground happened to be on a site which had been scheduled for a large new township. Fifteen years ago this would have been considered a most inconsiderate thing for the bird to do and no doubt the township would have been built there, but today the whole thing was replanned in order that the Noisy Scrub Bird should be left in peace and have its own reserve. These are the bright spots; but there are too few bright spots and too many dark ones.

Now, while pressing for conservation of animals in the wild state, there is something else we can do, and that is precisely why I formed my Trust. Many species have been saved from extinction by being taken into zoological gardens or parks and bred under controlled conditions. This, of course, is a last ditch stand, but at least it prevents the species from being completely wiped out and one hopes that, at some future date, the conservation rules and regulations will be enforced in their country of origin so that, having saved a nucleus breeding stock, it will be possible to release them once again in their native area. The list of animals that have been saved in this way is a long and impressive one. There is, for example, the Père David deer which became extinct in China during the Boxer rebellion. Fortunately, the then Duke of Bedford collected together all the Père David deer he could find in the zoological gardens of Europe and released them on his estate at Woburn where they flourished and bred. Now the herd has reached large enough proportions for pairs of this rare deer to be sent to zoos all round the world, and recently they have even been sent back to their place of origin in China. If the Chinese succeed in breeding them – and there is no reason why they shouldn't – they could set aside an area, a reserve, properly patrolled and run, and once more there would be Père David deer in their natural habitat. The Hawaiian goose is another example. This beautiful bird was almost extinct but, due to the sensible attitude of the Hawaiian authorities and the farsightedness of Peter Scott, it has been saved from certain extinction. There is quite a list of creatures that have been helped in this way, such as the European bison, the North American buffalo, the Saiga antelope, Przewalski's wild horse, and so on, but there are many more that desperately need such help.

The Trust I have created is trying to fulfil exactly this function. I realize that it is merely a cog in the complicated picture of protection today, but we hope that it is an important cog in its own way. It has not been created just to keep the animals in captivity. I look upon it as a reservoir – a kind of stationary ark – in which I hope that we can continue to keep and breed some of the species most urgently in need of protection. Then, at some future date, we can re-introduce them into their original homes. I would gladly see the Trust dissolved tomorrow were there no more need for it.

But at present I'm afraid there is a very great need and I wish I could see similar Trusts springing up all over the world.

As I have explained in this book, I have devoted my life to this work and I have spent a considerable amount of my own money on it, so therefore I do not feel embarrassed at asking you, the reader, if you will help. If you have read this book and enjoyed it; if any of my books have given you pleasure; may I point out that they could never have been written if it had not been for the wildlife of the world? Yet all over the world many of these same animals are in a desperate plight and unless they are helped they will vanish. I am trying to do what I can, but I cannot do it without your assistance, so would you please join the Trust, and try and get as many as possible of your friends – or, for that matter, enemies – to join as well?

Finally, may I just say that if you don't want to join my Trust, then I beg of you to join some sort of organization that is doing something to try and halt the rape of the world. Do anything you can: worry your local MP – or whatever the equivalent is in your country – into a nervous decline should you think there is going to be some unnecessary, ill-planned encroachment on a valuable piece of habitat, or that some plant or bird or animal is in danger and not receiving sufficient protection. Write indignant letters. It is only by lifting up your voices that the powers that be will be forced to listen. It is worked on the principle that if you shout loud enough and long enough, somebody is bound to hear. Remember that the animals and plants have no MP they can write to; they can't perform sit-down strikes or, indeed, strikes of any sort; they have nobody to speak for them except us, the human beings who share the world with them but do not own it.

AFTERWORD

THE END OF THIS BOOK isn't the end of Gerry's story. The various experiences you have just read about gave impetus and inspiration to his lifetime crusade to preserve the rich diversity of animal life on this planet.

Although Gerry died in 1995, his words in this and his other books will continue to inspire people everywhere with love and respect for what he called 'this magical world'. And his crusade goes on through the untiring efforts of the three Wildlife Preservation Trusts he created.

Over the years many readers of Gerry's books have been so motivated by his vision that they have been unwilling simply to close the books and forget. They have wanted to continue the story for themselves by supporting our Trusts. I hope you feel the same way today. I hope you want to meet the challenge Gerry put to all of us when he said 'Animals are the great voteless and voiceless majority, who can only survive with our help.'

Please don't let your interest in conservation wane when you put down this book. Write to us now and we'll tell you how you can become a part of Gerry's crusade to save animals from extinction.

Yours sincerely,

Lee Durrell

LEE DURRELL

For further information, or to send a donation, write today to:

Jersey Wildlife Preservation Trust
Les Augrès Manor
Jersey JE3 5BP
ENGLISH CHANNEL ISLANDS

BOOKS BY GERALD DURRELL

Dates given are for first editions. Many of the books have since been
reissued by different publishers.

1953   *The Overloaded Ark.* An account of the first collecting trip to the Cameroons (Faber & Faber).

1954   *Three Singles to Adventure.* Animal collecting in British Guiana (Rupert
Hart-Davies).

1954   *The Bafut Beagles.* A return visit to the Cameroons (Rupert Hart-Davies).

1955   *The New Noah.* A collection of stories for children about his trips to the
Cameroons, Guiana and Paraguay (Collins).

1956   *The Drunken Forest.* A collecting trip to Argentina and Paraguay (Rupert
Hart-Davies).

1956   *My Family and Other Animals.* The first of his three books about the
Durrell family in Corfu (Rupert Hart-Davies).

1958   *Encounters with Animals.* A selection of stories about animal collecting, a
result of requests from listeners to his BBC radio programmes (Rupert
Hart-Davies).

1960   *A Zoo in My Luggage.* An account of his third trip to the Cameroons,
resulting in the founding of the zoo in Jersey (Rupert Hart-Davies).

1961   *Look at Zoos.* A young person's guide to zoos (Hamish Hamilton).

1961   *The Whispering Land.* A major collecting trip to Argentina, resulting in
many new animals for the Jersey Zoo (Rupert Hart-Davies).

1962   *Island Zoo.* A children's guide, with photographs, about the first animals
to arrive at the Jersey Zoo (Collins).

1962   *My Favourite Animal Stories.* (Lutterworth).

1964   *Menagerie Manor.* The early years of the zoological park, culminating in the
founding of the Jersey Wildlife Preservation Trust (Rupert Hart-Davies).

1966   *Two in the Bush.* A visit to New Zealand, Australia and Malaya with the
BBC Natural History Unit (Collins).

1968   *The Donkey Rustlers.* A story for children (Collins).

1968   *Rosie Is My Relative.* A novel, which features an amazing elephant (Collins).

1969   *Birds, Beasts and Relatives*. A companion volume to *My Family and Other Animals* (Collins).

1971   *Fillets of Plaice*. A collection of short stories (Collins).

1972   *Catch Me a Colobus*. Further zoo stories and collecting trips to Sierra Leone and Mexico (Collins).

1973   *Beasts in My Belfry*. Experiences as a student keeper at Whipsnade (Collins).

1974   *The Talking Parcel*. A story for children (Collins).

1976   *The Stationary Ark*. A look at the role of zoological parks, in particular the one he created in Jersey (Collins).

1977   *Golden Bats and Pink Pigeons*. An account of two expeditions to Mauritius (Collins).

1978   *Garden of the Gods*. Companion volume to *My Family and Other Animals* and *Birds, Beasts and Relatives* (Collins).

1979   *The Picnic and Suchlike Pandemonium*. A collection of anecdotes (Collins).

1981   *The Mockery Bird*. A novel with a conservation message (Collins).

1982   *The Amateur Naturalist*. Written with his wife, Lee. A lavishly illustrated guide on how to become a naturalist (Hamish Hamilton).

1982   *Ark on the Move*. A look at Mauritius and Madagascar, based on the television series of the same title.

1984   *How to Shoot an Amateur Naturalist*. An account of experiences while filming *The Amateur Naturalist* (Collins).

1986   *Durrell in Russia*. An incredible journey through the nature reserves of the Soviet Union, illustrated with over 300 colour photographs (Macdonald).

1987   *The Fantastic Flying Journey*. An adventure story for children (Conran Octopus).

1989   *The Fantastic Dinosaur Adventure*. Another children's adventure story (Conran Octopus).

1990   *The Ark's Anniversary*. An update on the conservation work of the Jersey Wildlife Preservation Trust (Collins).

1990   *Keeper*. A boxer dog works as a zoo keeper in this story for children (Michael O'Mara Books).

1991   *Marrying Off Mother*. A collection of short stories (HarperCollins).

1991   *Toby the Tortoise*. A story for children (Michael O'Mara Books).

1992   *The Aye-Aye and I*. An account of a major collecting expedition in Madagascar (HarperCollins).

INDEX

Gerald Durrell would, traditionally, end his books like this:

'A world without birds, without forests, without animals of every shape and size, would be one that I, personally, would not care to live in.

If you have enjoyed this book (and perhaps some of my other ones, as well), please remember that it was the animals that made them possible and made them amusing. They are the great vote-less and voiceless majority who can only survive with our help.

It is up to everyone to try to prevent the awful desecration of the world we live in. I am doing what I can in the only way I know, and I would like your support.'

Gerry Durrell's Wildlife Preservation Trusts continue to expand his vision – working to preserve animals and their habi-tats for the future of our children and our world.

If you would like to hear more about this work, please write to one of these addresses:

Jersey Wildlife Preservation Trust
Les Augrès Manor
Trinity
Jersey JE3 5BP
Channel Islands

Wildlife Preservation Trust International
1520 Locust Street
Suite 704
Philadelphia
Pennsylvania 19102
USA

Wildlife Preservation Trust Canada
120 King Street
Guelph
Ontario
Canada N1E 4P8

Catch Me a Colobus

Gerald Durrell

'His best book for some time . . . only the Marx brothers could do justice to the chimpanzee breakout at Christmas dinner time'
The Times

A bloom of monkeys . . .

A big and rather beautiful tree grew a couple of hundred yards from the verandah just below us. There was a crash and rustle amongst the leaves. And then, suddenly, it seemed as though the whole tree had burst into bloom, a bloom of monkeys. They were Red and Black Colobus, and they were the most breath-taking sight.

'Another pot-pourri of animal anecdotes, based on hectic days at the author's Jersey zoo and his forays to various corners of the earth to rescue animal species in danger of extinction'
Sunday Telegraph

0 00 634462 3
£5.99

The Stationary Ark

Gerald Durrell

'. . . simultaneously funny, enthusiastic, unsentimental and compassionate'
Daily Telegraph

Gerald Durrell has been a zoo-maniac since the age of two when he started collecting everything alive, from minnows to woodlice. When, finally, he decided to set up the Wildlife Preservation Trust in Jersey, he determined that it would be different from those zoos – alas, the majority – to which parents reluctantly take children to ride an elephant and get sick on ice cream, and where animals are simply imprisoned. His would certainly be a place of entertainment, but it would be a research laboratory, an educational establishment and a conservation unit as well . . .

'. . . a flow of rib-tickling anecdotes'
Yorkshire Post

0 00 635000 3
£5.99

Two in the Bush

Gerald Durrell

'Delightfully readable and often very funny'   *Daily Mail*

'An account of Gerald Durrell's tour of New Zealand, Australia and Malaya in search of rarities . . . Easy to read, difficult to put down, with many vivid sidelights on the human side of the expedition. This absorbing narrative reveals the ardours, ironies and disappointments, the organizational miracles and the hilarious human mishaps . . .'   *Sunday Times*

'Mr Durrell has the knack of writing about animals and their antics with tremendous affection and enthusiasm, but without sentimentality'   *Sunday Telegraph*

'Will delight his fans and armchair naturalists everywhere'
          Evening Standard

0 00 634554 9
£5.99

Golden Bats and Pink Pigeons

Gerald Durrell

'. . . highly entertaining'   *Sunday Telegraph*

Mauritius, once the home of the ill-fated Dodo (symbol of
Gerald Durrell's Jersey Wildlife Preservation Trust), still has
among its fauna many unique but endangered species, among
them Mauritian kestrels, Telfair's skinks, Gunther's geckos and
Pink pigeons. When Gerald Durrell went to rescue some of
these creatures from extinction, he experienced danger, discom-
fort and exertion, but he enjoyed himself enormously. And
when the trip was over, he had many living trophies for his
Jersey sanctuary from where the progeny could, in time, be
restored to Mauritius.

'This is not only an enjoyable volume, it is also, in my humble
opinion, the best-written Durrell so far'   *Yorkshire Post*

0 00 635557 9
£5.99